Demographic Differences
in Organizations

Demographic Differences in Organizations

Current Research and Future Directions

Anne S. Tsui
and
Barbara A. Gutek

LEXINGTON BOOKS
Lanham • Boulder • New York • Oxford

LEXINGTON BOOKS

Published in the United States of America
by Lexington Books
4720 Boston Way, Lanham, Maryland 20706

12 Hid's Copse Road
Cumnor Hill, Oxford OX2 9JJ, England

British Library Cataloguing in Publication Information Available

Library of Congress Cataloging-in-Publication Data

Tsui, Anne S.
   Demographic differences in organizations : current research and future directions / Anne S. Tsui and Barbara A. Gutek.
      p.   cm.
   Includes bibliographical references and index.
   ISBN 0-7391-0056-4 (cloth : al. paper)
   1. Diversity in the Workplace.   I. Gutek, Barbara A.   II. Title.
HF5549.5.M5T75   1999
331.11'43—DC21   99-12741
                                                                  CIP

Printed in the United States of America

♾ ™ The paper used in this publication meets the minimum requirements of American National Standard for Information Sciences—Permanence of Paper for Printed Library Materials, ANSI/NISO Z39.48–1992.

Contents

Tables

Figures

Preface

Our book addresses the basic question, How do demographic differences between and among individuals in an organization influence their attitudes and behavior toward each other and toward the organization as a whole? We focus on the influence of one's demographic characteristics in relation to others' rather than one's own demographic profile per se. For example, how different are the social and psychological experiences of being male in an all-male organization from being male in an all-female or a mixed-sex organization? The issue is not about being a female, non-white, or older employee; it is about the reactions of people who are different from their coworkers in specific demographic attributes. The social units we consider here are the dyad, the interactive small group, the relatively large work unit, and the organization as a whole. This book is fundamentally social psychological in nature because it examines the way individual perceptions, attitudes, and behaviors are affected by the presence—physical, imagined, or implied—of others in a social unit.

Our book focuses specifically on the influence of the demographic characteristics of others in relation to one's own in the given social unit. It gives the reader an understanding of what demographic diversity means to individuals and provides insight into the reasons for the psychological and behavioral reactions of people at work who are demographically different from others in their work unit.

This focus on the reactions of all employees, rather than just the numerical or the social minority, is one of the major distinctions between this book and other books written on diversity. While a number of excellent books have been published in recent years on the subject of diversity in organizations, most were written for managers and emphasized the social status and psychological reactions of individuals who are in a "minority" category, such as blacks, women, or the physically disabled. The treatment (inferred or overt) of these individuals by others (usually members of the majority category) and the experiences of these individuals resulting from these treatments constitute the subject matter of these books. Their goal: understanding the nature and effect of diversity on these "minority" groups from the manager's perspective with the purpose of using such knowledge to manage diversity so that its benefits can be capitalized upon and its disadvantages minimized. By giving primary attention to the reactions and situations of individuals in the "minority" categories, these books have, however, ignored the reactions of a significant proportion of the work force. Our book gives equal attention to the effect of diversity on individuals in both the majority and the minority categories, defined both numerically and socially, and thus provides information on the way all categories of people experience diversity.

Another distinction between our book and others is the type of demographic attribute being analyzed. Diversity research and writing focuses primarily on race and sex as the major categories that affect people's experiences. However, research on organizational demography has shown that individual experiences and group processes are influenced by many demographic attributes beside race and gender. Demographic diversity is a multi-dimensional construct because individuals are a composite of multiple demographic attributes. We include a host of other demographic variables such as age, company tenure, level of education, and functional background. We even extend the analysis into the international arena by reviewing the emerging studies that focus on the role of particularistic ties or *guanxi* (e.g., common background) in business relationships in China.

Demographic Differences in Organizations aims to analyze the social psychology of diversity by drawing on relevant theories to explain when, how, and why certain individual reactions or responses will occur. The analysis and discussion draws heavily from the research literature on the concepts of similarity-attraction, self-identity, and self-categorization as well as other social psychological theories. In addition, we examine published research on diversity and demography conducted in both laboratory and field settings. Both sets of literature have produced valuable insight into the issue at hand and this is the first time that findings from both streams of research have been integrated and considered together.

We wrote this book for researchers, scholars, students, and consultants who wish to understand the influence of demographic diversity in organizations. We think managers also may find this book useful and important for learning what diversity means to different categories of employees, how their own employees may react to it, and what actions these employees and employers could take to adapt to such challenges. Finally, the most important reader is every individual who must learn to adapt to the reality that more and more of their fellow employees at work (including superiors, co-workers, and subordinates) are different from them in a number of demographic attributes. We hope this book gives our readers some insight into how diversity affects them and how diversity can be turned into a positive resource for both themselves and their organizations.

This book draws extensively on our own research and that of others who have published on the topic. Our research and the preparation of this book benefited from grants awarded to Anne S. tsui by the United States Office of Naval Research, the National Science Foundation, and the Research Grants Council of Hong Kong. Many colleagues and friends provided intellectual support, advice, encouragement, and assistance in preparing the manuscript. We thank our many research collaborators who contributed to our understanding and love for this topic. They include Charles O'Reilly, Katherine Xin, Terri Egan, and Larry Farh. Kim Gale at the University of California, Irvine, laboriously typed the first draft. John Hulpke provided valuable feedback on an early draft. Chung Mien Tsung at the Hong Kong University of Science and Technology and Lois Christ at the University of Arizona patiently went through many revisions in preparing the final manuscript. At the University of Arizona, Katie Lake's help was invaluable. To all of them, we are indebted. To our families and friends of both similar and different backgrounds, you have enriched our lives. We dedicate this book to you.

Chapter 1

Defining the Problem

The United States is in the midst of a grand experiment in equal opportunity in employment. On the basis of widespread support for equal opportunities to those who have talent and are willing to work, the United States has undergone a major shift in attitude. It has passed a variety of federal and state laws aimed at providing equal opportunity, redressing past wrongs, and punishing firms that discriminate on the basis of race, ethnicity, religion, sex, or age. No longer are want ads listed separately for men and women. No longer can someone be excluded for consideration because he is Jewish or she is over 40 years of age. We cannot force employees to leave their job when they marry, as airline attendants had to in the past. In the United States, we cannot—and for the most part do not want to—say as one can in Thailand, "No Chinese need apply" or as one can say in Central Europe, "No gypsies need apply."

This grand experiment in equal opportunity is not going smoothly, and there is a considerable amount of grumbling about *un*fair treatment and *un*equal opportunity. For example, a consultant of one of the most well-known management consulting companies recently called the first author:[1] "I read this briefing of your study on organizational demography. What you described in terms of white male reactions to workforce diversity is right on. White males do not like what is going on and they are having a tough time coping with this reality."[2] He went on to provide some examples of what white men and other people said about diversity in his consulting work with companies:

- "This company hires 'likes.'"
- "They try to avoid the race issue."
- "No blacks moving into upper ranks—only whites."
- "Why am I blamed for the wrongs of society/the company?"
- "Minorities get away with a lot: wasting time, sick days, coming in late and leaving early."

1

- "Minorities receive special attention. It is difficult to fire them because HR gets involved to minimize litigation. Managers do not want the hassle."
- "Company comes down harder on white people; bending over backwards too far."
- "They make us feel guilty about time with our families."
- "Why is everyone protected but me?"
- "Does anyone realize that I feel different too?"

Expressions such as these made by both ethnic minorities and the white majority, as well as by both men and women, are probably common in most work organizations today. Some of these expressions suggest that minority groups (i.e., females and racial or ethnic minorities) are not happy with management. Progress is not fast enough for them, they still perceive barriers to advancement, and for them, the "old boy network" continues to operate in selection or promotion decisions.

The tone of some of the other expressions indicates that the majority members (white men) are not happy with management either. They perceive women and ethnic minorities of both sexes as getting undue attention, special exclusionary programs aimed at them, and favorable treatment in hiring and promotion. Life is no longer the same at the work place for white men. They are not sure how to act or talk appropriately without worrying about offending someone. Some of them feel left out.

Below the surface of increased activities and some apparent progress in diversity efforts by companies lie feelings of discomfort, frustration, confusion, and even anger, among women and men, ethnic minorities and the white majority. How, with a variety of diversity initiatives, can management be losing the battle with both the minority and the majority? In this book, we will attempt to answer some of these questions by explaining the social-psychological dynamic created by increasing diversity among employees. In doing so, we will integrate the research on organizational demography with the research and writing on diversity. In the process, we hope to show that dealing with men versus women or minority versus majority workers is not all that different from dealing with marketing versus accounting or R&D versus manufacturing. By integrating the research on organizational demography with that of the writing on diversity, we expect to provide a framework for understanding diversity in organizations and to provide suggestions for managing diversity in a productive and effective manner.

This book addresses this basic question: How do demographic differences between and among individuals in an organization influence the individuals' attitudes and behavior toward each other and toward the organization as a whole? The focus is on analyzing the influence of an individual's demographic characteristics in relation to other individuals' characteristics rather than his or her demographic attributes per se. For example, a man in an all-male organization will likely have very different experiences than a man in a predominantly female or mixed-sex organization. The issue is not whether one is male, non-white, or over age 40. The basic demographic issue is the effect of diversity on the reactions and experiences of individuals who are different from others in a work setting and on those who are not different. In other words, this book explores people's interpretation of demographic differences and their own attitudinal and behavioral reactions to the presence, in their work setting, of people who are similar or different from them. It analyzes the experiences associated with demographic diversity by every employee and not just the minority members in a work setting.

Salient Dimensions of Diversity

Demography is the study of the inflow and outflow (immigration and birth; emigration and death) of broad social categories of people (based on age, race, ethnicity, sex, national origin). Demographic diversity refers to the mix of people along these broad social categories. Organizational demography refers to the study of broad social categories within organizations. The focus is on organizationally relevant characteristics such as functional specialty, job tenure, and organizational tenure as well as traditional demographic features such as age, race, ethnicity, and national origin. Organizational demographic diversity refers to the mix of people along any of these demographic or organizationally relevant characteristics. In fact, the concept of diversity has been applied to many dimensions, ranging from visible personal characteristics to less visible values and attitudes (Jackson, 1992b; Milliken & Martins, 1996). In practice diversity often refers to "womenandminorities"; that is, sex and race have been the focus of diversity efforts.

This book focuses broadly on diversity by including a broad range of social and demographic characteristics, including dimensions of organizational demography such as distributions of experience, tenure, occupation, and functional area of specialization. We do not consider attributes such as abilities, personality, values, or attitudes as demographic variables. Therefore, our focus is entirely on the sociological categories of demography, including both ascribed and achieved personal attributes that distinguish people in any group. By this definition, we are focusing more on what has been referred to recently as "surface" diversity than on "deep-level" diversity (Harrison, Price & Bell, 1998). Though Harrison et al. (1998) define surface diversity as those "overt, biological characteristics that are typically reflected in physical features" (page 97), we include sociological attributes such as educational level, occupation, and tenure.

Harrison et al. (1998) considered attitudes, beliefs, and values as potential deep-level diversity variables. We consider diversity in such psychological variables as possible outcomes of demographic diversity rather than as sources or types of diversity.

We intend to focus on both *ascribed* and *achieved* demographic characteristics. Ascribed characteristics are those we are born with or acquire and cannot generally change through our own efforts. An important principle underlying the United States' grand experiment in equal opportunity is the belief that no one should be disadvantaged because of characteristics they cannot control and which are not relevant to the job they hold or for which they wish to apply. A person over 40 should have the same opportunity for a job as a person under 40 and an Asian American should have the same opportunity as someone of European ancestry. A person who has a physical handicap should have as much access to any job that he or she can do as well as another person without that handicap. A person who is brilliant, however, should have a better than average chance at a job, even if brilliance is not under one's control, if, in fact, brilliance is associated with good job performance.

In contrast to ascribed characteristics, *achieved* characteristics—level of education, level of job experience, for example—are usually under a person's control. In general, we believe that it is usually wrong to discriminate on the basis of ascribed characteristics and acceptable—even desirable—to discriminate on the basis of achieved characteristics. Those applicants with more job experience or more formal education can and often should be given priority over applicants with no job experience or little formal education. The exception to the rule about discriminating on the basis of ascribed characteristics is a BFOQ (or bona fide occupational requirement). Height, age, ethnicity, national origin, religion, and sex are acceptable bases of discriminatory treatment if they are true job requirements.

Although we wish to focus broadly in our examination of demographic diversity, the available research does not focus equally on all the relevant characteristics. The demographic characteristics of age, sex, race, handicapped status, ethnicity, and national origin are especially important for several reasons: (1) These demographics are among the most visible features that distinguish individuals, people think they matter, and they influence the way people are treated. (2) The American workforce has become increasingly diverse in age, sex, race, handicapped status, ethnicity, and national origin. (3) Age, sex, race, handicapped status, ethnicity, and national origin are, as already mentioned, *ascribed* not *achieved* characteristics, i.e., we cannot improve or modify our age, sex, or national origin, the way we can modify our educational level, work experience, or work motivation. (4) Some of these characteristics, notably age, sex, and ethnicity/race constitute legally "protected classes" that require special attention in organizations.

There is, however, a more fundamental reason to emphasize social and organizational demography more broadly than these important categories. Diversity in demographic characteristics (social and organizational) create social categories which in turn lead to social psychological processes—in both the "regular" workers and the "diverse" workers—that can create feelings of isolation, discomfort, and confusion, as well as creative tension and diverse solutions to problems. This is because these social categories are potent sources of self-identity for people. Any social category—functional specialty and dialect as well as sex and ethnicity—is relevant if it serves as a basis for self-identification. Providing the reader with an understanding of the social psychological dynamics associated with demographic diversity is the primary reason for writing this book.

Before we begin, it will be helpful to clarify what we mean by a social category. Following Konrad and Gutek (1987), we suggest that five kinds of conditions identify social categories:

- Social categories of individuals (such as the physically handicapped versus the nonhandicapped, or young versus the elderly) may behave in systematically different ways.
- Conflict often exists between social categories of people (e.g., Catholics versus Protestants in Northern Ireland, Muslims versus Christians in Bosnia).
- Status differences often exist between social categories of people (e.g., managers versus subordinates).
- Institutional practices, such as having different work hours, wearing different clothing, or using formal versus familiar speech, often distinguish social categories of people.
- Social categories such as age, race, or sex are often easy to distinguish visually.

The strength of social categories varies depending on how many of these criteria apply. Some categories overlap; for example, gender may overlap with occupation (e.g., the engineers are men and the secretaries are women). Gender may also overlap with status (e.g., the engineers are higher status in the firm than the secretaries) and with institutional practices (e.g., the engineers can come and go as they please whereas the secretaries are expected to be at their desks from 8 A.M. to 5 P.M.). In this case, gender, occupation, and position in the firm foster social categorization and may be strong sources of self-identification that can affect one's own behavior.

Before we begin by providing an overview of the current U.S. labor force, we feel it will be helpful to clarify a few terms. For many years, while the majority of immigrants to the United States came from Europe and the majority of women were not employed, white men of European ancestry dominated the U.S. labor force. In essence, the quintessential organizational man is a white male of European ancestry. Even though today they no longer "dominate" the labor force by their numbers, they do still predominate in the executive ranks. Thus, in this book, we refer to them as the "majority" (unless otherwise specified). The "minority" or the "diverse" are those who are different from the white male majority, such as, women, African-Americans, Hispanics, Asian-Americans, immigrants from all countries, and the physically handicapped. For most other social categories such as age, tenure, or functional background, the terms of "majority" and "minority" do not carry any social meaning except to refer to their numerical proportions.

A Demographic Profile of the Contemporary U.S. Workforce

The U.S. workforce is growing fast—faster than the population. In short, a higher proportion of the population is in the labor force now than in the past; since 1950, the labor force has grown from a little over 62 million to over 132 million people (Table 1.1). The majority of adult Americans earn their livelihood by being in the labor force, not through government entitlement programs (such as Social Security), the accumulation of capital, being dependent on other adults, or living off the land (e.g., subsistence farming). Therefore, it is important that people in the labor force both believe and actually do have fair access to stable and significant means of livelihood (e.g., interesting, well paying jobs).

Table 1.1 shows that as of 1995, 66.6% of the almost 200 million adults (16 and over) who compose the civilian noninstitutionalized population of the United States are in the labor force, compared to 59.2% in 1950. Only a small percentage of the labor force—5.6% in 1995—is unemployed.

Table 1.1 The U.S. Labor Force

Year	U.S. Labor Force	Percent of Population in the Civilian Labor Force	Percent of Labor Force Unemployed
1950	62,208	59.2	5.3
1960	69,628	59.4	5.5
1970	82,771	60.4	4.9
1980	106,940	63.8	7.1
1985	115,461	64.8	7.2
1990	125,840	66.5	5.6
1995	132,304	66.6	5.6

Source: U.S. Bureau of the Census, *Statistical Abstract of the United States: 1996* (116th ed.), Washington, DC, 1996. Table No. 614, Employment Status of the Civilian Population: 1950 to 1995.
Note: U.S. Labor force in thousands.

Women as well as men, and ethnic minorities as well as whites, are active in the labor force as Table 1.2 shows. Teenagers, too, are active in the labor force; Table 1.2 shows that half of young men and women ages 16 to 19 are in the labor force. While women still lag behind men in being in the labor force, the magnitude of the difference is smaller among younger cohorts and is growing smaller over time (Table 1.2). The general trend is toward converging rates of labor force participation and this is true for black and Hispanic women as well as white women.

Table 1.3 shows that, while married men are more likely than either single men or other men (separated, divorced, or widowed) to be in the labor force, it is still true that married women are less likely than other women to be in the labor force. However, although married women are less likely

Table 1.2 Labor Force Participation

Race, Sex, and Age	Participation Rate (as percentage)			
	1980	1990	1995	2000 (projection)
Total	63.8	66.5	66.6	67.1
White	64.1	66.9	67.1	67.8
Male	78.2	77.1	75.7	74.9
Female	51.2	57.4	59.0	61.6
black	61.0	64.0	63.7	62.7
Male	70.3	71.0	69.0	67.4
Female	53.1	58.3	59.5	59.0
Hispanic	64.0	67.4	65.8	65.4
Male	81.4	81.4	79.1	77.6
Female	47.4	53.1	52.6	53.3
Male	77.4	76.4	75.0	74.0
16–19 years	60.5	55.7	54.8	53.1
20–24 years	85.9	84.4	83.1	82.1
25–34 years	95.2	94.1	93.0	91.9
35–44 years	95.5	94.3	92.3	92.0
45–54 years	91.2	90.7	88.8	88.4
55–64 years	72.1	64.8	66.0	66.0
65 years+	19.0	16.3	16.8	16.5
Female	51.5	57.5	58.9	60.6
16–19 years	52.9	51.6	52.2	51.2
20–24 years	68.9	71.3	70.3	70.5
25–34 years	65.5	73.5	74.9	75.3
35–44 years	65.5	76.4	77.2	78.7
45–54 years	59.9	71.2	74.4	78.2
55–64 years	41.3	45.2	49.2	53.4
65 years+	8.1	8.6	8.8	9.5

Source: U.S. Bureau of the Census, *Statistical Abstract of the United States: 1996* (116th ed.), Washington, DC, 1996. Table No. 615, Civilian Labor Force and Participation Rates, with Projection: 1970 to 2005.

8   *Chapter 1*

Table 1.3 Marital Status and Labor Force Participation

Marital Status and Year	Total Male Participation Rate	Total Female Participation Rate
Single		
1985	73.8	66.6
1990	74.8	66.7
1995	73.7	66.8
Married		
1985	78.7	53.8
1990	78.6	58.4
1995	77.5	61.0
Other*		
1985	68.7	45.1
1990	68.9	47.2
1995	66.2	47.4

Source: U.S. Bureau of the Census, *Statistical Abstract of the United States: 1996* (116th ed.), Washington, DC, 1996. Table No. 624, Labor Force Participation Rates, by Marital Status, Sex, and Age: 1960 to 1995.
*Other = widowed, divorced, or married (spouse absent)

to be in the labor force than single women, 61% of married women were in the labor force in 1995, an increase of 7 percentage points in a 10 year period. In contrast, the percentage of single women and men in the labor force has remained stable over the same 10-year period. If the current trend continues, women who are married may be as likely in the future to be employed as women who are not married.

One of the implications of 61% of married women being employed is that there are now substantially more two-earner families than one-earner families. Although not depicted in Table 1.3, among married-couple families there are over 22 million husband-and-wife earners versus 12 million husband-only earners in 1993. Furthermore, the increase in husband-and-wife earners relative to husband-only earners has been getting larger over time (compare with 19 million versus 15 million in 1980).[3]

The American workforce is fairly well educated. Table 1.4 shows that overall 28.3% of the labor force has graduated from college and only 10.8% of the labor force has received less than a high school diploma. Among the men in the labor force, 29.7% have a college degree or more and among the women, 26.6% have a college degree or more education. blacks and Hispanics in the labor force are less likely to have graduated from college than whites and 38.9% of the Hispanics in the labor force have less than a high school diploma. In general, the more educated the person, the more likely he or she is to be in the labor force and this is true for blacks and Hispanics as well as for whites. The last column of Table 1.4 shows the per-

Table 1.4 Labor Force Participation by Educational Attainment

	Less Than High School Diploma	High School Graduate, No Degree	Less Than a Bachelor's Degree	College Graduate	Total	% College Graduates in Labor Force
	1995 Percent of Civilian Labor Force					
Total	10.8	33.1	27.8	28.3	100%	
Male	12.2	32.3	25.7	29.7	100%	93.8
Female	9.1	34.1	30.2	26.6	100%	82.8
White	10.0	32.8	27.8	29.3	100%	88.8
black	14.1	38.6	29.6	17.7	100%	90.9
Hispanic	38.9	28.2	21.3	11.6	100%	87.9

Source: U.S. Bureau of the Census, *Statistical Abstract of the United States: 1996* (116th ed.), Washington, DC, 1996. Table No. 618, Civilian Labor Force and Participation Rates, by Educational Attainment, Sex, Race, and Hispanic Origin: 1992 to 1995.

centage of college graduates in the labor force. Among college graduates in 1995, 88.8% of whites, 90.9% of blacks, and 87.9% of Hispanics were in the labor force (as were 93.8% of men and 82.8% of women).

The information in Tables 1.1 through 1.3 suggests that women and minorities constitute an increasing share of the labor force. Table 1.5 shows this to be true: from 1980 to 1995, women went from 42.6% to 46.0% of the labor force; blacks went from 10.2% to 11.2%, and Hispanics went from 5.7% to 9.3%. Men decreased from 57.5% to 54.0% and whites decreased from 87.6% to 84.7% (though in absolute numbers men and whites increased over this period). These data converge on the basic idea: that the labor force has become more diverse over the 15-year period, from 1980 to 1995.

Women and ethnic minorities have also increased their share of managerial and professional jobs from 1983 to 1995. Women were 40.9% of professionals and managers in 1983 but were 48.0% in 1995; blacks went from 5.6% to 7.5% and Hispanics went from 2.6% to 4.4% of professionals and

Table 1.5 Changes in Labor Force Participation by Sex and Race

	Gender			Race			
Year	Male	Female	Total	White	black	Other	Total
1980	57.5	42.6	100%	87.6	10.2	2.2	100%
1990	54.8	45.2	100%	85.4	11.5	3.1	100%
1995	54.0	46.0	100%	84.7	11.2	4.1	100%

The percentage of people in the labor force of Hispanic origin (may be of any race) was 5.7% in 1980, 8.5% in 1990, and 9.3% in 1995.
Source: U.S. Bureau of the Census, *Statistical Abstract of the United States: 1996* (116th ed.), Washington, DC, 1996. Table 615, Civilian Labor Force and Participation Rates, with Projection: 1970 to 2005.

Table 1.6 Changes in Occupation by Sex, Race, and Hispanic Origin

	1983			1995		
	Female	Black	Hispanic	Female	Black	Hispanic
Total Employed Civilians	43.7%	9.3%	5.3%	46.1%	10.6%	8.9%
Managers and Professionals	40.9%	5.6%	2.6%	48.0%	7.5%	4.4%
Technical, Sales, and Administrative Support	64.6%	7.6%	4.3%	64.4%	10.2%	7.3%
Service Occupation	60.1%	16.6%	6.8%	60.0%	17.0%	13.0%
Precision Production, Craft, and Repair	8.1%	6.8%	6.2%	8.9%	7.9%	10.6%
Operators, Fabricators, and Laborers	26.6%	14.0%	8.3%	24.3%	15.0%	14.3%
Farming, Forestry, and Fishing	16.0%	7.5%	8.2%	19.9%	4.2%	18.1%

Source: U.S. Bureau of the Census, *Statistical Abstract of the United States: 1996* (116th ed.), Washington, DC, 1996. Table 637, Employed Civilians by Occupation, Sex, Race, and Hispanic Origin: 1992 to 1995.
Note: Percentages are percent female, black, or Hispanic in the total labor force, in managerial and professional occupations, etc.

managers (Table 1.6). African-Americans have also increased their share of technical, sales, and administrative support jobs, from 7.6% in 1983 to 10.2% in 1995. Hispanics have increased their share in many areas: service occupations (from 6.8% in 1983 to 13.0% in 1995); precision, production, craft, and repair jobs (from 6.2% to 10.6%); machine operator, fabricator, and labor jobs (from 8.3% to 14.3%); and farming, forestry and fishing jobs (from 8.2% to 18.1%)(Table 1.6). Overall women are over-represented in service occupations and technical, sales, and administrative support (where they are over 60% of workers, but 46% of employed civilians). Blacks are over-represented among machine operators, fabricators, and laborers (where they are 15.0% of these workers but 10.6% of employed civilians), and Hispanics are over-represented in service occupations and farming, forestry, and fishing. Hispanics are, for example, 40.3% of farm workers and 28.3% of private household cleaners and servants (not shown in Table 1.6) but they are 8.9% of civilian employees.

Another important feature of the labor force is the distribution of the kinds of jobs in which Americans are employed. Table 1.7 shows that in 1995, 28.2% of Americans were employed in managerial and professional specialties, 30.0% were employed in technical, sales, and administrative support, and another 13.6% were employed in service occupations. That leaves a mere 28.2% for agriculture and the production of goods. More specifically, 2.9% of the labor force is engaged in farming, forestry, and fishing; 14.5% are operators, fabricators, and laborers; and 10.8% are in precision production, craft, and repair jobs. The major change from 1983 to 1995, as Table 1.7 shows, is growth in managerial and professional jobs relative to other occupations.

It is important to note that although women and racial and ethnic minorities are an increasing share of the labor force, and are employed in a number of different occupations, does not imply that men and whites are losing jobs. Because the labor force is growing (see Table 1.1), the number of men, whites, and white men has increased in most occupational areas. Take managers and professionals, an area where women have shown a substantial increase (Table 1.6). Table 1.7 shows that the number of professional and managerial jobs has increased from about 23.5 million in 1983 to over 35 million in 1995. Of those professional and managerial jobs, men held about 13.9 million in 1983 and 18.3 million in 1995, an increase of over 4 million jobs. Women, by comparison, held about 9.6 million professional and managerial jobs in 1983 and 16.9 million in 1995. In contrast, whites and men *are* holding both fewer and a smaller percentage of jobs in 1995 in farming, forestry, and fishing, compared to 1983. This is an area in which the number of jobs is relatively small and declining (from 3.7 million in 1983 to 3.64 million in 1995), and the percentage of these jobs held by women and Hispanics has gone up while the percentage held by men (and blacks) has gone down (Table 1.6).

Table 1.7 Percentage and Number Employed by Occupation, 1983 and 1995

	1983		1995	
Managers and Professionals	23.3%	23,592	28.2%	35,318
Technical, Sales, and Administrative Support	31.0%	31,265	30.0%	37,417
Service Occupation	13.7%	13,857	13.6%	16,930
Precision Production, Craft, and Repair	12.2%	12,328	10.8%	13,524
Operators, Fabricators, and Laborers	15.9%	16,091	14.5%	18,068
Farming, Forestry, and Fishing	3.6%	3,700	2.9%	3,642
	100.0%	100,834	100.0%	124,900

Source: U.S. Bureau of the Census, *Statistical Abstract of the United States: 1996* (116th ed.), Washington, DC, 1996. Table 637, Employed Civilians by Occupation, Sex, Race, and Hispanic Origin: 1992 to 1995.
Note: Total employed in thousands. Numbers have been rounded.

In sum, the above set of tables shows that the U.S. labor force is increasingly diverse in sex, race, and ethnicity and supports the contention of Johnston and Packer (1987) that white men—the traditional U.S. labor force, and a continuing powerful component of the current labor force—will be only a small percentage of the net increase in the labor force. Johnston and Packer (1987) contend that by 2000, white men will constitute only 15% of the net increase in the labor force; everyone else will account for 85% of the net increase. The U.S. labor force is not only diverse in sex, race, and ethnicity, it is also diverse in age, with a majority of older teens (1–19) employed at least part time. In addition, about 10–15% of those over age 65 are employed.

Finally, the labor force is increasingly a white-collar workforce. The majority of Americans today are employed in white-collar professional, managerial, technical, and administrative support positions or in service occupations; as of 1995, 71.8% of the labor force was employed in these jobs. If anything, that percentage will increase as services continue to grow and manufacturing, like farming, forestry, and mining, is increasingly technology-intensive requiring fewer workers in the production process, and is done outside the United States.

Demographic Diversity in Organizations

Just as the labor force's diversity can be described, so also can an organization's diversity. In addition, some organizations are more diverse than others while other organizations are demographically homogeneous. Law firms, for example, often typify homogenous organizations. They are composed of lawyers, paralegal workers, and secretarial support workers, a small subset of all the occupations that make up the American labor force. The lawyers in the firm may be fairly homogeneous in age, especially if the firm has low turnover and does not grow in size. The secretarial staff may be more heterogeneous, but may also simply be younger if there is fairly high turnover among the staff. If the firm has not hired many lawyers in recent years, the lawyers are likely to be male, the paralegal and secretarial support workers primarily female. Most of the lawyers and paralegals are likely to be white and if there are many ethnic minorities, they are likely to be among the secretarial support workers. A modern hospital or a multinational manufacturing firm may be more diverse than the law firm, but it is not likely to reflect the diversity of the labor force as a whole. In fact, for a variety of reasons, almost all organizations are likely to be less diverse than the labor force as a whole.

What are the effects of diversity among workers in a firm on the organization, on the behavior and attitudes of individuals and groups, and on the interactions and relationships among individuals and work groups?

Why should these questions be of interest to anyone? The answer is simple. For a variety of reasons including immigration, differential birth rates, changing family dynamics, changing sex role expectations, and a variety of federal and state laws, the workforce of almost all organizations is becoming increasingly diverse or heterogeneous in terms of such demographic attributes as age, sex, race, ethnicity, and national origin (Johnston and Packer, 1987). This reality means that more individuals will be working with people who are different from themselves on one or more of these demographic attributes.

Social science research has found that demographic heterogeneity leads to a variety of social psychological and behavioral dynamics such as communication difficulty and interpersonal or inter-group conflict. At the same time, however, heterogeneity also has the promise of greater creativity and better quality decisions (Jackson, 1992b). These research results suggest that demographic diversity is both a problem and an opportunity for employers. For the employees, demographic diversity adds a level of complexity to their life at work. Furthermore, lack of demographic heterogeneity may expose organizations to charges of discrimination that can impair morale and entail considerable financial cost. This is especially true if a firm is faced with a class action charge, and is true whether or not the firm settles the case rather than undertaking the cost of litigation. For example, in 1997, Publix, a Florida-based grocery chain, settled a class action charge of sex discrimination for $81 million and Home Depot settled a class action charge of sex discrimination for over $100 million. (These costs were judged by management to be less than the costs of litigation.) As the quotations in the beginning of this chapter imply, most employees are poorly prepared to meet the challenges posed by demographic diversity.

Distinction between Demography and Diversity

How does the demography focus proposed here differ from most articles, books, and organizational programs on diversity? Organizational demography focuses on the distribution of worker characteristics along dimensions studied by other demographers (i.e., sex, race, ethnicity, national origin, age, migration, and emigration). But organizational demography also includes additional dimensions along which workers can be categorized, such as tenure in the organization, job tenure, occupation, or functional specialty. Migration and emigration translate into entry and exit from the organization. Organizations can be described along these dimensions as well. In brief, the demographic profile of an organization can be affected by a variety of processes such as rate of growth, skill requirements, complexity of the work, and turnover rate.

The diversity guru Roosevelt Thomas (1991) defines diversity as the configuration of a workforce on a variety of demographic dimensions, including age, race, gender, nationality, religion, ethnicity, tenure, functional or educational background, physical status, or sexual orientation. By his definition, there is virtually no difference between organizational demography and diversity. In practice, however, as already noted, diversity tends to focus on just a few of these dimensions. In addition, there are a number of other differences between demography and diversity research. These fall into two areas. First, the methods used by scholars studying diversity are quite different from those used by scholars analyzing demographic dynamics in organizations. Second, the purpose for the research and the writings by diversity experts is different from those held by organizational demographers.

Diversity research tends to focus on the employment experiences of individuals in the minority categories—women, individuals of nonwhite racial or ethnic backgrounds, or other historically disadvantaged groups. Research methods commonly used by diversity researchers are case studies of the employment experiences of individuals in the minority categories, field research, and laboratory studies using student samples. The research often compares the success of minorities and nonminorities at work. Some of this research assumes that any differential attainment is a function of the demographic status of the minority individuals while other research searches for contextual factors that might account for differential rates of success. Most diversity research focuses on "main effects," that is, how women or handicapped people are treated. Thus, these studies focus on the effects of being a woman, ethnic minority, or over age 55. This is valuable to the extent that "diverse" people have been understudied in the past, but it also can lead to backlash on the part of the "non-diverse" as the examples at the beginning of the chapter demonstrate.

In contrast, demography research focuses on the effect of demographic distributions or differences on *everyone*, not only on minorities. Further, demography research usually employs organizational samples (e.g., teams, work units, departments, divisions) and it assumes that differential employment outcomes are due to the social psychological dynamic associated with diversity rather than due to the demographic status of any particular group or individual.

A second important difference is the policy and practice orientation that characterizes diversity experts but not demographic analysts. The major objective of the diversity school is changing the practices of managers and organizations in order to improve the employment status of individuals in the minority categories. Thus, the research is not only descriptive, but also has a prescriptive overtone. It aims to describe and improve the experiences of those who are different (usually referring to the minority as defined by race, gender, etc.). The goal of the research is to provide valid and descriptive information about people who were unfairly treated in the past, and to inform and sensitize those who either have not thought about the experiences of those who are different from them or do not believe that being different matters. It is also to serve as a basis for designing programs that will provide equal opportunity or affirmative action in order to provide a "level playing field" for all.

According to Thomas (1991), diversity efforts in firms have progressed in three stages. The first stage concentrated on creating diversity in an organization's workforce through progressive policies on affirmative action and equal opportunity employment, or career development programs targeted at the historically under-represented groups. These efforts represented organizational responses to the civil rights movement of the 1960s and the women's movement of the 1970s. Efforts in the second stage emphasized valuing diversity. Once the historically under-represented groups have achieved access to the jobs from which they have previously been excluded, how will they be treated? Thus, the second stage is aimed at the "old-timers" in the firm, i.e., those who are not "diverse." An example is the Digital Equipment Corporation's "Valuing Differences" program, the underlying assumption of which is that differences are assets that bring synergy and creativity to the organization (Walker & Hanson, 1992). Therefore, organizations should value and use rather than ignore or suppress differences among employees. Most of the recent writings by diversity experts and practices by organizations represent this stage of development in diversity efforts (Jackson & Associates, 1992).

The third stage revolves around the idea of managing diversity. Here, the emphasis is on creating an environment so that every employee is able to contribute to the best of his or her ability. Thomas refers to this as "empowering or enabling employees." In all three stages, management is responsible for addressing the problems and challenges associated with diversity. The primary beneficiaries of these diversity efforts are those employees in the minority categories, but presumably, the whole organization should benefit, too.

Demography experts, on the other hand, seek understanding and explanation as the major objectives in their research and writing rather than a prescription for action or change by organizations. They focus on understanding the meaning of demographic diversity and analyzing the effects of such diversity on individuals, groups, and organizations. Demography analysts do not assume that any one group is necessarily advantaged or disadvantaged because of its demographic attribute. Rather, they assume that any individual or group could be affected, either positively or negatively, based on their demographic relationship to others in the social unit. The research on organizational demography tends to be theoretical, rather than descriptive, focusing on topics that strike researchers as interesting, whether or not they have immediate practical application. Furthermore, much effort has gone into finding and developing appropriate measures of homogeneity and heterogeneity as well as techniques for analyzing changes in demography over time (e.g., Blau, 1977; Teachman, 1980).

Improving understanding of the complexity of demographic diversity is our primary goal for creating this book. Diversity provides a good practical application for the theoretical and methodological focus of organizational demography. This understanding is intended for everyone and not only for researchers, managers, or employers. Further, it is for individuals in any demographic category and not only for those with historical, social, or numerical minority status. In other words, the philosophical underpinning of demography is that *diversity is everyone's business*, because as will be evident in the chapters to follow, demographic diversity affects everyone. Our premise is that the organization as well as every individual within it will benefit if everyone understands the dynamics of demography and participates in making the work place a comfortable and productive environment for one and all.

Outline of the Book

The next chapter introduces three different approaches to demographic analyses that are found in organizational demography studies. Chapter 3 reviews the research on demographic diversity. Chapter 4 provides a detailed discussion of the various theories associated with demography and illustrates how these theories are useful for understanding the dynamic of demographic diversity in organizations. The next three chapters focus on demographic diversity at different levels. Chapter 5 discusses the dynamic of demographic differences in pairs of individuals with special emphasis on superior–subordinate dyads. Chapter 6 focuses on understanding the demographic dynamic in work groups, reviewing published research on both relatively permanent and temporary task groups. The entire organization is the focus of Chapter 7 and it reviews published research on the relationship of employee demography to the structure and the culture of the company. Chapter 8 extends the demography idea to the international arena and describes research on this issue in the Chinese context. The dynamic of demographic diversity in indigenous Chinese firms and multinational corporations operating in China will be reviewed. Chapter 9 provides an integrative framework on the antecedents and consequences of demographic diversity and identifies interventions that may arrest the negative affects of diversity. Chapter 10 shifts the attention to action implications and deals with strategies for managing demographic diversity by an individual, a work group or team, or the organization as a whole. Chapter 11 identifies critical diversity issues that require further research as well as suggests research methods for studying the dynamics of demographic diversity in work organizations. Finally, Chapter 12 discusses the potential value of demographic diversity for both individuals and organizations that employ these individuals.

Notes

1. He was referring to the study that Anne Tsui published with Egan and O'Reilly in 1992.

2. He asked that his name and the name of the consulting company be concealed in order to protect the identity of organizations from which these quotes were obtained.

3. From Table No. 664. Families with Earners—Number and Earnings: 1980 to 1993. *Statistical Abstract of the United States 1996,* 116th edition.

Chapter 2

Three Approaches to Demographic Analysis in Organizations

"Demography," according to *Merriam-Webster's Collegiate Dictionary* (10th edition), refers to "the statistical study of human populations especially with reference to size and density, distribution, and vital statistics." Demographers are population specialists, and they concern themselves with problems of birth and mortality, migration patterns, population growth, and family structure as well as labor force participation rates and patterns. They provide population information and predictions that are inputs to the discussion and analyses of political, social, and economic development of a region. Organizational demographers perform similar analyses on the demography of an organization's employee population and assess the implication of demographic diversity for an organization's economic and social development or progress (Cox & Blake, 1991; Cox, 1993). Organizational demography research can be broadly classified into three approaches.

The Categorical Approach: Demography As Personal Traits

The following beliefs represent the categorical approach:

- "Young workers lack commitment."
- "Women value family more than career."
- "Asians are non-assertive."

Behavioral scientists have analyzed the effect of demographic characteristics of individuals on their work behavior and attitudes for many years. In the writing to date, the interest is in discovering differences in work behavior and attitudes among people with different demographic attributes. For example, do women behave differently than men at work?

19

Do black employees and white employees have similar career aspirations? Are employees with children absent more often than employees without children? Underlying these questions is the assumption that all individuals with these traits are similar in their work behavior or attitudes. The passage of the Civil Rights Act of 1964 drew attention to the importance of demographics such as age, sex, race, religion, and national origin. Attention turned to analyzing the attitudes, behavior, or decisions of managers as a function of the employee's or the applicant's demographic attributes. Do managers show bias against minority applicants for jobs or against women employees for higher level positions? Do older employees receive less favorable performance evaluations than their younger counterparts? Using the categorical approach to demographic analysis, researchers studied the effects of demographic characteristics on the individual's own attitudes or behaviors and on others' reactions to this individual. Tsui and O'Reilly (1989) use the term "simple demography" to refer to this approach. According to this approach, demographic characteristics are important because they provide information on how individuals in certain demographic categories are likely to behave and are likely to be treated by others in employment situations.

Researchers using this categorical approach have discovered that certain characteristics such as age, sex, race, and education could influence a person's work attitudes and behavior and treatment by others. For instance, some studies have shown that

- Older employees tend to be rated lower than young workers on performance (Waldman & Avolio, 1986)
- People with more education are more likely to leave a company than people with less education (Morris & Sherman, 1981)
- Under certain circumstances, women are evaluated less favorably than men (Nieva & Gutek, 1980)
- Under certain circumstances women tend to be absent more often than men (Johns, 1978)
- Individuals of minority racial categories are less likely to be hired than individuals who are majority members (McIntire, Moberg & Posner, 1980)

Research using this approach has continued into recent years. For example, recent studies show that women and minorities continue to run into obstacles in terms of promotion to executive level positions (Morrison & Von Glinow, 1990). Further, women and minorities are less likely than white men to receive developmental assignments that prepare them for higher level responsibilities (Ohlott, Ruderman & McCauley, 1994).

The basic premise of the categorical approach is that individuals in certain categories of a demographic characteristic (e.g., males) will have experiences at work that are different from others in a different category (e.g., females). The differential experience is due to the unique social-cultural perspectives or stereotypes presumed to be associated with the category of demographic characteristic being considered. For example, if people perceive Asians to be non-assertive and poor in communication skills, they are less likely to judge Asians as being suitable for executive leadership positions. In other words, the categorical approach treats the demographic attributes of the individuals as the primary source or cause of their work experiences. Much of the writing on this approach concludes that individuals in numerical minority categories, such as women, racial minorities, foreign nationals, or individuals with certain handicaps tend to have less favorable employment experience than other employees. The increased attention to managing diversity is not surprising given that people in these categories constitute more than 50% of the labor force.

The categorical approach, however, provides only a partial, and in fact a very incomplete understanding of the nature and effects of workforce diversity in organizations. It assumes that the experiences of specific categories of individuals are the same in all situations and for all individuals in that category. This assumption is a serious flaw in the research and reasoning underlying this approach. Research evidence abounds that individuals within a particular category have very different experiences and that the same individual may have different experiences in different settings. The categorical approach has ignored at least two important factors. First, there are variations in attitudes or behaviors among individuals belonging to the same category, e.g., not all Asians are equally non-assertive. Second, this approach has ignored the importance of the situational context, e.g., the same Asian may be outspoken in some settings but not in other settings. The demographic composition of a group may cause an otherwise assertive Asian person to be very shy and reserved. Focusing on the demographic composition of the group constitutes the second approach in demography research.

The Compositional Approach: Demography As Structural Properties of a Group

The following beliefs represent the compositional approach:

- "There is more conflict in diverse groups than there is in homogeneous groups."
- "Groups of men work together better than mixed-sex groups."
- "Organizations with mostly young employees are more creative and entrepreneurial."

These beliefs suggest that demography involves more than the personal traits of individuals. It is also concerned with the structural property of a social unit. This approach is similar to that used by population demographers. The term "compositional demography" refers to the distribution of basic attributes such as age, sex, educational level, length of service or residence, race, and so forth of a social entity that may be a work group, a department, or an entire organization. Pfeffer (1983) introduced the term "compositional demography" to refer to such distributional characteristics of an organization. Thus, an organization may be described in terms of its sex composition, its racial composition, its age or length of service distributions, and so forth. The basic issue is whether the experience of employees and the functioning of groups are affected by different compositions or distributions of specific demographic attributes. The assumption is that the social and psychological dynamic of units and among individuals in a unit will differ for units with different collective demographic profiles. The compositional demography approach, therefore, focuses on the relationship between the collective demographic profile and outcomes such as the work unit's internal processes and performance as well as the group members' behaviors or attitudes.

Demographic analyses based on this compositional approach may provide answers to questions such as these:

- Does the employment experience of women vary as a function of the proportion of women in an organization?
- What is the relationship between different distributions of employment service (i.e., company tenure) and employee turnover?
- Do men in work units with different proportions of women report different degrees of job satisfaction or organizational commitment?
- Do groups perform better or worse with a different mix of educational or functional backgrounds among members?

The basic premise underlying the compositional approach is that the distributional properties of a group's or an organization's demography are crucial in understanding the experiences of employees and group processes such as communication, conflict, commitment, or performance. Single descriptive statistics such as the mean, median, or proportion are useful, but they do not capture the more complex and situational properties of the group's collective demographic profiles. Therefore, measures that reflect the entire spectrum of a distribution are more appropriate than those that reflect only a specific category or level. For example, instead of comparing the commitment level of people with over 20 years of company tenure and people with less company tenure, the compositional approach compares the entire distribution of tenure across multiple units and analyzes the turnover pattern or turnover rates among units with different distributions of tenure. A number of different compositional demography measures are available for describing the collective demographic profiles of entire work units. Chapter 3 describes these measures in some detail.

The compositional approach, while providing further insight on the role of demography for a group's processes and outcomes, ignores the demography of the individual and treats the effect of the group's demographic distribution to be the same for all individuals in that group. It does not recognize that two individuals with different demographic profiles but in the same group may have different experiences in that group. For example, the young person in a group of mostly older individuals may feel different than an older person in the same group. In other words, the relationship of the individual's attribute to that of the group also may influence the individual in addition to the group's demographic profile as a whole. The relational aspect of demography is the focus of the third approach described below.

The Relational Approach: Demography As Social Relationships between an Individual and the Group

When people use demography to describe an individual's relationship to others, they are approaching demography from a relational perspective.

- "I like being the only woman in this group. It makes me feel special."
- "As the newcomer to this group, I am ignored."
- "Being old in this company is a curse. It is synonymous with incompetence."

The third approach in demographic analysis focuses on the relationship between an individual's demographic characteristics and that of the group. Tsui and O'Reilly (1989) introduced the term "relational demography" to refer to the difference between the individual's demographic attributes and those of the other members in the group. This approach combines the emphases of both the categorical and the compositional demography approaches. It is referred to as the "relational" approach because it emphasizes the relational aspect of demography in a social unit. The social unit may be a pair of individuals, a work group, or the organization as a whole. The basic premise of the relational approach is that the relationship of an individual's own demographic attributes to that of all the other members in a particular unit will have an impact on the individual's experience in that unit. For example, the experience of a woman in a group of all or mostly women will be different from that of another woman in a group of mostly men. In other words, the demographic makeup of the members of the group serves as the reference point in terms of the degree to which a particular demographic attribute may be salient for an individual. Clearly, being a woman is not a distinguishing attribute when the woman is among a group of women but this feature stands out when the same woman is among a group of men. Similarly, a young person would not recognize his or her youth in the midst of a group of young adults. The same person will be quite cognizant of his or her youth among a group of senior citizens. Finally, among a typical group of executives, their maleness and their whiteness are not salient, but may well be very salient to the new Asian woman promoted to the executive rank. These examples underscore the importance of the relational aspect of demography.

An individual may be similar to some members in a group on some demographic attributes but different from other members in the group on other demographic attributes. A measure can be used to capture the degree to which an individual is similar to or different from all other members or a subset in a given group on a specific demographic attribute. For example, a young person in a group with mostly older employees will have a larger value on this measure than all the other members of that group. One woman in a group will have a larger value on this measure than all men in that group or another woman in a group with many women. Chapter 3 describes the commonly used relational demography measures in detail.

Summary

In summary, relational demography focuses on the relationship between an individual's demographic profile and the group's collective demographic profile and the effect of the difference (or similarity) on the individual's behaviors and attitudes. Compositional demography, on the other hand, focuses on the effect of the collective demographic profile for either the entire unit or the members within the unit. It does not consider how the individual's attributes relate to the unit's attributes. Finally, categorical demography focuses on the effect of the individual's own demographic profile independent of the demographic makeup of the group. All in all, demography is much more than the simple attributes of individuals. In addition to a direct individual effect, it also has a group level effect depending on the nature of the collective demographic profile of the group. Further, it has a relational effect in that a particular attribute takes on a different meaning and significance for a specific individual depending on how similar or different that individual is on that attribute to the rest of the group. Relational demographic analysis explicitly considers the context embedding the individuals in order to assess the full impact of potential demographic effects.

Chapter 3

Research on Demographic Diversity

The workforce of organizations is becoming increasingly diverse or heterogeneous in sex, race, ethnicity, and national origin. This is a well-accepted fact among practicing managers and management scholars alike, a fact supported by data from the current population surveys conducted by the U.S. Bureau of the Census. Consequently, both managers and scholars are interested in understanding the effect of such diversity on the organization, and developing insights on how to best manage this increasingly diverse workforce. Fortunately, such knowledge is accumulating. Since the 1980s, two largely non-intersecting but related streams of work that deal with this topic have appeared in the organization and management literature. One stream, referred to here as *diversity research*, developed partly in response to the Hudson report on the nature of the U.S. work force by year 2000 (Johnston & Packer, 1987). A second stream, referred to as *demography research*, was inspired by Pfeffer's (1983) creative paper on organizational demography. These two publications stimulated a plethora of empirical and theoretical work analyzing the nature and effects of work force diversity or heterogeneity on individuals, groups, and organizations.

As we briefly discussed in Chapter 1, *diversity research* refers to the study of the effects of diversity on the employment experiences of individuals, usually individuals who are in the minority categories. Diversity research is driven by the social agenda of improving practices on managing a diverse workforce. In this research stream, at least six books appeared in the early 1990s (Cox, 1993; Fernandez, 1991; Jackson & Associates, 1992; Jameison & O'Mara, 1991; Loden & Rosener, 1991; Thomas, 1991). Many more have appeared in recent years (e.g., Chemers, Oskamp & Costazo, 1995; Cross & White, 1996; Hayles, 1997; Herriott, 1995; Jackson and Ruderman, 1995; Kossek & Lobel, 1996; Leach, 1995; Loden, 1996; Lynch, 1997; Newell, 1995; Prasad et al., 1997; Simmons, 1996; Tayeb, 1996; Thomas, 1996). These books document the effect of diversity on employment outcomes but with an emphasis on suggesting solutions to minimize the negative effects and enhance the benefits of diversity. In addition, a number of empirical and theoretical articles also have appeared that address the issue of diversity in organizations and work groups (e.g., Cox, 1991; Cox & Blake, 1991; Cox, Lobel & McLeod, 1991; Jackson, 1992a; 1992b; Jackson, Stone & Alvarez, 1993; Jackson, May & Whitney, 1993; Nkomo, 1992; Watson, Kumar & Michaelsen, 1993). A prominent feature of this stream of work is that much of the knowledge about the effects of diversity is based on case studies (e.g., Jackson & Associates, 1992) and qualitative interviews (e.g., Fernandez, 1991). Many are social psychological experiments using student samples (e.g., Hoffman, 1979; McGrath, 1984; Shaw, 1981; Watson et al., 1993) or are based on writers' own personal experience observation or viewpoints. The last approach dominates most of the recently published "how to" books on diversity management.

Demography research, on the other hand, refers to the study of both the causes and the consequences of the composition or distribution of specific demographic attributes of employees in an organization or units within it. Organizational demography researchers are interested in the effect of demography on everyone, not only the minority individuals. These researchers seek understanding of the demographic dynamics as a primary goal and deriving policy or practice implications as a secondary objective. Another major distinction between diversity and demography research is that the latter utilizes entirely organizational samples.

In this chapter, we focused on empirical studies that used demography as the *primary* independent variable. More specifically, we included only studies that use either compositional or relational approaches to measuring the nature of demography in the unit (which can be the dyad, the group, or the organization as a whole). We did not include any studies that utilize the categorical approach (see Chapter 2 for a definition of the categorical approach) or studies that measure diversity (or heterogeneity) using perceptions of members. For example, Eisenhardt and Tabrizi (1995) analyzed the effects of project team design on development time of new products in the global computer industry. They included a multifunctional team measure, which is a numerical count of the number of functions (e.g., marketing, manufacturing, purchasing, engineering, etc.) represented by the project team members. They found such a measure to be associated with accelerated product development. This study was not included in this review because demography is not its main focus and because the measure is not a compositional index. Campion, Medsker, and Higgs (1993) used three items to measure team members' perception of heterogeneity in membership in terms of areas of expertise, background, and abilities. Studies illustrated by this example also are excluded because we are interested in documenting the effect of heterogeneity based on actual differences in demographic variables. We found several studies that included measures of compositional demography but these studies failed to find any effects (e.g., Michel & Hambrick, 1992; Wiersema & Bantel, 1993). We excluded these few studies as well since they do not provide new insight on the problem (most studies failing to find demographic effects also failed to be published). We further excluded from this review many excellent papers that offer theoretical models of diversity (e.g., Pelled, 1996a; Priem, 1990). Several conceptual papers in Tolbert and Bacharach (1992) provide interesting discussions on different typologies of demographic structures as well as determinants of demographic composition and change in firms. These papers were excluded because they did not include any empirical tests of their models.

There are two excellent review papers on the topic (Milliken & Martins, 1996; Williams & O'Reilly, 1998). The scope of these reviews includes diversity studies using all three types of demographic approaches (i.e., categorical, compositional, and relational). Also, they included both published articles and work in progress. For example, about 15 of the 62 field studies reviewed by Williams and O'Reilly are either conference presentations or working papers. Many were not demography studies but reported some demographic effects. Our review includes only work with a primary focus on demography published in refereed journals. Thus, we excluded book chapters, working papers, or papers presented in conferences. This is to ensure that we include only research that has passed the rigorous scrutiny of the journal review process and also to ensure that readers can easily locate these published works. Consistent with the theme of this book, this chapter is devoted to an analysis of how "objective" demographic diversity of organizations affects individuals and groups, based on studies of "real" organizations and groups within them.

This chapter is devoted to reviewing and summarizing the published empirical studies on organizational demography that met our criteria for inclusion. The review begins with defining the conceptual and operational definitions of organizational demography. It then describes the specific demographic attributes studied and the specific effects analyzed in these studies, i.e., the outcomes are affected by the demographic composition in the group, the organization, or even between two individuals. Finally, the lessons learned from this review of published demography research are summarized.

A Review of Demography Studies

Our review resulted in 25 empirical studies that focused on intra-organizational demographic issues. They are listed in Table 3.1. The majority of these studies (9 of the 25) analyzed the nature and effects of demography in top management teams, followed by a focus on departments,

work units, or work groups (8 of the 25). Two studies analyzed demographic effects in project or new product teams. Five studies focused on
the operating units within very large organizations such as installations
of a government agency (Hoffman, 1985), divisions or manufacturing
plants of a multi-divisional corporation (Tsui, Egan & O'Reilly, 1992), hospitals (Alexander, Nuchols, Bloom & Lee, 1995; Pfeffer & O'Reilly, 1987)
and law firms (Ely, 1994). The smallest unit of analysis is the supervisor–
subordinate dyads, all from a large private corporation (Tsui & O'Reilly,
1989). The primary focus of these 25 empirical studies is on investigating
the impact of demographic composition on a variety of outcomes at the
individual, group, and organizational levels. Even though the study by
Ely (1994) focused only on women's experience rather than relating a composition measure directly to the experience of all members of an organization, we included it because it illustrates how composition at one level
could influence experience at another level.

It is important to note that there was no comparative study of the demographic composition of an organization's entire workforce. The study by
Alexander et al. (1995) and the study by Pfeffer and O'Reilly (1987)
focused only on the nursing staff in the hospitals. The study by Ely (1994)
focused only on women attorneys. The study by Tsui et al. (1992) treated
each business division, manufacturing plant, or hospital as a separate organizational unit. Given that most companies have computerized personnel
information systems and that the methodology is developed on how to
index the demographic distribution of an employee population, the lack
of research on organizational level demography is rather surprising.
Another interesting observation from Table 3.1 is that there is no empirical research on what "causes" demographic diversity in organizations.
Mittman (1992) has noted that, "only a small number of studies have
focused directly on the origins and determinants of demographic patterns
and their trends in organizations" (p. 5). We could find only a few such
articles (Baron, Mittman & Newman, 1991; Haveman, 1995; Keck &
Tushman, 1988; Tolbert & Oberfield, 1991). Haveman (1995), for example,
found organizational foundings, mergers, and resolutions to have important effects on the tenure distributions of organizations. This lack of
research attention to antecedents of demography is quite consistent with
the diversity research where demographic composition and trends are also
treated as given. Since the purpose of this book is on analyzing the effect
of demographic diversity, studies that analyzed the cause or determinant
of diversity are not included in this review. However, they will be considered in Chapter 9 where we introduce an integrative model of demographic diversity including a consideration of the antecedents of diversity.

A further observation from Table 3.1 is that only one study analyzed
demographic diversity in modern high-involvement teams. Given the

Table 3.1 Twenty-five Demography Studies Using Organizational Samples

SUPERVISOR–SUBORDINATE DYADS
1. Tsui and O'Reilly, 1989 — 272 dyads in a Fortune 500 firm

TOP MANAGEMENT TEAMS
2. Bantel, 1993 — 80 state-chartered and national banks
3. Bantel and Jackson, 1989 — 199 chartered and national banks
4. Hambrick, Cho & Chen, 1996 — 32 major airlines
5. Jackson, Brett, Sessa, Cooper, Julin, & Peyronnin, 1991 — 93 bank holding companies
6. Murray, 1989 — 89 of the Fortune 500 companies
7. Smith, Smith, Olian, Sims, O'Bannon & Scully, 1994 — 53 high-technology firms
8. Wagner, Pfeffer & O'Reilly, 1984 — 31 Fortune 500 companies
9. Wiersema & Bantel, 1992 — 87 Fortune 500 firms
10. Wiersema & Bird, 1993 — 40 Japanese firms

WORK GROUPS OR WORK UNITS
11. Harrison, Price & Bell, 1998 — 39 units (groups) in a hospital and 32 grocery stores in a regional grocery chain
12. Konrad, Winter & Gutek, 1992 — 89 work groups (49 So. California organizations)
13. Magjuka & Baldwin, 1991 — 72 employee involvement teams in two organizations
14. McCain, O'Reilly & Pfeffer, 1983 — 32 academic departments (one large university)
15. O'Reilly, Caldwell & Barnett, 1989 — 129 employees in 20 convenience stores (in a national chain)
16. Pelled, 1996 — 42 blue-color groups in one company
17. Pelled, Eisenhardt & Xin, 1999 — 45 work teams in three companies
18. Riordan & Shore, 1995 — 98 work groups in a life insurance company

PROJECT OR PRODUCT TEAMS
19. Ancona & Caldwell, 1992 — 45 new product teams (five high-technology firms)
20. Zenger & Lawrence, 1989 — 19 project groups (one electronic firm)

ORGANIZATIONS
21. Alexander, Nuchols, Bloom & Lee, 1995 — 398 U.S. community hospitals
22. Ely, 1994 — 8 law firms
23. Hoffman, 1985 — 96 installations (Federal Civil Service Commission)
24. Pfeffer & O'Reilly, 1987 — 298 hospitals (national random sample)
25. Tsui, Egan & O'Reillly, 1992 — 151 operating units (three large organizations)

importance and increasing use of self-managing work teams in organizations (Lawler, Mohrman & Ledford, 1992), more research on the effect of diversity in fully or semi-autonomous work teams is both possible and desirable.

Conceptual and Operational Definitions of Organizational Demography

The compositional and relational approaches involve different definitions of demography, different levels of analysis, and different operational measures. We have briefly described the difference between these two approaches in Chapter 2. Pfeffer argued that the distributional properties of demography of the organization, not merely single descriptive statistics such as the mean, median, or proportion of the workforce with a given length of service, can be crucial in understanding the effects of demography on organizational processes and outcomes (1983, p. 307).

Therefore, measures that reflect variations in the entire length of service distributions across organizations or organizational sub-units are more appropriate than those, for example, that reflect only a specific category of length of service. Following Pfeffer's definition, those studies (e.g., Finkelstein & Hambrick, 1990; Katz, 1982) that use the mean of the variables are not considered as demographic diversity research. Even the proportion of a specific range in a distribution does not capture variance or distribution (e.g., Pfeffer & Moore, 1980). Studies (e.g., McCain, O'Reilly, and Pfeffer, 1983) that include measures on pre-defined cohorts and on the number of gaps between cohorts are consistent with Pffeffer's definition because they capture a distribution pattern. It is this emphasis on distributions and variations in these distributions across units that distinguish Pfeffer's composition theory of demography from that proposed by Kanter (1977) and Blau (1977). Both Kanter and Blau focused on the impact of proportions on individuals, using race and sex as primary examples for such categorization. For example, they both would predict that individuals in the numerical minority category will have different social experiences from those who are in the numerical majority category. Pfeffer, on the other hand, focused on length of employment distributions, and the concept of majority or minority is less relevant in this type of demographic patterns.

Compositional measures.

Several operational definitions of compositional demography have been used in the empirical studies that follow Pfeffer's definition. The most common index for measuring distribution of continuous variables like age or tenure is the coefficient of variation, defined as the standard deviation divided by the mean. Allison (1978), in a thorough review of measures of inequality, observed that the coefficient of variation provides the most direct and scale-invariant measure of dispersion. In fact, all of the studies (listed in Table 3.1) that include a demographic attribute measured on a continuous scale employed this index in capturing distribution on that variable. For categorical variables, four indices were found in the various studies. They are the Blau index (1977), the diversity or heterogeneity index (Teachman, 1980), the Gini index (Blau, 1977), and the Shannon index (1949).

The formula for the Blau index is (1-Sum Pi2) where P is the proportion of group members in a category and i is the number of different categories represented in the group. The Blau index also has been referred to as the Herfindal-Hirschman index (Hambrick, Cho & Chen, 1996). The Shannon index (1949) is of the form 1-Sum log(1/Pi), where Pi has the same meaning as the Blau index. In either case, if all members of the group are in one category, a situation of complete homogeneity, the measure takes on a value of zero. The Gini index is widely used by economists and sociologists as an index of inequality. Blau (1977) suggests the following computational formula:

$$G = \frac{2 \; Sum \; [SiPi \; (Pbi - Pai)]}{2 \; Sum \; [SiPi]}$$

where Si is the mean of the category Pi, Pi is the proportion of population in category i, Pbi is the proportion of population below Pi and Pai is the proportion of population above Pi.

Although popular, the Gini index has problems, including the upper limit that is related to the number of categories and a sensitivity to the underlying frequency distribution that results in an overweighting of left-skewed distributions (Allison, 1978). Because of these limitations, others (Taagepera & Ray, 1977; Teachman, 1980) recommend a diversity index (also referred to as the heterogeneity index) based on the concept of entropy. This measure, originally developed by Shannon (Shannon & Weaver, 1949) has a flat sensitivity to transfers in the underlying distribution. This means that it "does not have diminishing marginal utility or where its utility of value (if any) is irrelevant" (Allison, 1978, p. 869). Thus, it may be more appropriate for indexing distribution of demographic variables. This measure is defined as:

$$H = -\underset{i=1}{\overset{s}{Sum}} \; Pi \; (ln \; Pi)$$

Among the four, the diversity index is the most widely accepted measure for providing information in an empirical distribution (Allison, 1978). While the four diversity indexes capture the pattern of the entire distribution, the most conceptually simple approach to measure categorical variables is the use of proportions. Kanter (1977) proposed various proportions as representing different types of composition patterns, ranging from skewed to balanced. This approach is usually used to measure distribution based on gender and race.

Table 3.2 summarizes the 20 (out of 25 reviewed in this chapter) studies that have employed one or more of the five compositional demography measures. Each measure captures the distributional pattern of the group and focuses on the group or the organization as the unit of analysis. As shown, the most popular index is the coefficient of variation for continuous measures and the Blau index for categorical variables. In addition to the coefficient of variation, one study (Hambrick, Cho & Chen, 1996) also included the standard deviation (SD) as a measure of distribution, though SD is already a component in the coefficient of variation index (SD/mean). For this reason, we did not include SD in Table 3.2. Four studies (Ely, 1994; Hoffman, 1985; Konrad, Winter & Gutek, 1992; Riordan & Shore, 1995) used the proportion index. For example, Riordan and Shore (1995) classified a group as most white if it was composed of 60% or more white. The

Table 3.2 Compositional Measures of Organizational Demography

Study	C/V	BI	DI/HI	GI	SI	P
1. Alexander et al., 1995			x			
2. Ancona & Caldwell, 1992	x		x			
3. Bantel, 1993	x	x				
4. Bantel & Jackson, 1989	x	x				
5. Ely, 1994						x
6. Harrison, Price & Bell, 1998	x	x				
7. Hambrick, Cho & Chen, 1996	x					
8. Hoffman, 1985						x
9. Jackson et al., 1991	x	x				
10. Konrad, Winter & Gutek, 1992						x
11. Magjuka & Baldwin, 1991			x			
12. Murray, 1989	x	x			x	
13. O'Reilly, Caldwell & Barnett, 1989		x				
14. Pelled et al., 1999	x		x			
15. Pfeffer & O'Reilly, 1987			x	x		
16. Riordan & Shore, 1995						x
17. Smith et al., 1994	x	x				
18. Wagner, Pfeffer & O'Reilly, 1984	x		x			
19. Wiersema & Bantel, 1992	x	x				
20. Wiersema & Bird, 1993	x	x				

Top header spanning: Compositional Demography Measures

Note: C/V = Coefficient of Variation; BI = Blau Index; GI = Gini Index; DI/HI = Diversity Index or Heterogeneity Index; SI = Shannon Index; P = Proportions.

group was classified as 50/50 white and minority group if it had between 40% and 60% white. If a work group was less than 40% white, it was classified as a minority group. A similar approach was used in the other three studies.

One study (McCain, O'Reilly & Pfeffer, 1983) used two cohort measures to capture demographic distribution. One is the size and number of gaps between cohorts and the second is the relative size of a pre-determined cohort. This study was conducted before the various diversity measures became popular and this approach was never used again in subsequent demography research. Therefore, we did not include this approach in Table 3.2.

Relational Measures.

A second approach in demographic analysis is the relational demography idea that was originated in the study by Wagner, Pfeffer, and O'Reilly (1984) and later formalized by Tsui and O'Reilly (1989). Relational demography refers to "the comparative demographic characteristics of members of dyads or groups who are in a position to engage in regular interactions" (Tsui & O'Reilly, 1989, p. 403). The definition was subsequently revised (Tsui, Egan & O'Reilly, 1992) to simply refer to an individual's similarity to or difference from others in a group on specific demographic attributes. Interpersonal interaction is no longer assumed to be necessary for demographic effects to occur. This approach is used to analyze demographic effects on individuals in the context of a group. Table 3.3 shows eight studies that employed the one or more forms of the relational demography measure.

The single most frequently used operational definition of relational demography is the Euclidean Distance Measure. Computationally, it is the

Table 3.3 Relational Demography Measures

	Relational Demography Measures		
Study	Total Group	Subgroup	Dyad
1. Jackson et al., 1991	X		
2. O'Reilly, Caldwell & Barnett, 1989	X		
3. Pelled, 1996	X		
4. Tsui & O'Reilly, 1989			X
5. Tsui, Egan & O'Reilly, 1992		X	
6. Wagner, Pfeffer & O'Reilly, 1984		X	
7. Wiersema & Bird, 1993	X		
8. Zenger & Lawrence, 1989		X	

Note: The primary index is the Euclidian Distance measure.
Total Group = distance between one individual and all others in a pre-specified unit;
Sub-group = distance between one individual and a subset of other individuals in a pre-specified unit;
Dyad = distance between two individuals.

average root mean square distance to the members in the group. It is a network analog for representing social similarity or, conversely, isolation (Burt, 1982). It has the advantage of being applicable to groups of any size. For large groups, a subset of the group may be used in deriving the distance measure (e.g., Wagner et al., 1984). Another variation of this distance measure is the use of the denominator in the equation. Two studies (Jackson et al., 1991; Zenger & Lawrence, 1989) used the number of individuals in the group minus one $(n-1)$ as the denominator. Four studies used the total number of individuals (n) including the focal person whose distance score is being computed (Pelled, 1996; Tsui & O'Reilly, 1989; Tsui et al., 1992; Wagner et al., 1984). Tsui et al. (1992) provided an explanation of the difference in assumptions and results using (n) versus $(n-1)$ as the denominator in computing the distance score. According to Tsui, et al., using (n) rather than $(n-1)$ provides a metric that captures both the size and the composition effects. For example, one woman in a group within nine men would have a distance score of .95 (square root of $9/10$). One woman in a group with 99 men would have a distance score of .99 (square root of $99/100$). If $(n-1)$ were used, the distance score for the first women would be 1.00 (square root of $9/9$) and for the second women 1.00 also (square root of $99/99$). This example illustrates the advantage (and perhaps the accuracy) of using (n) over $(n-1)$ as the denominator in calculating the distance score. At the dyad level, the squared difference in the values for the demographic variable between the two individuals was used (e.g., Tsui & O'Reilly, 1989). Table 3.3 shows the types of distance measures used in the studies on relational demography.

An important observation on the measurement of demography is that the measures are all related to a single demographic attribute. Studies (e.g., Jackson et al., 1991; Tsui et al., 1992) that used multiple demographic attributes treated them as independent effects in regression models. Only one study (Murray, 1989) attempted to develop an aggregate measure that combined scores over multiple variables. Unfortunately, the author did not describe in the paper how these aggregate scores were formed. They appeared to be factor-loading weighted composite scores. Another study (Judge and Ferris, 1993), not a primary demography study, summed the standardized absolute differences on age and job tenure between the supervisor and the subordinate. No logic was offered for why this summed scale is meaningful. Developing an understanding of the relationship among multiple demographic measures (both compositional and relational) is a fruitful avenue for future research.

Demographic Attributes Studied

Table 3.4 summarizes the attributes included in the 25 demography studies as well as the specific effects analyzed. Tenure or "date of entry" was the most often analyzed attribute in terms of tenure with the entire company and tenure with the team or the group. One study (Tsui & O'Reilly, 1989), in addition to company tenure, also analyzed the difference in job tenure between the supervisor and the subordinate. Age is the next most frequently studied demographic attribute. Usually age and tenure were included as independent variables in the same study. Studies on age and tenure were designed explicitly to test Pfeffer's tenure demography theory (1983). Other frequently studied demographic factors include educational level, job level, functional background, specialization. Sex and race were included in only 8 of the 25 demographic studies.

Table 3.4 clearly shows that demographic analyses have focused primarily on age and company tenure. These two variables are important, especially for outcomes such as turnover, but the relatively small number of studies on other attributes suggests the opportunity for much more work in this area. The major challenge is the lack of diversity in certain populations. Most top management teams, for instance, are composed primarily of Caucasian males. There is little and often no variance in sex and race. Many laboratory studies, on the other hand, have focused on diversity on these two attributes. Jackson (1992b), however, questioned the generalizability of results from diversity research based on student samples. Research using management teams at lower levels where there is more variation in race and sex may be invaluable in providing insight into the effects of these demographic configurations on interpersonal dynamics and decision processes.

An interesting attribute that was studied only once is diversity on the prestige of the universities attended by members of the top management team in Japanese firms (Wiersema & Bird, 1993). This variable was not considered in any of the studies using U.S. samples. To the extent that alumni network is a power source of influence and identification, the potential importance of this variable even in the United States must be underscored.

Demographic Effects Analyzed

The outcome that has been studied most often is turnover. These studies provided robust findings on the effect of age and tenure distributions on turnover in management teams (Jackson et al., 1991; McCain et al., 1983; Pfeffer & O'Reilly, 1987; Wagner et al., 1984) and work units (O'Reilly et al., 1989). In addition to age heterogeneity, Jackson et al. (1991) also found heterogeneity in educational level, curriculum, and experience outside industry to predict individual turnover in executive teams.

The hypothesized mediating process that links demography to turnover is social integration, and the relationship between demography and social integration was analyzed in six studies. O'Reilly et al. (1989b) directly measured social integration in the work unit and found it to be related to

Table 3.4 Attributes and Effects Analyzed in Twenty-four Organizational Demography Studies

Study	Attributes Studied	Outcomes Analyzed	Effect Size
Supervisor–Subordinate Dyads			
1. Tsui & O'Reilly, 1989	age, gender, race, education, job tenure, company tenure	(rated) performance, supervisory affect, role ambiguity, role conflict	R^2 = .04 to .08
Top Management Teams			
2. Bantel, 1993	functional background, educational major	planning formality	r = .26
3. Bantel & Jackson, 1989	age, company tenure, function, education	technical innovation, administrative innovation	R^2 = .10
4. Hambrick, Cho & Chen, 1996	function, educational background, company tenure	action response, company performance	r = .09 to .26
5. Jackson, Brett, Sessa, Cooper, Julin & Peyronnin, 1991	age, company tenure, educational level, college alma mater, curriculum, experience outside industry, military experience	turnover, promotions	R^2 = .04 to .22
6. Murray, 1989	age, company tenure, team tenure educational major, occupation	firm performance	r = .11 to–.22
7. Smith, Smith, Olian, Sims, O'Bannon & Scully, 1994	functional background, experience (company and industry), educational level	return on investment, sales growth	R^2 = .33
8. Wagner, Pfeffer & O'Reilly, 1984	age, company tenure	turnover	r = .20 to .43
9. Wiersema & Bantel, 1992	age, company tenure, team tenure, functional specialization	change in diversification strategy	R^2 = .13
10. Wiersema & Bird, 1993	age, company tenure, team tenure, university prestige	turnover	R^2 = .11 to .16
Work Units and Work Groups			
11. Harrison, Price & Bell, 1998	age, race, and sex (interaction with time)	group cohesiveness	R^2 = .08
12. Konrad, Winter & Gutek, 1992	sex	isolation, sexism, dissatisfaction	R^2 = .02 to .04

Study	Attributes	Outcome	Statistic
13. Magjuka & Baldwin, 1991	job level	subjective assessment of team effectiveness	r = .60
14. McCain, O'Reilly & Pfeffer, 1983	company tenure (gaps in cohort)	turnover	R^2 = .10 to .25
15. O'Reilly, Caldwell & Barnett, 1989	age, group tenure	social integration, turnover	R^2 = .13 to .38
16. Pelled, 1996	race, gender, tenure	emotional conflict	R^2=.03
17. Pelled et al., 1999	age, gender, race, company tenure, functional background	task conflict / emotional conflict	r = -.27 to .14 / r = -.45 to .27
18. Riordan & Shore, 1995	gender, race, tenure	perception of group productivity, commitment, cohesion, and advancement opportunities	R^2 = .02
Project or New Product Teams			
19. Ancona & Caldwell, 1992	team tenure, function	group process, external communication, technical innovation, performance (rated), adherence to budget and schedule	r = -.27 to .40
20. Zenger & Lawrence, 1989	age, company tenure	technical communication	R^2 = .02 to .12
Organizations and Operating Units			
21. Alexander et al., 1995	tenure, education, employment status	turnover	r = .19 to .26
22. Ely, 1994	gender	social relations with female coworkers and senior-level women	Not Available
23. Hoffman, 1985	race	interpersonal communication, organizational communication, inter-organizational communication	r = .23
24. Pfeffer & O'Reilly, 1987	company tenure	turnover	R^2 = .04 to .10
25. Tsui, Egan & O'Reilly, 1992	age, company tenure, sex, race, education	psychological commitment, absenteeism, intent to stay	R^2 = .04 to .06

Note: Statistically significant effects were found on those attributes and outcomes printed in bold.

R^2 = proportion of variance in the dependent variable accounted for by the set of diversity attributes (either in the compositional or relational forms).

r = zero-order correlation between the composition or relational demography variable and the outcome, where unique contribution by the set of demographic variables is not reported in the regression.

group-level tenure distribution. Konrad et al. (1992) found sex composition to be systematically associated with two measures of social integration, isolation and dissatisfaction. Pelled (1996) found a positive effect of race diversity on emotional conflict. Another study by Pelled et al. (1999) also confirmed the relationship between demographic diversity and conflict. Tsui et al. (1992) found demographic distance of sex and race to be associated with low levels of organizational attachment. The study by Harrison et al. (1998) had an unusual finding. It found that sex diversity was associated with low group cohesion only for those groups where members had spent a relatively short amount of time together. Finally, at the dyad level, demographic dissimilarity on gender, education, and job tenure was associated with the supervisor's low level of liking for the subordinate (Tsui & O'Reilly, 1989). In this case, interpersonal liking may be considered a form of social integration at the dyad level.

Communication was the focus of three studies. Hoffman (1985) analyzed the frequency of communication as a function of race composition in 93 supervisory teams. He found that increasing race ratio in the group (i.e., more blacks) was associated with increasing organizational-level communication but decreasing within-team communication. Zenger and Lawrence (1989) found project members who were similar in age to others on the project team tended to engage in more technical communication with team members inside the team. Those who were similar to those outside the project team on both age and organizational tenure tended to communicate more with outsiders. Smith et al. (1994) found a heterogeneity effect on informal communication.

Ancona and Caldwell (1992) found that the greater the functional diversity of the new product team, the more team members communicated outside the team's boundary. In the same study, they also found such external communication to be associated with managerial ratings of team innovation. Innovation was the dependent variable in one other study. Bantel and Jackson (1989) found that the more innovative banks were managed by more educated teams who were diverse with respect to functional areas of specialization. It is unclear, however, whether innovation associated with diversity improves performance. For example, Ancona and Caldwell (1992) found both tenure and functional diversity to be negatively associated with team-rated performance. It may be that even though diversity may enhance creativity, it may impede implementation of innovations generated by that creativity due to the lower coordination capacity of heterogeneous compared to homogeneous work teams. The study by Magjuka and Baldwin (1991), however, found diversity in job level among members in employee involvement teams to be associated with a high level of effectiveness as rated by both supervisors and team members. Perhaps the inclusion of different levels in such teams ensures the power bases and experience for making decisions that are relevant for team effectiveness.

While Ancona and Caldwell (1992) and Magjuka and Baldwin (1991) analyzed performance at the team level, other studies focused on performance at the individual and organization levels. Tsui and O'Reilly (1989) found differences in gender and job tenure between the superior and the subordinate to be associated with low performance ratings of the subordinate by the superior. Murray (1989) discovered a negative relationship between occupational heterogeneity and firm efficiency (earnings ratios) but a positive relationship between temporary heterogeneity (defined by age and tenure variance) and firm adaptiveness (stock price ratios). A study by Hambrick, Cho, and Chen (1996) found heterogeneity on function, educational background, and company tenure to have a significant effect on airlines' growth in market share and growth in profits. Smith et al. (1994) also found heterogeneity in years of education to have a positive effect on the firm's return on investment and sales growth. The importance of diversity in the functional background of top management teams for corporate strategy, and especially for strategic change, was found in another Fortune 500 study (Wiersema & Bantel, 1992).

Other dependent variables studied include promotion of lower status team members (Jackson et al., 1991), improved task processes such as clarifying group goals and setting priorities (Ancona & Caldwell, 1992), perceptions of group productivity, commitment to the team, and advancement opportunities. Studies also have focused on role ambiguity by subordinates (Tsui & O'Reilly, 1989), and the experience of sexist stereotyping by women in male-dominated groups (Konrad et al., 1992).

From this list of dependent variables, it appears that the primary focus of organizational demography research has been on testing the effect of heterogeneity on communication, cohesion, and turnover. A majority of the studies focused on these relationships, which are reasonably well supported by the aggregate findings. A secondary focus of organizational demography research is the effect of diversity on performance at the various levels. Underlying this focus on performance outcomes is the assumption of distributed resources or expertise among individuals with different demographic profiles or backgrounds. For example, tenure is considered a proxy for experience while job level and educational or functional background represent different types of knowledge base or expertise.

Magnitude of Demographic Effects

The review of published demographic studies shows clearly that diversity matters. A variety of demographic diversity measures are related to, or influence, a variety of outcomes at the individual, group, and organizational levels. The next logical question is, how much do they matter? In other words, what is the magnitude of their effects? The last column in

Table 3.4 provides the information to answer this question. Most of the studies report the net effect of the demographic diversity measures (i.e., after controlling for the effects of other non-demographic diversity variables), though a few studies did not report this information separately. The R^2 refers to the net amount of variance in the dependent variable that can be explained by one or more of the demographic diversity measures. (We refer to this as the "effect size"). When a variable can fully explain variations in another variable, then the effect size would be 100%. This is rarely if ever obtained in behavioral science research. Often, given a reasonable sample size, a statistically significant effect could be obtained with an effect size of 2 or 3%.

A number of studies did not report the net effect accounted for by demographic diversity variables (i.e., change in R^2). For these studies, we reported the simple correlation (r) between the demographic diversity measure and a dependent variable. The "r" is not a precise measure of the effect size but it gives some idea of the potential magnitude. One study (Ely, 1994) did not report a statistic that can be directly translated into a magnitude index.

The information in column 4 of Table 3.4 suggests that the effects of demographic diversity are quite substantial in some studies. For example, Jackson et al. (1991) found that diversity among the top management team on age, educational level, and experience outside the industry explained almost 22% of the variance in the turnover of team members. McCain et al. (1983) also reported an effect of similar magnitude (25%) in their turnover study. O'Reilly et al. (1989b) reported an even greater effect (38%) in predicting social integration among employees in a set of convenience stores, as a function of diversity in age and group tenure. Smith et al. (1994) found that diversity indices explain about 33% of the variance in the firm's return in investment.

In most of the studies, the effect is modest, with the effect size of less than 10%. However, an effect size of even modest magnitude could be meaningful if it provides additional information and understanding of factors that may influence the variety of work outcomes that were examined in this set of research. Given that both researchers and practicing managers often do not consider the possibility that demography will have *any* impact on group processes or outcomes, even a small effect is potentially meaningful. Furthermore, small effects could accumulate and lead to non-trivial consequences. For example, a small tendency for the most different to leave groups can, over time, result in increasingly more homogeneous groups as one moves up the organizational hierarchy. In general, the effect sizes obtained from the list of studies included in this review, many of which are more than merely modest, suggest that demographic diversity is an organizational reality that should not be casually dismissed.

Lessons from Demography Research

What have we learned about diversity in organizations from demography research using organizational samples? We summarize the learning into three lessons. The first lesson involves the domain of demographic attributes. Attributes analyzed in demography research are different from those studied in the diversity stream. However, multi-attribute research is limited in both streams. The second lesson relates to the results on the effects of demographic diversity. The findings on process outcomes corroborate those discovered in the laboratory studies while results on performance outcomes are as inconclusive as those found in the diversity research. The third lesson entails the meaning of specific demographic attributes. Results from demography research suggest that demographic interpretations may be both individually determined and situationally induced. The three lessons lead to the overall conclusion that diversity is a situation-dependent issue and that understanding of diversity in organizations in general and demographic processes in specific will be incomplete without incorporating the context in the framework.

The Domain of Demographic Attributes

Based on the review in the preceding section, we may conclude with some degree of confidence that age and tenure diversity have an effect on turnover, communication, and cohesion. Interestingly, age and tenure diversity were seldom studied in the diversity research stream. Most of the case analyses and experimental studies have focused on gender and race composition. Experimental studies by diversity researchers rely almost exclusively on the use of college students where the variance in age is limited. Except in those rare instances when a longitudinal research design was used, the idea of (group) tenure also is irrelevant. The results on age and tenure distribution in organizations have provided important knowledge about one aspect of diversity that has not been addressed sufficiently in diversity research.

Demography research also introduced the idea of the demographic profile, arguing that individuals are a composite of multiple attributes (e.g., Tsui & O'Reilly, 1989). The dynamic of interaction among individuals and consequently the effect of demography on the group and individuals may differ in non-trivial ways with different compositions on multiple demographic attributes. Diversity research tends to focus on one or at most two attributes. A man is not only a man, he may be a white man, an old man, a well-educated man, a man of certain religious beliefs, or a man of distinguished family background. All of these attributes are likely to interact in influencing the perceptions of others about him or his interaction with others. The importance of including multiple attributes in the analysis is one area where demography and diversity researchers concur. What is needed is the development of multi-attribute measures.

A related question is on the relationships among the multiple attributes or their reduced dimensions. Are the effects cumulative or interactive in nature? Are there non-linear patterns or configurations of attributes that may be associated with different process and performance outcomes? We encourage explorations on various configurations of demographic attributes and their consequences for individuals and groups (Meyer, Tsui & Hinings, 1993). Developing creative methods to capture demographic configurations or profiles seems essential.

In addition to considering the importance of multiple attributes, organizational scholars may find that the dynamics associated with particular patterns of demographic heterogeneity differ depending on the level of analysis. For example, there might be a different dynamic associated with age diversity in supervisory–subordinate dyads, in work teams, and in the organization as a total entity. In supervisory–subordinate relationships, superiors are generally expected to be older than subordinates. A large age difference in a dyad may lead to different interactional patterns and outcomes, compared to when there is a small age difference in the dyad. However, in work teams age heterogeneity might be tolerated more than in dyads. Here power is generally equally distributed and the correlation between power and age may be less strong. Therefore, societal norms regarding power distance and age heterogeneity may not be a critical issue at the work team level. In summary, the level of the analysis is an important consideration in assessing the dynamic of demographic attributes.

Results on the Effects of Demographic Diversity

Most demography research focuses on process outcomes such as communication, cohesion, and commitment or turnover. The findings from these studies corroborate those conclusions derived from social psychological research in laboratory settings. Jackson (1992b) reviewed this stream of research and provided a summary of these research findings summarized in Table 3.5. According to Jackson (1992b), the evidence from laboratory studies is quite conclusive regarding the influence of attitude and demographic homogeneity on group cohesiveness. Less conclusive, however, are the results on performance outcomes, despite the fact that diversity research has had a predominant focus on group performance. Jackson (1992b) concluded that the only clear evidence is that groups with heterogeneity on personal attributes and ability outperformed homogeneous groups on tasks requiring creativity or judgmental decision making. There is no strong or conclusive evidence on the influence of heterogeneity on production or intellectual tasks, i.e., tasks with known solutions. A similar conclusion may be drawn from demography research. Heterogeneity on certain dimensions, especially functional background, was associated with innovation (e.g., Ancona & Caldwell, 1992; Wiersema & Bantel, 1992) and there is some evidence of demographic effect on overall firm performance. However, there is a paucity of research on performance effects in operating work groups involving production tasks.

The lack of studies on performance outcomes at the production level may be due to the inadequate specification of the relationship among the variables of demography, group process, and performance. A recent diversity study provides a good illustration of the complex relationship among these three variables. Watson, Kumar, and Michaelsen (1993) conducted a longitudinal study, using student subjects, comparing both process and performance outcomes between (racially) heterogeneous and homogeneous teams (composed of Caucasians) over 17 weeks divided into four time periods. They found that there was greater process and performance improvement in heterogeneous than in homogeneous teams over time. Initially, homogeneous teams outperformed the heterogeneous teams on all the measures. By the end of the fourth period, however, the heterogeneous teams outperformed the homogeneous teams on two of the five performance measures with no difference on the remaining performance measure and one process measure. These results suggest that, while

Table 3.5 Summary of Social Psychology Research Results for Group Heterogeneity Effects

Types of Outcomes	Types of Composition Variables	
	Personal Attributes	Abilities and Skills
Performance tasks	Few studies with mixed results. No clear effect of group composition on performance	Heterogeneity of types and levels of ability seem beneficial, but few studies
Intellective tasks	Too few studies to draw conclusions; some evidence that mixed-sex groups outperform same-sex groups	Almost no directly relevant research
Creativity and judgmental decision making	Evidence is fairly consistent in showing that heterogeneous groups outperform homogeneous groups	Moderate amount of evidence indicates that heterogeneity of ability levels is beneficial
Cohesion and conflict	The consequences of personality homogeneity are unclear. Attitude homogeneity and demographic homogeneity are related to group cohesiveness.	

From Jackson (1992b). Reprinted by permission of Sage Publications, Inc.

heterogeneous teams may require more time to work out process issues, they may have greater promise for overall performance than homogeneous teams once these process issues are resolved. In this case, time, a context variable, plays an important role in explaining and analyzing both process and performance outcomes. This study demonstrates the importance of research design and appropriate choice of the unit in demography research. Results from research using a cross-sectional design or executive teams provide only limited knowledge for understanding and managing diversity at the production levels.

In summary, the results on the dependent variables from demography research have provided confirming evidence on the effect of heterogeneity on process outcomes but have not produced sufficient knowledge about performance outcomes in work groups at the production level. These results suggest that understanding diversity in organizations would be improved by demography research using quasi-experiments with ongoing organizational work groups and a longitudinal design that permits the tracking of process and performance change over time.

The Meaning of Demography

Findings from demography research also suggest systematic and subjective differences in the interpretation of meanings of different demographic attributes. Jackson, May, and Whitney (1993) distinguished between readily detectable attributes (such as race, gender and age) and underlying attributes (such as abilities or values). They further organized the readily detectable attributes into task-related (e.g., age or occupation) and relation-oriented (e.g., gender or race) categories. While such distinctions are a useful first step toward providing some clarity on the meaning of demography, categorizing an attribute as either task-related or relation-oriented may restrict rather than expand our understanding of the issue. For example, it is possible that an attribute, e.g., being a lawyer or an accountant, may convey both task-related and relation-oriented information. To some people, lawyers not only possess specialized expertise but also some particular values. Occupation, therefore, contains information that may be potentially relevant for both task performance and relationship in the group. It is possible that most attributes may have both task and relationship implications. In part, this may be the reason why demography researchers often use the same set of variables such as age, sex, race, or education, to predict both relation-oriented (e.g., turnover and cohesion) and task-related (e.g., performance, innovation) outcomes.

Demographic variables may differ in terms of their relationship to various outcome variables, depending on the underlying meaning or subjective interpretation by team members. For example, demographic variables that convey attitudes and values but not ability and skills (e.g., religion) may be more strongly associated with conflict and cohesion than with performance in a group. On the other hand, demographic variables that convey abilities and skills but not attitudes or values (e.g., education) may be more strongly associated with performance than with cohesion and conflict. The outcome is probably less predictable if the attribute conveys both types of information.

Some research evidence exists to suggest that people may ascribe different meanings to the same demographic attributes. For example, in the study by Tsui et al. (1992), males and whites reacted strongly to increasing proportion of females and non-whites in the work unit while females and non-whites did not react to gender or race composition in terms of attachment to the organization. Therefore, sex appeared to be a more important social category for males than for females; and race appeared to be a more important source of identity for whites than for people of color. In addition to individual differences on the subjective meaning of demography, meaning may also be affected by situational cues. For instance, research has shown that males reacted differently when they were in the minority than when they were in the majority (Wharton & Baron, 1987), implying that the situation has modified the meaning or salience of the attribute.

Currently, researchers (e.g., Jackson, May & Whitney, 1993) seem to assume that individuals attach the same meaning to specific demographic attributes. This fundamental assumption may be problematic. Based on social identity and self-categorization theories (Tajfel, 1982; Tajfel & Turner, 1986; Turner & Associates, 1987), individuals derive self-identity from social categories and different social categories are meaningful for different individuals. Thus, future research on assessing the effect of demography in small groups should ideally include the cognitive processing of demographic information as well as potential subjective connotation and interpretation of demographic attributes by individuals in that social unit. Chapter 4 offers a detailed discussion and analyses of the multiple meaning of demography for individuals.

Summary

Based on the lessons we learned from demographic research, we came to the conclusion that the issue of demography is much more complex than would be suggested by most previous research. Demographic attributes are multiple and interdependent with potentially differing results depending upon the level of analysis being considered. In addition, organizations are dynamic social systems. Results from snap-shot demographic research may lack generalizability, and they may be non-conclusive or misleading. Further, the preliminary results from this stream of research suggest that a demographic attribute may mean different things to different people and that meaning may be affected by situational cues.

In essence, demography is about the relationship between a particular context and the demographic elements within it. Similarly, diversity is about the experience of being different from others in a specific setting having a particular set of social–structural features. Therefore, analysis of demographic effects must incorporate the influence of the context in situ. The organization and its associated cultural attributes represent a context that may be particularly relevant for understanding the dynamic of demographic diversity in organizations. This context is incorporated into a model of demographic diversity that we will propose and describe in Chapter 9.

Conclusions

Research on organizational demography is still in its early stage, and our knowledge of the effects and results of diversity in organizations is quite limited. Our review of the demography research suggests that much more work is needed in understanding and interpreting the effect of demographic diversity on performance outcomes at all levels of analysis: dyads, work teams, and the entire organization. Longitudinal and cross-level studies of the differential impact of different demographic dimensions and multi-dimensional patterns of demography should be important topics for future research.

Clearly, demography is much more than the simple attributes of individuals. It is a group-level variable. It is also a relational variable. Further, its meaning and effects are affected by situational cues. Therefore, theories of diversity in general or of organizational demography in specific need to take into account the effect of the organizational context embedding the individuals and groups. The organization and its associated cultural attributes is one relevant context variable that impacts the meaning of demographic attributes and shapes the social identity of groups and individuals. Demography in essence is both a dynamic and a context-based phenomenon. There is no one single correct interpretation of any particular demographic variable. Understanding of its meaning and evaluation of its effect depend on who is interpreting the demographic variable, at what level, and in what context. Finally, research in organizational settings with organizational samples will be invaluable for providing an ecologically valid understanding of the nature and effects of demographic diversity in organizations. In Chapter 11, we will discuss some of these issues as directions for future research.

Note

This chapter is based on the paper by Tsui, Egan, and Xin (1995a) but the content has been updated to include recent research on this topic.

Chapter 4

The Multiple Meanings of Demography

The term "demography" refers to the relatively permanent and immutable personal and background characteristics of the individual. Individuals are not able to change race, sex, national origin, place of birth, or year of birth without extraordinary effort. However, demography also refers to personal attributes that can be changed with some deliberate effort. Examples are tenure in an organization or a work unit, educational background and level, religion, occupation, marital or parental status, place of residence or membership in professional, social or recreational organizations. This collective set of attributes, whether relatively permanent or relatively mutable, are useful in describing an individual and are usually the bases for an initial understanding or impression of an individual. In other words, demography is a source of information about people.

Demographic factors are, however, more than information. They also are important sources of self-identity for individuals. Some individuals derive their core identity from their religion, for example, whereas others are proud of their Harvard degree. Some people think of themselves as a parent first, and a lawyer second. Others define themselves in terms of their professional involvement rather than their roles as family members or friends. In other words, the relative importance of various demographic factors differs for each individual. This chapter discusses the multiple meanings of demography for individuals and groups. The theories of social identity and self-categorization are the focal topics of this chapter. The British social psychologist Henri Tajfel (1981, 1982) developed social identity theory and John C. Turner (1982, 1985, 1987), an Australian social psychologist, developed self-categorization theory.

Demography As Social Information about People

Some of the most easily available sources of information about others, without engaging in actual communication with them are the social stereotypes associated with membership in specific categories such as religion, occupation, ethnic background, or country of origin. Stereotypes are shared beliefs in that most people in a particular society will agree that members of a specific social category possess the same qualities. Stereotypes put a boundary around a category of people and differentiate the social category in question from other social categories. For example, stereotypes that Irish are slow, that blacks are irresponsible, that women are emotional, and so forth, still exist despite the presence of many exceptions in recent history (e.g., John Kennedy, Martin Luther King, Margaret Thatcher) as well as exceptions we regularly encounter in our daily lives. Stereotypes serve a useful function in that they allow people to "simplify" the otherwise highly complex social environment. In other words, stereotypes are, as Walter Lippman (1922) noted, simplified pictures of the social world.

Categorization and Stereotyping

Stereotypes, therefore, are the qualities or characteristics associated with a social category of people. To stereotype an individual begins with categorizing an individual. When we first meet a stranger and before conversation begins, we already engage in a process of categorization. What is the basis for this initial categorization? There are multiple visible cues readily available. The demographic characteristics are the most visible and research has found that the gender and race (i.e., skin color) are noticed before anything else (e.g., Bem, 1981; Laws, 1979). Another readily visible trait is the person's approximate age. Clothing and demeanor also may provide cues about the person's background or identity. A person's educational background, occupation, and place of origin provide further information. Categorization brings the person into sharper focus and satisfies the perceiver's basic need for simplicity at a cognitive level. (An excellent discussion of stereotyping and categorization processes can be found in Hogg & Abrams, 1988).

Depending on the person's social categories, different stereotypes about the person's likely attitudes, behavior, beliefs, and actions are invoked. Categorization, therefore, precedes stereotyping. Without categorization, stereotyping does not occur. For example, an applicant who is an older Asian man with a Harvard degree may be perceived differently by different recruiters, depending on the primary social category to which the applicant is perceived to belong. The assumptions or inferences that are made about the applicant's abilities and attitudes when the applicant is categorized by ethnic background are different from those made when the applicant is categorized by educational background, age, or gender. Stereotypes provide the first level of information about an individual, information that may or may not be accurate about the specific person in question. Social psychological research has firmly demonstrated that first impressions, regardless of accuracy, have lasting effects.

Of all the possible categories as shown by the applicant/recruiter example, what determines which category is most salient? There are two factors that may contribute to an initial determination. First is the demographic make up of the perceiver. Second is the amount of stereotypic information that is available to the perceiver about a specific category.

The first factor suggests that the categorization process is as much a function of the perceiver as it is a function of the perceived. This is consistent with the relational demography idea discussed in Chapter 2. Categorization of people does not occur objectively and dispassionately but occurs with reference to self. In other words, people are classified on the basis of their similarities and differences to self. Others are perceived either as members of the same category as self or as members of a category different from self. Take the example of the applicant above. If the recruiter is also an Asian, and assuming that the recruiter has a strong Asian identity, the applicant is likely to be perceived or classified as Asian first and along any other categories second. For a variety of reasons, ethnicity probably dominates all other categories. Since one consequence of categorization is the accentuation of the positive features or stereotypes of members who belong to the same category (referred to as in-group members), the Asian candidate is likely to be perceived more positively by the Asian recruiter than other candidates who are not Asian. If, however, the recruiter is a Hispanic who also went to Harvard, and we further assume that the Harvard degree is an important source of pride for the Hispanic recruiter, the Asian applicant may be classified as a Harvard graduate first and as an Asian or an older individual second. In other words, the perceived will likely be categorized as a member of the social group with demographic attributes that are important sources of identity for the perceiver.

The second factor that may determine the categorization of others is the amount of stereotypic information the perceiver has about different social groups. In some cultures, there are well-developed stereotypes about people with a certain socio-economic background, gender, or occupation. For example, in the United States, most people are aware of stereotypes of males, females, Republicans, Democrats, Asians, New Yorkers, lawyers, blue collar workers, investment bankers, Jews, or fundamentalist Christians. These stereotypes are communicated via the mass media, books, and conversations at schools, at home, or at work. The more information one has about the stereotype of a social category, the more likely an individual classified in that category will be viewed stereotypically. By extension, individuals who belong to categories with well-developed stereotypes are more likely to be stereotyped than individuals in groups with less well developed stereotypes. Also by extension, stereotypes are only employed when individuals have (even if only some) knowledge about them. For example, if an individual has never met or heard about Jews or Hispanics, he or she is not likely to have stereotypes of Jews or Hispanics. Stereotypes serve as a source of information only when such information is known or available.

Self-Categorization and Self-Stereotyping

So far, we have focused on the categorization and stereotyping of others, and we have described the importance of the self in providing a reference point for categorizing others. The self, however, is important, not only for categorizing others but also for understanding how one perceives oneself in relation to others. Individuals have a tendency to categorize themselves also. Turner and Associates (1987) provide a thorough discussion of the self-categorization theory and process. One outcome of self-categorization is that people will use social stereotypes to describe themselves, particularly stereotypes associated with social categories salient to them. They may even describe themselves more stereotypically than uniquely, in effect "depersonalizing" themselves just as others do when they stereotype. Depersonalization means that we are more likely to behave or believe according to what the stereotypes suggest than we truly would behave or believe if we had not categorized ourselves as such.

Recent social psychological research has demonstrated the power of depersonalization caused by self-stereotyping (Steele & Aronson, 1994). In several carefully controlled experimental studies, African-American students were found to perform poorly on advanced verbal tests in comparison to white students when the students were asked to indicate their race on a test form before the test began. The test performance of the two groups was not different when the students were not asked to indicate their race on an identical test form. Evidently, indication of racial identity on the test form appeared to have invoked the stereotypes of African-Americans among these students. These students presumably had categorized themselves using race as a social category. Knowledge of the stereotypes associated with this social category served to constrain the true ability or beliefs of these students. Their test results were more consistent with the racial stereotype than with how they actually performed when racial stereotypes were not invoked.

Another series of four experiments showed that women also are susceptible to this predicament (Spencer & Steele, 1994). Women college students performed poorly compared to equally qualified men students on an advanced math test when they were told that gender differences have been shown on the test. The performance of women and men was equivalent when they were told that the test has shown no gender difference in performance. These results suggest that in situations where the stereotype applies, individuals may characterize themselves according to the stereotype. Thus, when the social category is made salient to the individuals that fit the category, they come to believe that the related stereotypes are true of themselves and behave accordingly. Where this social category is not salient, these individuals (e.g., blacks or women) tend to behave in a manner similar to individuals in the social category without the negative stereotypes (e.g., whites or men). Further experiments showed that lower performance is not due to lower self-expectations or motivation. These students are equal in all other measures of ability and aptitudes—just the knowledge that individuals in a category to which they belong perform poorly in general is sufficient to depress their true ability. The vulnerability to self-stereotype occurs relatively easily and its effects are incredibly strong.

A second outcome of self-categorization is a tendency to emphasize the similarities between oneself and other in-group members (those sharing a social category) and the difference between self and out-groupers. This explains why people have a tendency to express more favorable opinions and actions toward members of the "in-group" than toward members of the "out-group." As a result, positive traits of in-group members are exaggerated and negative traits of out-group members are emphasized.

Summary

In summary, demographic factors influence our perceptions and judgments not only of others but of ourselves as well. This is because demographic factors are sources of social information about people and they are made available or salient through the processes of social categorization and stereotyping. Stereotypes are developed over a long period of time in a social–cultural context, and they allow an individual to simplify the socially complex world by compartmentalizing people into categories with distinctive qualities. This is a normal, natural process in which we all engage.

Some stereotypes are positive while others are highly negative. People have a tendency to exaggerate the positive stereotypes of people classified in the same social category as self (in-groups) and to emphasize the negative stereotypes of people classified in a social category different from self (out-groups). Because of this simplifying tendency and the accentuation effect, the information about an individual derived from the categorization process may be highly inaccurate. Yet, our perception and judgment of others are formed almost immediately from our obser-

vation of other individuals. The importance of visible demographic factors in influencing our judgment of people and our relationship to those
who are different from ourselves is far greater than we might wish to
assume to be true.

Figure 4.1 provides a representation of the information function of
demographic factors. It shows that demographic cues influence the initial impression of an individual through the process of social categorization and stereotyping. Based on the demographic cues, individuals
are placed into social categories. Categorization of others occurs with reference to self, and individuals also categorize themselves. Stereotyping
of a target person depends on the category in which the target is placed
and the amount of stereotypic information available to the perceiver
about a target category. Categorization further leads to the accentuation
of differences between the in-group and the out-group. The in-group is
subject to positive stereotypes while the out-group is subject to negative
stereotypes. As a result, based on demographic cues, the initial impression of a target person in the same social category as oneself is likely to
be viewed relatively favorably. A target person in a different social category as oneself is likely to be viewed more unfavorably than the target
person may deserve.

Figure 4.1 The Information Function of Demography

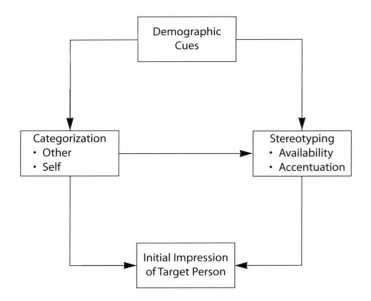

Demography As a Source of Identity for the Individual

The social categorization process described above is important not only for providing information about others (and ourselves!), it is also important because it is closely related to the formation and protection of positive social identities for individuals. According to social psychologists, there are two components to an individual's identity, a personal component derived from the individual's personality, values, and physical or intellectual traits; and a social component derived from the individual's membership in social categories such as sex, race, class, and nationality (Ashforth and Mael, 1989). Brewer and Miller (1984) captured the importance of demography-based social categories in their discussion of social identity, "An individual's personal identity is highly differentiated and based in part on membership in significant social categories, along with the value and emotional significance attached to that membership" (p. 281). Developing and maintaining positive self-identities is a fundamental motivation of human beings. Positive social identity is protected or enhanced through accentuated differentiation. Inter-group differences are exaggerated by the dual process of an emphasis on (1) the positive features of a social category in which one claims a membership, and (2) the negative features of the social category to which one does not belong. In other words, positive social identity is based to a large extent on a comparison between the in-group (e.g., males) and some relevant out-group (e.g., females). Therefore, the social categorization process not only is responsible for stereotyping a target person (other or self), it also is important for preserving an individual's self-esteem. In general, social categories with a positive social status in a particular society will be more useful in enhancing an individual's self-esteem than social categories with a low social status. It is esteem enhancing to be white, male, well educated at a prestigious university, and employed as a high-level manager or professional.

When Out-Groups Are Favored

The above discussion suggests that groups do not universally display in-group favoritism, but under some conditions, out-groups are favored over in-groups. Hinkle and Brown (1990) provided a good discussion of the conditions when out-group favoritism will occur. The important factor involved here is the social status of the group in question. In situations where there are clear status differences between groups, members of the low-status group will find their own group to be less attractive than the high-status group. In other words, they may view the out-group more favorably than the in-group. A number of research studies have confirmed this tendency to engage in out-group favoritism. For example, it has been reported that women preferred men rather than women as supervisors.

An illustration is Liden's (1985) study of female bank tellers. Hinkle and Brown (1990) provided discussions of many such studies conducted in Europe. Other studies have found token males to be treated much more favorably than token females. Both Schreiber (1979) and Fairhurst and Snavely (1983) found token men to be socially well integrated into female work groups. Kanter (1977) and Yount (1991) found token women to frequently be isolated. Favoritism of the out-group with high status does not, however, imply a corresponding increase of the same magnitude of negative evaluation of the in-group with low status. This behavior is understandable, especially when category membership is based on gender, age, race, or national origin. Since these attributes cannot be easily changed, the members are not likely to degrade their own category. To do so would be inconsistent with the basic need to protect or maintain one's social identity, part of which is related to membership in these demographic categories.

Depersonalized Attraction in Psychological Groups

When a social category is a meaningful source for social identity, an individual will have strong social identification with the category. That category becomes a meaningful psychological group, i.e., common identity provides a sense of togetherness among people who may be widely dispersed geographically. In the media today, a psychological group is sometimes referred to as a "community," as in the black community, the business community, or the immigrant community.

An important consequence of group identification is the attraction of members in one's psychological group. This group-based or depersonalized attraction is quite different from interpersonal attraction in that the liking is based on group membership rather than on friendship between the two individuals. There are at least three reasons why depersonalized attraction of other group members occurs. First, this attraction is generated due to the accentuation of similarities among members of the same group. Thus, the target person will be perceived to be more similar to oneself than might be true in reality. Research has firmly established the link between similarity (be it perceived, assumed, or real) and attraction (Bryne, 1971; Bryne, Clore & Smeaton, 1986; Baskett, 1973). Second, attraction also is generated because of the tendency to evaluate the in-group favorably and, by extension, to evaluate favorably all members of that group. Third, attraction is generated because the positive self-evaluation associated with self-categorization is extended to others in the same social category. These ideas are discussed in Hogg and McGarty (1990). For example, a common stereotype of Asians is that they are hard-working. "I am an Asian and you also are an Asian. I am hard working and therefore you are, too. And I like you even though I do not know you personally because I like hard-working people like me. Since we are the same, to not like you is the same as not liking myself."

In total, social attraction among members in a psychological group is high, and this accounts for the high level of social cohesion and group solidarity in homogeneous groups. This attraction is extended even to "strangers" (i.e., those about whom one does not have personal knowledge or with whom one does not have a friendship) as long as they claim membership in the same group. This tendency may explain why members of some ethnic groups (e.g., Jews) engage in extensive helping behavior toward those entirely unrelated to themselves except by a common membership based on the demographic category of ethnicity.

Clearly, a second important function of demographic factors is their influence on the social identity of an individual. (The first important function is the provision of information through social categorization and stereotyping). A positive social identity is derived from membership in social groups that afford a high status to the individual. These groups become meaningful psychological groups. Some group memberships are acquired at birth. If these groups do not command a high status in a social setting, an individual may not evaluate it favorably. However, to protect self-esteem, while individuals may show out-group favoritism, they are not likely to evaluate their own groups too negatively. As a rule, the generally recognized status level of a social category is an important factor in determining when social identity will be enhanced through group membership and when it will not. However, where explicit status difference among certain groups does not exist, there is a tendency to accentuate the positive features of the in-group and the negative features of the out-group. This accentuation of inter-group distinction is important for the enhancement of social identity associated with the group membership. Both self-esteem and group identification will be strong when group membership contributes to a positive social identity. What results is a high level of social attraction among members, and high social cohesion and solidarity in the group. Favorable actions are extended toward members of the in-group. All these may occur among individuals who are otherwise unknown to each other on an interpersonal level. Figure 4.2 shows graphically the role of social identity in explaining the relationship between demographic factors and in-group favoritism through the processes of self-categorization and social attraction. Turner and Associates (1987) is an excellent reference for further reading on the theory related to the self-categorization process.

Social Categorization and Interpersonal Attraction

The social categorization process described above suggests that favorable evaluation and actions are extended to people in the same social category even if there is no real friendship between individuals. However, it is quite

Figure 4.2 The Function of Demography-Based Attraction

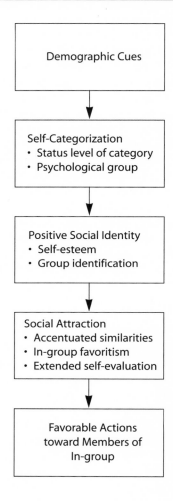

reasonable to expect that the opportunity to develop a friendship will be greater among members of the same social category than among members of different social categories. Commonality on some demographic factors, through the categorization process, not only leads to in-group (depersonalized) attraction but also facilitates interpersonal interaction. People are more likely to interact with people whom they perceive to be similar to themselves (e.g., on some demographic factors) and about whom they have a favorable first impression (through social categorization and stereotyping). Interpersonal interaction enhances further communication and friendship development. The attraction that results is based on personal

Figure 4.3 Demography and Two Types of Attraction

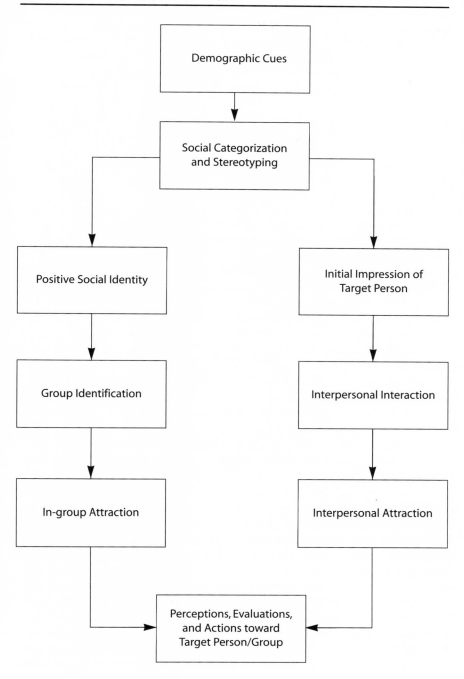

friendship and is qualitatively distinct from the in-group attraction that results from group identification.

In summary, social categorization based on demographic factors not only produces depersonalized in-group attraction but also facilitates interpersonal attraction, and the development of personal friendships through increased interpersonal interaction. Figure 4.3 provides a graphic summary of how demography is related to these two types of attraction.

The Relative Importance of Different Demographic Categories for Social Identity and Social Categorization

Individuals are a composite of demographic factors. Each factor is a potential source of identity. Clearly, not all factors are equally meaningful or important for an individual, and the same factor may not be equally meaningful for all individuals. For some people, religion is a major part of their self-identity, for others, it is ethnicity or occupation. Those demographic factors that are central or core to the individual's self-identity are considered as primary categories and those that are less central or less important (i.e., peripheral) to the individual are considered as secondary categories.

We can expect that the primary categories are especially likely to be used in self- and other-categorization. In the applicant/recruiter example discussed earlier, the Asian recruiter is more likely to categorize the applicant as an Asian first and as a Harvard graduate or an older person second. In other words, an individual will express more in-group favoritism toward those individuals cbelonging the social category that is core to the individual's self-identity. Thus, knowing the core (social) identities of an individual, it is possible to predict the group to which this individual is likely to be favorably predisposed. An extreme example of a demographic factor serving as a source of core identity is the group of self-declared white Extremists. Race is clearly the major demographic factor these individuals use to categorize themselves and others. Indeed, it is often difficult for people to understand the strength and depth of meaning of social categories salient to others but not to self. Americans who categorize Protestants and Catholics as Christians will have a difficult time understanding the continuing conflict in Northern Ireland; Americans who identified a region of Central Europe as Yugoslavia will have a difficult time understanding the conflict, genocide, and mayhem that has characterized that region in recent years. And at a much more local level, workers who refer to the management as "the suits" may have a difficult time understanding conflicts between two business units.

A primary demographic category (on which is based an individual's core identity) will not necessarily be used to categorize another individual if that individual is not distinct on that factor. If that other individual is distinct on a different demographic factor, that factor may be used for social categorization, even if it is only secondary to the perceiver's self-identity. To return to the example of the Asian recruiter given at the beginning of the chapter, being Asian might be very salient in a U.S. firm but not at all salient in an Asian firm. In the latter case, some other common social category—such as similarity in age or an MBA from Harvard—will be used for social categorization, even though it is generally secondary to the perceiver's self-identity.

The importance of a social category is determined not only by the individual's own predisposition. Social psychological research has shown that the setting surrounding the individual also influences the salience of a social category. Setting refers to both the demographic profile of other persons in the group and the primary demographic characteristic of the group itself. If either another individual in a group or the group itself is distinctively different from self on a particular demographic dimension, that dimension will become more salient and will be used for social categorization. For example, one study found that a comparison between Russia and America made American subjects' national identity more salient than when a comparison was made between Canada and America (Buss and Portnoy, 1967). Similarly, a demographic group that has high social-cultural distinctiveness (e.g., African-Americans in the United States) may draw attention and an individual with that demographic background may be categorized with this demographic factor due to its social distinctiveness. Along the same vein, the only old individual in a group of young people will stand out if age is used as a category for social categorization by members of that group. The setting also may influence salience of a category for in-group formation. A large number of experimental studies has found that groups created along minimal or near minimal categorization engage in in-group favoritism and out-group degradation (Tajfel, 1982). For example, in one study (Brewer, 1979), group members perceived out-group members as less trustworthy, honest, and cooperative than members of their own group that was created using an arbitrary criterion (e.g., red group versus green group). These studies are quite convincing in showing that it is possible to create a strong group identity to dominate inter-group behavior and relationships.

Summary

In summary, demography is both a source of information and a base for self-identity. Information resides in the stereotype associated with a social category. The social category is self-identity enhancing through the process of accentuation of positive features of the "in-group" and negative features of the "out-group." The relative importance of a demographic factor as a basis for social categorization (of both self and others) depends on both the importance of that factor to an individual's self-identity and the distinctiveness of the other person or group on that factor. Turner and Associates (1987, Chapter 6) contains a good discussion of the conditions in which different social categories are more or less important for social categorization. Research in social identity theory also shows that group identity, and the accompanying tendency toward in-group bias, could be created relatively easily through the formation of groups based on minimal categorization (e.g., height, hair color). These findings suggest two things: first social categorization is ubiquitous, and second, group identity can be created through deliberate categorization.

Finally, it is important to remind ourselves that the emphasis on demographic factors in analyzing interpersonal and inter-group relationships within the organization is not intended to imply that they are the only factors important for organizational outcomes. Rather, the purpose here is to increase our understanding of how demographic differences can affect individuals and groups in the organizational context. On the basis of the theoretical perspectives presented in this chapter and supporting empirical evidence to be presented in the following chapters, we believe that the grand social experiment in equal opportunity in the American workplace is long overdue.

Chapter 5

Understanding Vertical and Horizontal Pairs from a Demographic Point of View

According to both the social identity and the self-categorization theories (described in Chapter 4) and the relational demography point of view (described in Chapter 2), the fundamental unit of analysis is the dyad. A dyad consists of two people who each occupy some formal role or position and interact in the course of enacting their roles. In organizations, the two people can form a vertical dyad (i.e., when one is a supervisor and the other a subordinate) or they can form a horizontal dyad (when they are peers). Another dyad, increasingly important in the burgeoning service economy, is the customer–provider pair. A service provider–customer dyad does not fall neatly into either a vertical or a horizontal dyad because in some circumstances the customer is "king," in others the provider may have higher status, and in yet others, the two are more like peers. Thus, these dyads will be considered separately.

The two members of a dyad can be the same on some social category or different. They can be the same sex or different sexes, hold the same occupation or different occupation, be at the same level in the organizational hierarchy or at different levels. Thus, in examining the effects of demographic diversity on dyads, similarity and difference are the focus. Are there more positive outcomes when dyads are similar rather than different?

This chapter is divided into three sections: vertical dyads, horizontal dyads, and provider–customer dyads. It is divided this way because we expect to see different outcomes of similarity and difference in these three areas. Vertical dyads are by definition different in at least one attribute: hierarchical level. Simply by virtue of that difference, it may follow that other differences are desirable or expected that would not

61

apply to horizontal dyads. Provider–customer dyads also typically differ in that the provider often has some expertise, service, or goods that the customer does not. We begin our analysis with vertical dyads. We also wish to point out that because we are focusing on the influence of demographic diversity in dyads we are ignoring many other factors that influence dyads. This is not because other factors are unimportant, but because our goal is to understand the effects of demography on dyads.

The Nature of Demographic Differences in Vertical Dyads

An employee's relationship with his or her immediate supervisor is probably the most important relationship that employee has at work. Often, the supervisor represents the organization to an employee. The supervisor not only offers the employee an opportunity to do a job, he or she determines the quality of the employee's life at work. An employee may stagnate under one supervisor and be perceived as a mediocre employee, but blossom under another to become a productive contributor. Conversely, the supervisor is dependent on the employee for contribution to the productive activities of the work unit. The high level of interdependence between the two members of this vertical dyad suggests that this relationship is of paramount importance to the supervisor as well as to the subordinate. Given this, it is not surprising that supervisors spend more of their work time interacting with subordinates than with any other groups, including their own supervisors, peers, or customers (Mintzberg, 1973).

Inherent in supervisor–subordinate relationships is the fact that each supervisor typically has a number of subordinates whereas each of those subordinates usually reports to a single supervisor. This leads to a difference in attention directed toward the other. Supervisors are likely to attend to subordinates less than subordinates are to supervisors for at least three reasons (Fiske, 1993). First, as just mentioned, each subordinate attends to one direct supervisor whereas each supervisor has a number of subordinates to whom he or she must attend. Second, supervisors often control outcomes valued by subordinates—like pay increases, promotions, favorable work assignments, interesting tasks, opportunity for training. It makes sense to attend to the person controlling valued outcomes whereas it is not as important to attend to those who do not, especially when there are so many of them (i.e., subordinates). Third, Fiske (1993) found that some people in supervisory positions are particularly sensitive to power issues, which tends to focus their attention on those higher in the hierarchy, not those lower like their subordinates.

Not surprisingly, research has shown that there is wide variation in the quality of the relationship between the supervisor and each of his or her subordinates (Graen & Cashman, 1975). In other words, a supervisor may have a good relationship with one subordinate but a poor one with another. He or she may find that one subordinate provides more dependable and higher quality performance than another. He or she also may provide more consideration and support to one subordinate than to another. A number of factors contribute to the development of this differential quality of the supervisor–subordinate relationship. In this chapter, we focus on the function of demographic differences or similarities between the two members of this vertical dyad. We will argue that these factors probably play a more important role than we realize or are willing to admit. Further, we will demonstrate that demographic factors continue to influence the quality of the supervisor–subordinate relationship. This occurs because other factors such as interpersonal communication and interaction serve to reinforce initial impressions rather than modify them.

Initial Impressions Form Quickly

As the supervisor and the subordinate first begin working with each other, each has expectations about the other. The subordinate probably has expectations about the type of work the supervisor will assign, the types of contribution the supervisor expects him or her to make, how well she or he will be treated by the supervisor, and the types of rewards the supervisor will provide. Similarly, the supervisor is likely to have expectations about the quality of work the employee performs, how dependable or reliable the employee is in general, and the types of rewards the subordinate seems to value. Many of these mutual expectations are discussed explicitly in the employment interview or during the first few days at work. It is likely, however, that some expectations may remain unspoken because neither thought of them, one or both members of the dyad were reluctant to mention them, or one or both members held unconscious biases. For example, a supervisor may stereotype non-native-born Asians as having poor communication skills. While a particular Asian employee might have demonstrated fluency in English during the job interview, the supervisor might still retain an element of doubt about the new employee's ability to relate to customers or make sales presentations. Such expectations occur because the new employee has been categorized as an Asian rather than evaluated as a unique individual. Similarly, a new employee who is skeptical of any woman's ability to negotiate resources or influence decisions in an organization dominated by males may begin the job with a lack of confidence in a female supervisor. In this case, the subordinate's judgment of the female supervisor is influenced by her gender, or categorization based on gender.

Initial expectations based on social category influence future information processing about and evaluation of the other. In other words, subsequent information search, evaluation, and integration are often used to confirm rather than disconfirm initial impressions or expectations. Unless a person is motivated to pay attention to stereotype-disconfirming evidence when it is presented to them, they are likely to rely on category-based impressions (Fiske, 1987). The entire process can become a cycle of self-fulfilling prophecy, perpetuating the initial impression formed (Hogan, 1987; Sutton & Woodman, 1989). The fact that initial impressions tend to be reinforced explains in part why it is so difficult to change stereotypes. Interactions with dissimilar others do not necessarily lead to new knowledge because people seek out and attend to information that is consistent with prior beliefs rather than attend to stereotype-disconfirming evidence.

What Determines Initial Impressions in Dyads?

How are the initial expectations formed? According to the social categorization process described in Chapter 4, initial expectations are influenced by stereotypes associated with the social categories that describe the other member of the dyad. If the subordinate is perceived as belonging to the same social category as the supervisor, the evaluation and expectations of the subordinate are likely to be positive and favorable, other things being equal. Conversely, if a subordinate belongs to a different social category, the subordinate is likely to be evaluated less positively or favorably by the supervisor. Similarly, supervisors belonging to the same social category as the subordinate will, other things being equal, be found to be relatively attractive to subordinates, and more attractive than supervisors belonging to a different social category. Presumably, similarity on demographic factors leads to an inference or assumption of similarity in beliefs, values, and attitudes and perhaps knowledge, skills, and abilities as well. The presumption of knowledge of the other's abilities and attitudes leads to a sense of predictability, comfort, and confidence regarding the other's behavior in the future. These beliefs foster relationships of trust and reciprocity. The supervisor who is similar to the subordinate will, other things being equal, have a higher level of confidence in the subordinate and may well provide more support to that person than to other, dissimilar subordinates. The subordinate will likely have a higher level of trust in the supervisor and perceive a higher level of trust from the supervisor, motivating the employee to provide a high level of performance on the job. Employees typically do not want to disappoint a supervisor who has confidence in them. These outcomes further solidify the quality of the relationship between the two members of the vertical dyad.

Both Similarities and Differences Matter

The supervisor and the subordinate can vary on a number of demographic attributes. We have just reviewed the process, consistent with the social categorization theory, by which similarity contributes to in-group bias, and by extension, more trust, support, and favorable evaluations for similar others. On other attributes, however, differences may be desired. Sociologists have suggested that in most societies, both roles and status may be attached to age, education, or gender categories (Linton, 1940 and 1942; Parsons, 1942). Certain tasks or privileges may be reserved for those who have reached a certain age, or are one gender or the other, or have received special training. Researchers also have proposed that there are norms regarding when an individual ought to attain a certain status level. There are norms, for example, about the appropriate age at which to reach the executive level in a firm. The Young Presidents' Club is reserved for those who achieve a high rank earlier than the norm would suggest. Once a person reaches a certain age, he or she may be perceived as too old to become an executive.

People who advance faster or slower than the norm are viewed more negatively than people who advance according to the norm (Lawrence, 1988). The notion that there are norms about age and attainment is consistent with the categorical demography idea described in Chapter 2: Supervisors ought to be older. However, the relational demography idea (also described in Chapter 2) suggests that there are also norms about the age of the supervisor in relation to the age of the subordinate. In other words, the supervisor should be older than the subordinate. When the supervisor is older than the subordinate, it implies that the supervisor has, relative to that of the subordinate, more work experience, better skills, and greater knowledge of the work and of the organization. Older age implies greater capacity to lead in general. Capacity to lead also may be inferred from attributes such as educational level (suggesting skills and expertise), organization tenure (suggesting knowledge of and connections in the organization), or job tenure (suggesting knowledge about the nature of the work to be performed in the unit and in the job held by the subordinate). According to this line of reasoning, it is the relative differences along these demographic factors, rather than similarities, that may contribute to a positive relationship between the supervisor and the subordinate. The older supervisor, though a member of the out-group based on social categorization on the basis of age, relative to that of the subordinate, would, other things being equal, be viewed more favorably than a younger supervisor. In other words, the supervisor satisfies the "normative fit" criterion according to the social identity theory (Turner & Associates, 1987). Therefore, difference attracts. This is a prediction consistent with social identity theory.

Difference, per se, is not always desirable, but must be in the direction consistent with norms. A 50-year-old supervisor with a 60-year-old subordinate is not consistent with the relational norm. By having a younger supervisor, it implies that the older subordinate is less capable and/or has for some reason been passed by. This presents a delicate situation for both the younger supervisor and the older subordinate. Similarly, if male leadership is the norm, it may appear that the men were judged to be poor super-visory material if they were "passed over" for a woman. And like the situation of the young manager supervising an older subordinate, a woman manager supervising men may encounter resistance from some of the men and may need to be especially sensitive to her subordinates' concerns.

Demographic differences in the vertical dyad that are incongruent with the normative fit criterion may be interpreted in one or more of the following ways. The "older" subordinate may be perceived as "slow" in terms of advancement and development or as lacking new business knowledge. The "younger" supervisor may be perceived as an exceptional individual. The "older" or "better-educated" subordinate may perceive the "younger" or "less-educated" supervisor as having attained a position that he or she does not deserve, or that he or she does not have the level of wisdom, training, experience, or knowledge necessary to be a leader. Each of these interpretations will influence how the subordinate will behave toward the supervisor, or vice versa. The older subordinate may be predisposed to be less cooperative and supportive of the younger supervisor. The younger supervisor may be predisposed to negatively evaluate the older subordinate. In other words, both members can contribute to a poor-quality relationship.

When the supervisor is a woman, and if she also is young relative to the subordinate, she may be viewed by the subordinate as an "Affirmative Action promotion." She may be viewed as someone undeserving of the position, promoted to make the company "look good" by having a positive record on diversity. If the new supervisor is the "first woman" or the "youngest African-American" to attain a particular level or position in the organization, this puts extra pressure on the nontraditional supervisor to prove she or he really deserves the position (see Kanter, 1977; Steele, 1997). This special attention and an attribution of incompetence on the part of subordinates associated with a counter-normative difference or differences between supervisor and subordinate can severely strain their relationship (see, for example, Heilman, Block & Lucas, 1992), making it difficult for both parties to enjoy a good relationship.

In summary, in a vertical dyad, similarity on some demographic attributes along with differences consistent with normative fit on other demographic factors may contribute to a high-quality relationship between the supervisor and the subordinate. Below we present research evidence on the effects of some of these demographic factors in the vertical dyad.

Implications of Relational Demography in the Vertical Dyad: Research Findings

One of the major findings from the research on the vertical dyad is that the quality of the relationship is determined very early. In some laboratory studies, the supervisors decided on their favored subordinates within the first ten minutes of their interaction with the subordinate. Dockery and Steiner (1990) provided a good summary of these research studies. Other studies have found that as early as the second week, supervisors categorized some newly hired employees as low performers. In other words, these employees were perceived (or stereotyped?) as poor performers from the very start (Graen, Orris & Johnson, 1973). Research has further found that the quality of the supervisor–subordinate relationship, once determined as either good or poor, tends to persist long after the initial stage. For example, one study reviewed the relationship between 166 newly hired employees and their supervisors (Liden, Wayne & Stilwell, 1993). The study found that leader perceptions during the first week were generally consistent with the relationship assessed six months later. Similar findings were obtained in another study of 192 hospital employees (Vecchio, Griffeth & Hom, 1986). In a study conducted in Japan over a 13-year period, many managers who succeeded in their career were identified early in their career as having a high-quality relationship with their supervisors and were given preferential attention (Wakabayashi, Graen & Uhl-Bien, 1990).

Accumulated research evidence is quite convincing that subordinates are categorized as in-group or out-group members very early in the relationship by the supervisor and that subordinates engage in a similar process with respect to their supervisors. At this time, early in the relationship, not much informational or behavioral exchange has occurred between the two members. These findings support the argument presented in Chapter 4 that the physical and visible personal and background characteristics of the two members in the dyad can play a critical role in the formation of initial impressions. Further, the quality of the relationship is maintained over time, supporting the argument that initial impressions have lasting effects.

Taken together, the available studies suggest that the vertical dyad's initial impressions of each other may be influenced by demographic factors. Several studies have analyzed the relevance of specific demographic attributes in the relationship between members of the vertical dyad. We will first present research findings on the effects of demographic similarities in the dyad that are consistent with the similarity-attraction process and then summarize research findings on the effects of demographic differences that are consistent with dissimilarity-attraction process, i.e., the "normative fit" idea, as described in the section above.

Similarity-Attraction Effects.

Research studies have found that supervisors tend to favor same-gender subordinates. For example, one study involving 272 supervisor–subordinate dyads in a Fortune 500 corporation (Tsui & O'Reilly, 1989) found that, in dyads of the same gender, the supervisor expressed more liking toward the subordinate and rated the subordinate higher in overall performance than supervisors whose gender differed from their subordinates. In the same study, the subordinates in the mixed-gender dyads also reported a higher level of role ambiguity and role conflict. This may be due to a lower level of interaction and communication between the two members who differ in gender. Another study found that, in fact, female supervisors communicate with female subordinates somewhat differently than they do with male subordinates (Fairhurst, 1993).

Similarity-attraction is not limited to gender only. Other demographic factors also matter. Using a sample of 81 registered nurses and their supervisors in the nursing services department of a Midwest hospital, the study reported that supervisors expressed a high level of liking for subordinates when the latter were similar to the supervisors on age and job tenure (Judge & Ferris, 1993). The effect of similarity in job tenure also was found in the study of 272 dyads mentioned above. Subordinates who were similar to their supervisors in job tenure were liked better, received higher overall performance ratings, and expressed a lower degree of role ambiguity. Furthermore, similarity in educational level led to slightly higher supervisory affect toward the subordinate and lower job ambiguity by the subordinate.

Similarity in gender or in race affects performance ratings as well, especially in terms of the subordinates' voluntary actions to help the organization (citizenship behavior). This finding was reported in a study of 394 vertical dyads in ten companies (Tsui, Egan & Porter, 1994). The effect of similarity in age was particularly strong in this study. When subordinates were similar to their supervisor in age, compared to those who were different, they were rated higher on performance on basic tasks as well as various forms of citizenship behavior.

In total, research evidence thus far suggests that, other things being equal, similarity along the demographic attributes of gender, race, age, educational level, and job tenure is associated with favorable perceptions and evaluation of the subordinate by the supervisor. The effect of race similarity is generally weaker than similarity on these other demographic attributes. The lower level of role ambiguity and role conflict reported by the subordinates in the similar dyads, relative to the dissimilar dyads, suggests that similarity may be associated with more interaction and communication between dyad members. Table 5.1 summarizes the research findings that are currently available on the outcomes associated with similarity in the vertical dyad on a variety of demographic factors.

Table 5.1 Outcomes Influenced by Demographic Similarity in the Vertical Dyad

Similarity on		Outcomes
Age, Gender, Job Tenure, Educational Level	⇨	High supervisory liking toward subordinate
Age, Gender, Race, Job Tenure	⇨	High overall performance rating of subordinate by supervisor
Age, Gender, Race	⇨	High ratings on subordinate's organizational citizenship behavior by supervisor
Gender, Job Tenure, Educational Level	⇨	Low role ambiguity by subordinate
Gender	⇨	Low role conflict by subordinate

Dissimilarity-Attraction Effects.

There are fewer research studies on the effect of the attraction associated with demographic dissimilarity, i.e., showing that people like and evaluate positively those who are dissimilar. This is because most of the research on organizational demography has focused on similarity and has assumed that differences will yield only negative results. Some clues to the dissimilarity-attraction effect are found in Tsui and O'Reilly (1989). In that study, subordinates with less education or less job tenure than their supervisors were liked better by the supervisors than subordinates with more education or more job tenure than their supervisors. These findings are highly consistent with the notion of normative fit discussed earlier in this chapter. In addition, black supervisors expressed a higher degree of liking for the white subordinates than for the black subordinates. This finding is supportive of the idea of out-group favoritism discussed in the previous chapter. It is consistent with the self-stereotyping tendency discussed in Chapter 4 as well. Black supervisors (as well as white supervisors) can categorize black subordinates. Stereotypes of blacks can influence their perceptions and evaluation. Lower social status attached to this social category (black) does not contribute to a positive social identity by the supervisors. Therefore, other things being equal, black subordinates were liked less well than the white subordinates, even if the actual behaviors of both black and white subordinates were similar.

The strongest evidence for the dissimilarity-attraction effect is found for age (Tsui, Egan & Porter, 1994). Based on the actual distribution of age and differences in the age between the supervisor and the subordinate, Tsui, Egan, and Porter (1994) created three groups. One group consisted of supervisors who were on the average 16 years older than the subordinates.

These were "older-supervisor" dyads. A second group consisted of supervisors who were about the same age as the subordinates (on the average only four years older). These were the "similar-age" dyads. A third group consisted of supervisors who were about 14 years younger than the subordinates, on the average. These were the "younger-supervisor" dyads. In a mailed survey, the supervisors rated the subordinates on four performance dimensions, basic tasks, and three forms of organizational citizenship behavior: helping the organization, helping others, and self-learning (e.g., attend non-required outside functions to help the organization and research new ideas). The ratings could range from 1 (low) to 7 (high). The average ratings given by supervisors of each of these three groups of dyads are summarized in Table 5.2.

As shown in Table 5.2, subordinates with younger supervisors consistently were rated much lower on all performance dimensions than subordinates in the other two groups. Subordinates with older supervisors were generally rated higher though the differences in ratings between these subordinates and the subordinates with similar-aged supervisors were not statistically significant. These findings support the argument, consistent with the perspective of normative fit, that difference in age in the vertical dyad is desirable. Further analyses showed that subordinates in the 49 or older age category with supervisors younger than 38 years old were rated the lowest among all the subordinates. The difference in age in this group of dyads was most incongruent with the expectations associated with normative fit.

There are a number of reasons why a young supervisor may give an older subordinate lower ratings than an older supervisor may give a younger subordinate. It could be age bias or stereotypes about older people who have not advanced as quickly in the hierarchy. It could be that the older subordinate perceives that the younger supervisor does not deserve the status at such a young age, which makes the older subordinate respond less favorably to requests and assignments, in effect performing

Table 5.2 Average Ratings of Subordinate Performance in Vertical Dyads with Age Differences (from Tsui, Egan & Porter, 1994)

Performance Dimension	Superior Age Relative to Subordinate Age		
	Older (93 dyads)	Similar (197 dyads)	Younger (92 dyads)
Basic tasks	5.45	5.27	4.83
Helping the organization	5.33	5.16	4.83
Helping others	4.95	4.86	4.53
Self-learning	4.43	4.29	3.96

Note: Performance ratings range from 1 (low) to 7 (high). There are a total of 394 dyads from 10 companies.

more poorly than he or she would with an older supervisor. We need further research to provide a better understanding of the social dynamic that is triggered by this difference in age that is inconsistent with normative fit. The current research findings, however, support the basic argument that both similarity and differences on demographic factors influence the quality of the relationship between the supervisor and the subordinate in organizations.

Summary

In general, the research findings reported above consistently show that demographic dissimilarity in a specific direction in the vertical dyad is associated with positive outcomes such as liking between the two members and supervisory perceptions of subordinate performance. The demographic factors that appear to be important are job tenure, educational level, and age. In all cases, the dyadic relationship is more positive when the supervisor has longer job tenure and more education and is older than the subordinate. These preliminary research findings are consistent with normative fit as well as with the idea that the supervisor, by virtue of his or her status, belongs to a different social category than the subordinate. That is, after all, what a "vertical dyad" is; the two people are in different hierarchical categories. Stereotypic expectations associated with the supervisor's social category may, therefore, influence the perceptions of the subordinate. Conversely, stereotypic expectations associated with individuals in the subordinate role may influence the perception of the supervisor as well. People who do not fit these normative expectations are viewed more negatively than those who do. These explanations are quite consistent with the available research results.

Demographic Differences in Horizontal Dyads

Compared to vertical dyads, much less is known about the role of relational demography in horizontal dyads. However, based on the social categorization process described in Chapter 4, we would expect that, in general, due to the equal status of peers, demographic similarity would be more relevant in producing attraction than demographic difference. Categorization could occur along many demographic factors, including age, gender, race, education, functional background, or occupation. The inter-group conflict between different functions (e.g., marketing versus manufacturing) in the organization is well known.

However, the current focus is the horizontal dyad, or two individuals not in a direct reporting relationship. At the interpersonal level, do demographic factors influence the relationship between two individuals who are not in a supervisor–subordinate relationship? and what are the outcomes that might be influenced? Earlier research on similarity-attraction has found that similarity on any number of dimensions can increase interpersonal attraction (Baskett, 1973). One study found similarity in hobbies and interests to predict friendship and attraction (Werner & Parmelee, 1979). Another study found similarity in gender, age, and education to influence friendship ties (Lincoln & Miller, 1979). Similarity in social-economic background also has been found to predict liking (Bryne, Clore & Worchel, 1966).

Similarity in Gender and Race

One recent study of work and friendship networks found gender similarity to be important in the friendship networks for both male and female employees (Ibarra, 1992). The major finding was that both men and women have more friends of their own sex than the other sex. In general, homogeneity in gender appears to be important for providing social support, and research studies have confirmed this importance in the development of friendship ties.

A further finding was that, while men's work networks (referred to as instrumental networks in the study) consisted primarily of men, women's instrumental networks tend to have more men than women. Given that more men than women occupy high-level positions in organizations, women generally cannot have networks of high-status people without some men but men often can have high-status networks without any women.

Most of the organizational research on similarities in dyads has studied mentoring relationships. Several studies, while not studying demography explicitly, have, nevertheless, examined protégé outcomes for same-sex and cross-sex or same-race and different-race dyads. In a study of mentor–protégé relationships among health care professionals (Koberg, Boss & Goodman, 1998), those protégés with same-sex mentors reported more psychosocial mentoring (i.e., social support) relative to those with other-sex mentors (means of 4.34 and 3.86 on a five-point scale). Ragins and McFarlin (1990) found that cross-sex mentor–protégé dyads spent less time in after-work social activities than same-sex mentor-protégé dyads. In addition, protégés with same-sex mentors, especially women, were more likely than other protégés to view their mentor as a role model.

There is some evidence that similarity in race is important for the provision of social support to individuals as well. One study on mentoring reported that African-American protégés with same-race mentors were more satisfied with their career advancement than African-American protégés with white mentors (Murray, 1982). Race may be a positive source of social identification in same-race mentoring relationships, an explanation consistent with the social identity theory described earlier. Another study of mentoring involving over 300 mentoring relationships reported that protégés in cross-race relationships indicated that they received much less psychosocial support from their mentors than protégés in same-race relationships (Thomas, 1990). Yet another study (Koberg et al.) found that psychosocial mentoring was higher in same-race than in cross-race dyads (means of 4.38 and 2.94 on a five-point scale). Since mentoring usually involves two people not directly related in a direct reporting relationship, the research findings from these peer relationships are quite consistent with the race-based similarity-attraction process.

In a study that directly tested the similarity-attraction hypothesis in horizontal dyads, Tsui and Ashford (1991) also found race to be an important factor for interpersonal communication of a specific sort. This study involved over 1,000 pairs of peers who worked in the same company. One of the hypotheses was that demographic similarity would lead to a higher tendency to seek feedback from peers on one's performance on the job. This is because of the greater degree of liking, comfort, trust, and confidence in peers who are similar to self on a variety of demographic factors. Individuals were especially less likely to seek information that was negative about one's job performance from peers who were different from them in race. In other words, they sought feedback about how they could improve more often from peers who were similar in race than from peers who were different. The results indicate that non-white managers reported seeking negative feedback more often from peers who were also non-white than from peers who were white. This finding, along with the finding from the mentoring studies, supports the importance of similarity in race for the development of supportive relationships and friendship among horizontal dyads.

Research evidence supports the importance of gender and race similarity for interpersonal attraction and friendship in horizontal dyads. Gender similarity may also increase the probability that the mentor will be viewed as a role model by the protégé. Some earlier studies suggest the relevance of age similarity as well. The importance of age and company tenure for group cohesion is well established, as will be described and discussed in the chapter to follow. However, more research is needed on examining the influence of demographic similarity and difference on a variety of outcomes in the horizontal dyad, including outcomes such as friendship, helping behavior, communication, and cooperation.

Provider–Customer Dyads

For service organizations, the effectiveness and performance of the service provider and customer dyad is very important. There is a burgeoning research literature on service interactions and service providers, and some of this research focuses on both the service provider and the customer (see, for example, Leidner, 1993; Rollins, 1985; Schneider & Bowen, 1985; Schneider et al., 1980). The extent to which customer-provider similarity and difference affects provider performance, customer satisfaction, sales, return business, and the like is an interesting issue which so far has received little attention. There is some anecdotal evidence that companies such as Avon have successfully bolstered their performance by matching the ethnicity of their sales force to their customers. This practice suggests that demographic similarity may be a relevant factor for competitiveness. The general notion that a customer will look at a product or service more favorably when the customer-contact worker shares a salient social category with the customer is consistent with the social identity theory.

One factor that will probably affect the importance of similarity on demographic factors is whether or not the customer interacts with a provider who is a stranger or whether the customer receives service or goods from a regular service provider, i.e., the provider with whom they have a service "relationship" (Gutek, 1995). The customers have a service "encounter" if they transact with someone they have never met before and do not expect to meet again in the future. The interaction is brief as it is for many service encounters (e.g., fast food, bank teller, store clerk, check-out clerk). In this case, demographic similarity may enhance the customer's experience but it may also be less important than the context in which the interaction takes place. For example, an Asian customer who lives in an Asian neighborhood and buys fast food in that neighborhood restaurant may care relatively more about whether the restaurant employs a significant number of Asians overall, and care relatively less about the ethnicity of the person who waits on him.

While customers may not be fussy about who waits on them in one-time encounters, they may be more selective about the provider they choose for long-term service relationships. Customers may feel more comfortable selecting a hairstylist, manicurist, or dentist who is similar in social categories that are important to the customer. On the other hand, once the relationship is established and the customer is satisfied with the work of the provider, the provider's competence and concern about the customer may be more important than similarity on demographic characteristics. Gutek (1995) hypothesized that, in service encounters, both customer and provider would engage in more stereotyping of the other (because neither has a base of experience or any information other than that provided by visible social categories) than customer and provider in relationships. Much of this stereotyping will be based on social categories because of a lack of experience with or knowledge of the person. Thus, although not minding if the provider is a different race, ethnicity, or sex, customers may still stereotype the provider by race or sex or age when they are searching for an explanation for the provider's behavior (e.g., she miscounted my change because women aren't good at math). The same is true of providers in encounters; while expected to wait on all customers, in the absence of information about their customers, they may engage in category-based attributions (e.g., customers who are senior citizens always take "forever" because they don't have anything to do).

Service relationships provide more opportunity for differential treatment than encounters. A female patient can usually select a female physician over a male physician if she wants to and a white physician can fairly easily claim to be too busy to take on new patients if he or she does not want a Hispanic patient. But it would be very difficult indeed for a McDonald's counter worker or an emergency room physician to reject a patron who was a different race, age, or sex. Each is expected to provide service to the next customer (or patient) waiting in line. Similarly, a customer who might want a physician (with whom he or she intends to interact in the future) of the same race probably would not care if the hamburger server (a stranger with whom he or she will not interact in the future) was a different race. Talking to a dissimilar (say, much younger) stock broker one time at a discount brokerage is not the same as having a regular long-term broker who is much younger and therefore perhaps viewed with less trust. It is also more likely that a provider and customer will develop a friendship when they interact in a service relationship than in a service encounter and that such a relationship is more likely to develop when the dyad is similar on social categories with which they identify. In other words, if the service relationship is a successful one, the customer and provider will probably discover areas of similarity because of their increased interaction and communication (Gutek, 1995). Research focusing explicitly on how gender matching and ethnicity matching influence customer satisfaction is lacking, although some is underway (Kulik & Holbrook, 1998).

Summary

A relationship between two members of a dyad can be influenced by both demographic similarities and differences. The importance of relational demography in the vertical dyad is quite well established. The quality of the relationship in the supervisor–subordinate dyad appears to be determined very early and is relatively resistant to change over time. This relationship appears to be determined, in part, by similarity in age, gender, job tenure, and race, as well as educational level. Subordinates who are similar to their supervisors on these factors seem to enjoy a better relationship than subordinates who differ from their supervisors. The relationship is further complicated by findings that dissimilarity in age may be advantageous if the supervisor is older than the subordinate. Older subordinates are generally perceived to perform, more poorly when they have younger supervisors but not when they have same-age or older-age supervisors.

In horizontal pairs (i.e., two employees not in a direct reporting relationship), friendship and social support seem to be especially likely to occur between individuals similar in gender, race, age, functional background, or company tenure. Mentors who are the same sex may also be more effective role models. At this point, we do not know much at all about the effects of similarity and dissimilarity between service providers and customers.

Note

Much of this chapter is adapted from an earlier paper by Tsui, Xin, and Egan (1995b).

Chapter 6

Understanding Demographic Diversity in Groups

Groups are different from dyads. Relationships arising from similarities and differences are more complex than those in dyads. Fortunately, we know relatively more about the effect of demographic diversity in small groups than in dyads (focus of Chapter 5) or the organization as a whole (focus of Chapter 7). This is because there is by far more research on demographic diversity in small groups. In a long tradition of experimental studies, social psychologists interested in various types of diversity, including race, gender, attitudes, skills, or personalities, use student samples to study group process and performance. Jackson (1992a, 1992b) provided succinct summaries of findings from this stream of research. In this chapter, we shall focus only on research findings involving demographic background rather than personality, interest, attitudes, or skills. Studies of demographic diversity of the types emphasized in this book began only recently. These research studies use natural groups in organizations such as R&D teams (e.g., Ancona & Caldwell, 1992), top management teams (e.g., Bantel & Jackson, 1989; Smith et al., 1994; Hambrick, Cho & Chen, 1996). They also include project teams (Zenger & Lawrence, 1989), work groups (Konrad, Winter & Gutek, 1992; Pelled, 1996; Riordan & Shore, 1995) or "high involvement" teams (Magjuka & Baldwin, 1991).

With the exception of studies that analyzed student teams over the course of an entire academic term, the groups in most of the experimental studies were asked to perform a task for a duration that may range from ten minutes to an hour or so. At best, these groups may be considered temporary task groups. Groups from organizational samples may be appropriately considered relatively permanent work groups. The relevant question here is whether demography would influence group processes and outcomes similarly in both temporary and permanent groups. This chapter will address this question and review the research on the influence of demographic diversity on both temporary and permanent work groups, with a primary focus on permanent organizational groups. Research using student subjects will be reported in the section in order to compare the effects of diversity in permanent and temporary work groups.

Nature of Demographic Diversity in Work Groups

A work group is defined here as comprising three or more individuals whose members engage in regular work-related interactions. (Two-member groups are defined as dyads in this book.) Here, the dynamic of demographic diversity extends beyond the dyadic level. It is the composition of the entire work group on some demographic attributes that are of interest. As described in Chapter 1, the composition along demographic lines is rapidly changing in the U.S. workforce.

First, a large percentage of women are now in the labor force. As was shown in the first chapter, women were 46.1% of the labor force in 1995 and by the year 2000, some observers expect that the labor force will be almost completely gender-balanced (Johnston & Packer, 1987). Further, gender-based occupational segregation is declining as well. For example, as of 1995, women held 42.7% of the administrative and managerial jobs (*Statistical Abstract of the United States, 1996*, Table 637, p. 405). Women are beginning to appear in top management teams and on corporate boards. Racial and ethnic minorities, too, have increased their proportion of managers. The proportion of managers and administrators that was black increased from 4.7% in 1983 to 7.2% in 1995, and the proportion Hispanic increased from 2.8% in 1983 to 4.8% in 1995 (*Statistical Abstract of the United States, 1996*, Table 637, p. 405). In the next decades, it is also projected that there will be a steady increase in the number of non-white racial/ethnic groups and white or non-white immigrants entering the U.S. workforce. The workforce will continue to increase in diversity in terms of ethnicity and national origin as a result of these trends. Diversity in ethnicity and nationality also is influenced by the increasing globalization of businesses. Transnational teams for project design, operations, and marketing will most likely become more prevalent in the near future (Kanter, 1991).

Another variable worthy of study is age. Some employers are hiring people of very different age groups to do the same job. For example, it is now more common to see college students, middle-aged women (mostly mothers working part time), and retirees working side by side in McDonald's than it was years ago. Also, with the rapid change in the technology of production and doing business in many fields, employers are substituting higher education (mostly younger employees) for job experience (possessed by older workers). As a result, more young individuals (elite MBA grads especially) are hired into higher level jobs that previously were accessible only to people with many years of actual work experience. The net effect of these changes is that in some firms age diversity is increasing in many work groups at all levels.

A trend in the managing of contemporary organizations in the context of extremely high competitive pressure is the increasing use of semi-autonomous work teams comprising individuals from different functions and with different skills. Lawler, Mohrman, and Ledford (1992) surveyed the use of such teams in Fortune 1000 companies. The impact of diversity in functional background on these natural teams is largely unknown. Should this trend of managing by teams continue, more and more employees will work in close contact with people who are different from them on a number of demographic dimensions, in addition to functional expertise or specialization.

The composition of the work group can vary along a spectrum of demographic factors such as race, gender, functional background, company tenure, age, ethnicity, national origin, and educational background and level. Any of these factors may be a basis for social categorization by team members, resulting in either group cohesion or the creation of subgroups, leading to inter-group or interpersonal conflict along demographic lines. Take, for example, an academic department in a university. Older and senior faculty members tend to coalesce, and some conflict between them and the junior colleagues is quite common. The business school provides a more vivid illustration. Faculty in finance and economics commonly engage in explicit conflict with the management or marketing faculty who come from behavioral disciplines such as psychology or sociology. The conflict in this case is not at the interpersonal level but is based on the areas of expertise, which serve as a basis for social categorization and social identity by members of both sides. Inter-group conflict is understandable, almost inevitable.

The demographic diversity of the group can range from entirely homogeneous to highly heterogeneous. Chapter 3 describes a number of measures used to capture the relative degree of diversity or heterogeneity on one or more demographic attributes. For example, on attributes that involve only two levels or categories (e.g., gender), the highest degree of heterogeneity is 50% of each category. On attributes measured by continuous scales (e.g., age or company tenure), heterogeneity is measured by a variety of indices, the most common of which is the coefficient of variation (a measure of the spread of the distribution, adjusted by the average for that distribution). The actual metric is the standard deviation of the attribute among group members divided by the group mean on that attribute (see Chapter 3 for a detailed discussion of these measures). Most of the earlier research on diversity, as presented by the studies on tokenism, focused on the effect of diversity on the numerical minority. However, the compositional approach emphasized in the more recent demography research focused on the influence of demographic diversity on the entire group and all the members of the group, regardless of their numerical status. In other words, the numerical majority may be influenced by different degrees of demographic diversity as much as the numerical minority. Diversity potentially affects everyone.

In the next section, we shall summarize the research studies that provide some knowledge about the way demographic diversity influences the internal processes and work performance of relatively permanent work groups in organizations. Most of the research was conducted in organizations with groups at various levels and performing varying functions.

Implications of Demographic Diversity for Relatively Permanent Organizational Groups: Research Findings

The most frequently studied work group in organizational demography research is the top management team. Most of these teams were drawn from Fortune 500 companies. Several studies used operating work groups or departments where members are likely to engage in interactions. A third type of group studied is the new project team where members work collaboratively in the creation of new ideas, processes, or products. Since these three types of groups differ in terms of their tasks and scope of responsibility, we shall discuss the research findings on the influence of demography in each type of group separately.

Top Management Teams

Few organizations are run by a single person at the top. Instead, it is a team of top managers who are responsible for making critical decisions facing the firm. Hambrick and Mason (1984) wrote the first major article arguing that the composition of the top team can greatly influence firm outcomes. These teams define the mission and strategies of the entire organization (as well as for separate business units in multi-divisional firms). Jackson (1992a) provided an interesting theoretical discussion of group composition and the interpersonal dynamics of strategic issue processing by top management teams. These teams seek novel solutions to issues and the issues often involve many equally viable or effective solutions. These teams engage in creative thinking and judgmental decision making. The ambiguous nature of the tasks that they tackle makes it difficult to know which of the team members has the best solution or most knowledge. Since each decision may have great consequences for the organization, consensus in decision making is often desired so that no one is fully responsible for any one decision.

Given the characteristics of the problems and tasks that this kind of team faces and the potential impact of an error in a strategic choice, there is pressure to form teams in which members feel relatively comfortable with one another and feel they can trust each other. This social dynamic can easily explain the relative homogeneity of most top management teams, including homogeneity on gender and race. Interestingly, of the published studies that analyzed top management teams, not one included the race or the gender of the team members. Diversity on these two attributes at the executive level simply does not exist, or, if it does, there are not sufficient numbers for a meaningful comparison.

Though relatively homogeneous on race or gender, diversity on other demographic dimensions does exist. The demographic attributes that were studied most often are age, company tenure, educational level, functional background, industry experience, and tenure on the team. The outcomes that were analyzed include turnover (of team members) innovation, adaptation, and change; and firm performance.

Turnover.

Using longitudinal data over a five-year period, one study analyzed the turnover of top management team members in 31 Fortune 500 companies (Wagner, Pfeffer & O'Reilly, 1984). It found higher turnover in teams with more variations in company tenure among team members. Further, managers dissimilar in age to other members in the team were more likely to turn over. Turnover was one of the several outcomes examined in another study of 93 top management teams in bank holding companies (Jackson et al., 1991). This study analyzed turnover data over a four-year period. A variety of demographic factors were included, in addition to age and company tenure. The study found team turnover to be significantly related to team heterogeneity in age and experience outside the banking industry (reflecting lack of common work background). Members who were most different from other team members on educational level, college major, and experience outside of the banking industry were most likely to leave.

Turnover was the focus of a third study of 220 executives in 40 Japanese companies (Wiersema & Bird, 1993). Each team averaged 5.6 members. In addition to age and team tenure, the researchers also included a measure that reflected the relative prestige of each team member's alma mater. Coefficient of variation was used to measure heterogeneity on these three demographic factors. Turnover at the individual and team level was measured three years after the measurement of the heterogeneity indices. The findings were consistent with the two previous studies reported above: the more diverse the members' tenure on the team, the higher the number of exits from the team. Further, diversity in university prestige was also associated with turnover. These results were obtained after taking into account factors such as average team age, company performance, and industry.

These three studies together suggest that demographic diversity could cause executives to turn over. Specifically, executives most different from others in the team were more likely to leave the team. The relevant factors appear to be lack of similarity in age, team tenure, industry experience, educational background, and type of universities that the executives attended. All these factors may be meaningful categories for social identification. Team members who are least similar to others on any of these factors are most likely to have low identification with the team and thus are least socially integrated. Thus, they are most likely to leave the team due to the low social integration and low identification.

Innovation, Adaptation and Change.

The types of diversity described in the above section also are sources of different knowledge, information, and perspectives. Therefore, teams with demographic diversity should be more likely to introduce change and have more new ideas. Four studies focused on innovation, organizational change, or adaptation as outcomes of the demographic composition of the top management team.

The first study analyzed the effect of diversity in the functional background of top management teams on the technical and administrative innovation of 199 banks (Bantel and Jackson, 1989). Results indicate that, after considering other factors that may influence innovations (e.g., bank size, team size, average education level of team members), more innovative banks are managed by teams that are diverse with respect to the members' functional areas of expertise.

A second study analyzed diversity in functional background of executive team members and a firm's willingness to adopt new strategies (Wiersema and Bantel, 1992). This study was conducted in 87 Fortune 500 companies. It found firms more likely to undergo changes in corporate strategies when their top management teams were diverse in educational specialization. The educational specializations measured in this study were arts, sciences, engineering, business and economics, law, and so on. It appears that differences in educational disciplines (often related to functional or occupational specialization, which was not measured in this study) represent diversity in information resource and perspectives. This diversity in cognitive perspective facilitates the discovery and adoption of new ideas.

A third study focused on the action response of the top management teams in a sample of 32 major airlines using data over an eight-year period (Hambrick, Cho & Chen, 1996). Their study included diversity in functional background, educational curriculum, and company tenure as the independent variables. A version of the Blau index was used to measure heterogeneity. Several types of action responses were measured, including the propensity to act and to respond to competitors' moves, the magnitude of the actions or responses, and execution speed. Heterogeneous teams were found to have a greater propensity to take actions than the relatively more homogeneous teams. Further, both their actions and their responses were strategic in nature and of substantial magnitude. Strategic actions included making substantive investments in fixed assets, people or structure any making decisions that are of greater scope. While diversity increased action propensity and decision magnitude, diverse teams also were slow in executing their actions and in responding to their competitors' initiatives.

A fourth study focused on the background of the team and the team's strategic planning process (Bantel, 1993). The author found heterogeneity in functional background to be associated with a more formal planning process. The author reasoned that such teams have representation from a broad range of functional viewpoints. This brings a thoroughness and richness to the planning process. Such teams can be more comprehensive in information gathering and are also in a better position to see the big picture. These four studies provided reasonably robust evidence that diversity in functional or educational background and in company tenure could facilitate innovation and strategic change due to the cognitive resources associated with such diversity. Diversity in team tenure, however, seems to slow the process of adaptive change and the speed of executing new ideas. The lack of stability in teams with diverse team tenure has been consistently found to be associated with turnover of team members. This could have contributed to the relative slowness in executing actions and responses.

Firm Performance.

As described in Chapter 3, a number of studies have examined the relationship between top management team characteristics and the firm's financial performance. The general belief is that top managers determine major strategic decisions, and these should influence the firm's financial performance. The research reported in the previous section on innovation and change provided some support for this belief. Diverse teams made decisions of greater magnitude than non-diverse teams. These decisions benefited from a variety of perspectives and cognitive resources associated with demographic diversity. Therefore, diversity may contribute to firm performance through the increased cognitive capacity of the team. However, the extant research has not specifically addressed the mediating role of cognitive capacity or decision quality. There are several studies that examined the direct effect of diversity on firm performance. We describe three such studies that provided confirming evidence on the effect of top management team diversity on firm performance.

The first study used a sample of 84 Fortune 500 companies in two industries, food and oil (Murray, 1989). Data were obtained over 12 years (from 1969 to 1981). Two types of management team composition were obtained. One is a composite of heterogeneity in age, tenure in the company, and tenure in the top team (referred to as temporal heterogeneity in the study). Another is a composite of heterogeneity in occupation and educational background (referred to as occupational heterogeneity in the study). Firm performance was measured as earnings ratio (considered a measure of short-term performance) and stock price ratio (considered a measure of long-term performance). A positive relationship was found between temporal heterogeneity and the firm's long-term performance. A negative relationship was found between occupational heterogeneity and the firm's short-term performance. These findings were obtained for companies in the oil industry but not for companies in the food industry.

These findings suggest that the relationship between top management team demography and firm performance is highly complex. It depends on demographic factors being considered, the performance dimension being evaluated, and the industry in which the firm operates. No simple conclusion can be drawn from this study. It appears, however, that the top team may make a bigger difference in industries where there is a rapid rate of change with unpredictable contingencies. In such industries (as was the case with the oil industry in the period of this study), top management has to manage these critical contingencies. In the relatively stable industries (as was the case with the food industry in this study), the impact of the top management may be more limited since the firm could operate quite smoothly with established policies and routines. The study by Murray (1989) was useful in showing that the relationship between demography and performance is complex. Also, the negative relationship between the occupational heterogeneity index and short term firm performance is puzzling in light of the positive relationship found between such diversity with innovation and adaptive actions. The study used composite indices on both the diversity and the performance variables. These composite indices may have masked the relationship between each diversity variable and each performance index. Therefore, further studies in dynamic industries using individual diversity and performance indices would be desirable.

The study by Smith et al. (1994) improved upon these areas. It was conducted in 53 high-technology firms in industries undergoing rapid changes. Three team diversity indices were obtained: tenure on the team, years of education, and functional background. Separate analyses were performed on each individual diversity index. This study also measured the processes that may link diversity to firm performance. These processes include social integration among team members, extent of informal communication, and frequency of communication. Firm performance was measured by return on investment (ROI) and sales growth.

The results showed a positive relationship between team diversity on educational level and both ROI and sales growth. Diversity on team tenure, however, has a negative effect on ROI but no effect on sales growth. Further, diverse teams in terms of team tenure and functional background experienced a lower level of social integration than the relatively more homogeneous teams. Social integration, in turn, has a positive effect on both performance measures.

This study provided further information on the complex relationship between team demography and firm performance. Unlike the Murray study described above, in this study we know how each diversity variable is related to each performance index. In this case, diversity in team tenure makes it difficult to develop cohesion. These teams may encounter conflict in decision making that may delay the team's ability to respond quickly to external conditions. Therefore, tenure diversity not only contributes to turnover but also appears to hinder firm performance. Stability in the top management team appears to be important for both cohesion and firm performance.

Diversity in educational level is a positive factor for firm performance, and it has no relationship to cohesion or communication. It appears that these firms have benefited from the diversity of cognitive ability and knowledge among members with different educational qualifications. It is interesting that diversity in functional background has no direct effect on performance in this study, though other studies have found a positive effect on innovation and strategic change.

A third study analyzed the direct effect of diversity in functional background, education, and company tenure on two measures of company performance: changes in market share and growth in profits (Hambrick et al., 1996). Results confirmed the positive relationship between the three measures of diversity and both measures of firm performance. These findings are consistent with some of the findings in the Murray study (1989) for the oil industry where competition was high, as it was for the airline industry during the period under study. This is precisely the condition when top management team heterogeneity is expected to be advantageous (Hambrick & Mason, 1984). Thus, in a highly turbulent setting, diverse top management teams, despite their relative slowness in taking action, have superior competitive and adaptive capabilities, resulting in improved performance. Further, unlike the Murray study (1989), the three types of diversity studied in Hambrick et al. (1996) showed considerable consistency in their effects on the firm's competitive behavior and performance.

In general, there is evidence to support a direct effect of top management team demography on team performance, especially for firms in competitive industries where diversity in knowledge base and perspectives could facilitate high quality decisions. The relevant demographic diversity factors are functional and educational background, and tenure in the company. Diversity could influence firm performance directly but also indirectly through low turnover and high team cohesiveness associated with homogeneity.

Summary.

The demography of top management teams affects three types of outcomes: (a) team member turnover; (b) firm innovation, adaptation, or change; and (c) firm performance. Innovation includes creation of new technical and administrative processes, adoption of new business strategies, introduction of new structures to adapt to external demands, and responses to competitor initiatives. The research findings suggest the importance of five demographic factors: age, team tenure, company tenure, functional background (including educational and occupational specialization), and educational level of the team members. Diversity in age and team tenure lead to a higher turnover among team members but diversity in team tenure also leads to a lower level of adaptive changes and firm performance. Adaptive change, planning formality, and innovation, however, are high in organizations where top management teams are diverse in functional or educational background.

These findings in total suggest that age and tenure in the team may be relevant factors for social categorization and that diversity on these categories leads to lower intra-group cohesion (hence higher turnover). Diversity in functional or educational background may represent cognitive resources that are valuable for new ideas and may offer different perspectives on any given issue. Organizations gain from the improvement in cognitive resources as shown in improved performance. However, cognitive diversity may not always lead to improved performance, perhaps due to the lower group cohesion or greater interpersonal conflict among people who are demographically different. Therefore, ability to manage team process is necessary in order to realize a performance gain. We will discuss these skills in Chapter 10 on strategies to manage demographic diversity.

Operating Work Groups

These groups focus on real production tasks, including the design of products, manufacturing or processing of goods, or delivering of services. In operating work groups, it is usually possible to identify a solution that is better than alternatives. Jackson (1992b) distinguished among three types of tasks that groups perform: production, intellectual, and creative problem-solving tasks. Examples of natural and relatively permanent work groups that have been studied in demography research are academic departments in universities, small convenience stores, administrative units, professional units, and clerical or production teams. Gender and race composition in work units is more commonly studied at the operating level than at the top management level. Age and company tenure are two other factors that have received considerable attention, but here the focus is on the influence of the distribution of such factors on work group processes or outcomes. The outcomes that have been analyzed include turnover, conflict, social cohesion or integration, and performance or effectiveness. Social integration reflects group members' attraction to the group, satisfaction with coworkers, and high social interaction among members.

Social Integration, Conflict, and Turnover.

Using a sample of 20 convenience stores, which had on the average four employees each, one study analyzed heterogeneity in group tenure and several group outcomes (O'Reilly, Caldwell and Barnett, 1989). Tenure diversity was associated with low levels of group cohesion and social integration, which, in turn, was related to turnover of group members five years later. Furthermore, individuals most different from others in tenure were most likely to turn over. Age diversity also influenced turnover, in the same direction as tenure diversity. Turnover was highest in the groups with the most diversity in the age of the members, regardless of the degree of social integration in the group. Evidently, even in groups with a high level of social integration, the members most different from others in age are likely to turn over. This finding is quite consistent with the results of studies on the top management team where age and tenure diversity were usually associated with high turnover of team members. Harrison et al. (1998) did not find a main effect of gender diversity on group cohesiveness but they did find an interaction of gender diversity with time. Gender diversity is negatively associated with group cohesiveness in groups where members had spent a relatively shorter amount of time together. This relationship did not exist for groups where members had spent a longer amount of time together. This finding is in support of the dyad-level research where demographic effects generally occurred early in the relationship. However, in dyads, such effects maintained over time. In groups, other processes appear to neutralize the effect of gender diversity over time.

A second study (Konrad, Winter & Gutek, 1992) analyzed the effects of different-sex compositions on the experiences of isolation, dissatisfaction, and sexism in 89 workgroups in 49 companies (74% services and 26%

manufacturing) in the Southern California area. Being in the minority in the work group (defined as 35% or fewer members of one's sex) was associated with greater social isolation and more sexist stereotyping, but for women only and not for men. In addition, an analysis was performed of sub-samples where women held superior or higher-level job titles to men and where men held superior or higher-level job titles to women. The results showed that, in those work groups where women were not only in the minority but were also in higher-level positions than men, the women reported the most social isolation and sexist stereotyping. There were no significant compositional effects when men held superior positions to women. These findings on social isolation and stereotyping might help explain the fact that, when women who are in non-traditional jobs leave those jobs, they tend to move into female-dominated jobs, rather than into other male-dominated jobs, other things being equal (see Jacobs, 1989). This study, along with that by Harrison et al. (1998), suggests that the effect of gender diversity is quite complex. Context (such as the gender composition of the group or time) may either enhance or neutralize the effect of such diversity on individuals.

Though it is not typical to consider academic departments in universities as work groups, faculty members in an academic department generally have opportunities to interact with each other during faculty meetings or research seminars. Also, it is not uncommon to find that some academic departments have a more collegial climate than others. Diversity in age, gender, race, length of service, and disciplinary backgrounds may affect the overall social cohesion of the unit. The only study in this area suggests the importance of diversity on tenure (or date of entry to the department) for faculty turnover. From two campuses of a large state university, 32 departments were analyzed (McCain, O'Reilly & Pfeffer, 1983). A variety of disciplines were represented by these 32 departments, including anthropology, art, chemistry, economics, geology, mathematics, history, and psychology. The tenure (date of entry) profiles of the department assessed in one year were related to faculty turnover in the following five years. The analyses controlled for departmental size (in that larger departments will have more turnover in absolute numbers) and resources (in that departments with fewer resources might experience more turnover). It was found that departments with the largest number of tenure gaps (suggesting distinct cohorts entering in irregular periods rather than continuous infusion of new members in regular intervals) experienced the highest turnover.

This research finding suggests that a common entry date (a cohort) provides a basis for group identity. Others in the department who entered in different times do not share a common experience or identity and thus are likely to be categorized as out-group members, both by themselves and by others. Inter-group conflict between different distinct cohorts is likely to exist, leading to lower cohesion in the entire department. Higher turnover among members in these departments is not surprising.

Studies have confirmed the intervening process of lower commitment and higher conflict in diverse groups. Riordan and Shore (1995) found commitment to the group to be lower among white employees in the groups dominated by minorities. Pelled (1996) reported in a study of 98 work groups that employees most different from others in the group in terms of gender and tenure reported the highest level of emotional conflict with other members in the group. In a study of 45 work groups in three different companies, Pelled, Eisenhardt, and Xin (1999) found a positive relationship between functional background diversity and task conflict. They also found that diversity in age and company tenure diversity were associated with a high level of emotional conflict. Age diversity, interestingly, was associated with a low level of emotional conflict. Perhaps there is less social competition among peers who are at different career stages, which correlates with age.

These studies in general provide evidence in support of the social identity and social categorization processes. Conflict is higher and cohesion is lower between individuals who do not share similar social categories. However, conflict is not always bad for the team. Pelled et al. (1999) found that task conflict is positively related to performance. Task conflict brings out the different perspectives. These ideas in turn are beneficial to team performance. Several studies explicitly focus on the direct effect of diversity on group performance.

Work Group Performance.

Magjuka and Baldwin (1991) evaluated the effectiveness of 72 high-involvement teams in two organizations. Effectiveness of the teams was measured by subjective assessment by supervisors and the team members themselves. The significant predictors were the extent to which the teams have access to information about their own or other departments, team size, and degree of heterogeneity in the job functions performed by the team members. The job functions were managerial, salaried professional, salaried nonprofessional, and hourly. These functions could also be considered as job levels. The Blau index was used to measure diversity. Diversity reflects the involvement of both professionals and managers in the activities of the team. Perhaps this broad level of involvement facilitated team performance. Both team members and supervisors rated these teams as being more effective than teams without such a broad level of involvement. However, this study is limited in that it does not provide insight on the specific processes that link this particular type of diversity to effectiveness.

Using new project teams, one study (Ancona & Caldwell, 1992) found diversity in team tenure and functional background to be negatively associated with team performance on budget and schedule. Tenure diversity also was associated with performance ratings provided by the team members. Functional background diversity, however, had a positive effect on these performance ratings. Another study using workgroups in a life insurance company (Riordan & Shore, 1995) found ratings of work group productivity to be higher in the groups dominated by whites than in the groups with a higher proportion of non-whites. Members of groups with mostly minorities gave the lowest ratings. This study is interesting in that it does not support the theory (e.g., Bullock, 1976; Giles & Evans, 1986; Longshore, 1982) that outcomes would be most negative in the most diverse groups (groups with equal proportion of all categories rather than being dominated by one group).

It appears that diversity's negative effect may be reversed if there is a constructive group process. An experimental study (Watson, Kumar & Michaelsen, 1993) using student samples provides evidence to support this idea. Even though this study did not utilize actual organizational groups (and therefore was not included in the list reported in Table 3.1), it shows how heterogeneous teams may outperform homogeneous teams over time. Each of the 36 teams had four or five members, and team members remained in the same group for 17 weeks. During this period, group members had frequent opportunity to interact as they engaged in a wide variety of group activities. Two types of groups were created. The ethnically homogeneous groups consisted of white American students. The ethnically heterogeneous groups contained a white American, a black American, a Hispanic American, and a foreign national from a country in Asia, Latin America, Africa, or the Middle East. There were 17 homogeneous groups and 19 ethnically heterogeneous groups. These teams worked on several tasks and each task consisted of completing a structured analysis of a case that described situations prevalent in real companies. Three different instructors graded these case analyses independently (without knowledge of the names of the students on the team). Average of three grades was used as the performance measure of the groups. The team members also rated the interaction process among team members four times throughout the seventeen weeks. After each assessment (of both the interaction process and the performance on the case analysis), the group was provided feedback on their team process and their cases analyses (without revealing the specific grade).

The results of this study are rather intriguing. Initially, homogeneous groups scored higher on both group process and performance than heterogeneous groups. Over time, both types of groups improved on both group process and performance. By week 17, there was no difference in group process or overall performance. However, the heterogeneous groups scored higher on the number of different perspectives and alternatives members brought to bear on the task. In other words, heterogeneous groups seemed to do better in producing more ideas.

This study is particularly important in showing two things. First, demography may affect new groups more than on-going groups. Second, over time, the dysfunctional aspect of diversity can be overcome when (and only when) heterogeneous group members learn to interact with each other. This study has important implications for the management of demographically diverse teams, a topic that will be addressed in detail in Chapter 10. One limitation of this study is that it compared the most homogeneous to the most heterogeneous group along ethnicity lines. In work groups in organizations, there is probably a range of diversity along ethnicity. The extreme type of diversity represented by these student groups is probably unusual today but is, nevertheless, becoming more common in contemporary organizations.

Summary.

To date, the research on the effects of demography on (relatively permanent) operating work groups has focused primarily on social cohesion, turnover, and conflict with some studies focusing on performance. It may be that performance of work groups is often difficult to measure or quantify. Furthermore, it may be difficult if not impossible to derive a common performance measure for groups performing different tasks (e.g., administrative versus technical units). However, where performance can be measured, there is some evidence that both group and individual performance may be negatively affected by diversity on some demographic dimensions, unless the group learns how to manage the negative dynamic associated with diversity.

Most research has focused on demographic factors that influence group identity (e.g., age, tenure, race, or gender) and less on the factors that suggest diversity in cognitive resources (e.g., educational or functional backgrounds). Clearly, there is a great need and a huge opportunity for more research on organizational groups in terms of demographic effects on any number of factors involving many different types of outcomes. With increasing use of various types of self-managing or high-involvement teams (with the goal of improving performance), it is both possible and desirable to conduct more research on understanding how diversity can hinder or facilitate the realization of performance goals by these types of organizational groups.

Project or New Product Development Teams

The tasks of project or new product development teams are qualitatively different from those of the top management teams (determining the business strategies and policies of the entire organization) and those of the operating work groups (implementing new ideas, processes, or policies). These teams must create new ideas about products or processes. How should such teams be formed? Conventional wisdom would suggest that these teams would benefit from members who have different backgrounds and expertise. The unique knowledge or expertise of each member will contribute to new idea generation. Communication among team members is important for sharing of expertise and ideas. Furthermore, because these teams benefit from the latest ideas or developments in an area, communication with outsiders also is desirable. The situation, however, is not that simple. Diversity in functional expertise may in fact lead to less intra-team communication. Communication may also be affected by diversity in age or in company tenure. This section will present the research findings that focused on new product and project teams and how diversity may affect communication and team process and performance.

Communication.

As described in Chapter 4, according to the social categorization process, people tend to interact and communicate with those who are similar to themselves. Using 19 project groups that ranged in size from three to nine members from a research division of a medium-sized U.S. electronic firm, one study directly examined the relationship between age and tenure diversity and technical communication, both inside and outside the project groups (Zenger and Lawrence, 1989). The team members were research and development engineers and engineering managers in the organization. They conducted development work, as opposed to basic research or technical service. Most project groups met informally once a week.

This study focused on the similarity in age or tenure between each engineer and all other engineers on the project team or other employees in the entire organization. A relational demography index (discussed in Chapter 3) was created for each demographic variable. The findings showed that both age and tenure similarity are important for communication. Engineers who were similar in age to others on the project team tended to communicate more with team members than engineers who were less similar. Engineers who were similar in age to others in the company were more likely to communicate outside the project team than engineers who were less similar to others. This finding suggests that these engineers who are similar in age to more people have developed more friendship ties in the company than engineers who are similar in age to fewer other people. These findings suggest that age is a very important variable for self-categorization and friendship formation.

In addition to age, similarity in tenure also contributed to communication. Engineers who are more similar in company tenure to other employees were more likely to engage in communication outside the project teams. This finding suggests that individuals who join an organization at the same time may develop a similar understanding of the organization and may have similar perspectives about the technology involved in accomplishing work. Therefore, being part of a tenure cohort contributed to the development of a group identity. The group identity leads to inter-personal interaction and communication.

Another study using new product teams found that communication also is affected by similarity in functional background (Ancona and Caldwell, 1992). It is probably easier to talk to others who are in the same occupa-tion, function, or discipline than to others who are dissimilar on these attributes. Therefore, it is reasonable to expect that the functional diver-sity of a group may lead to a lower level of intra-group communication and a higher level of inter-group communication. Results from this study of 45 new product teams in five high-technology companies confirmed the relationship between functional diversity of the team and communication outside the team. These teams were responsible for developing a proto-type product and transferring the new idea to manufacturing and mar-keting groups. The average team size was 10, and each team consisted of employees from engineering, research and development, and marketing and manufacturing. Thus a functionally diverse team would be composed of members from all four groups while a functionally homogeneous team would consist of individuals from only one function. The finding was that the greater the functional diversity of the team, the more the team mem-bers communicated with outside groups such as marketing, manufactur-ing, and top management.

This study also found that diversity in company tenure was related to greater frequency of communication with people outside the team. Diversity in company tenure among the members of a team means that each team member may be a member of a cohort outside the team. Therefore, individuals on teams with a diverse distribution on company tenure are more likely to have friends outside the team. On the other hand, team members who have similar company tenure may have formed friendship with teammates who belong to the same tenure cohort. Therefore, intra-team communication is higher and outside team com-munication is lower among these team members.

Task Process, Innovation, and Performance of Project Teams

The group literature and the study by Watson et al. (1993) described in the previous section on operating work groups suggest that a group's task processes are important for group performance. Task processes refer to the group's organizing behavior and approach to getting the work done. Examples of task process behaviors are goal setting, developing work plans, and prioritizing work activities. The study of 45 new product teams by Ancona and Caldwell (1992) also described earlier found team diversity to affect task process, team performance, and innovation. Both functional and tenure diversity were positively related to task processes. Furthermore, the more functionally diverse teams were rated by both managers and the team members themselves as being less innovative and performing less well than the functionally more homogeneous teams.

These findings are somewhat different from those found in the research on top management teams. There, it was found that functional diversity of the top management team led to greater innovation of the firm, though tenure diversity tended to relate to negative outcomes such as low social integration (Smith et al., 1994). It could be the case that identification (i.e., self-categorization) by functional background may be stronger among project team members when they are functional experts. Most top managers have progressed beyond being functional experts. Therefore, functional background serves to provide different ideas and expertise but may not serve as a basis for self-categorization and identity. The negative relationship found between functional diversity of the team and the team's innovativeness or performance is noteworthy. These findings reinforce the idea that the negative dynamic of diversity can make it difficult for teams to benefit from the different cognitive resources and perspectives that diverse individuals bring to the team.

Summary.

In the case of project or new product teams, diversity on demographic factors such as age, company tenure, and functional background may have both positive and negative consequences for the team. Diversity on any of these factors leads to more communication outside of the team. This may lead to the infusion of more new ideas for product design and may facilitate the transfer of completed designs to other groups for implementation. However, diversity also may lead to less intra-team communication, which may hamper the creative process. Functional diversity may be particularly important for product development teams where such diversity may benefit both product design and successful transfer to manufacturing and marketing. Functional diversity may substitute for diversity in company tenure. Since both facilitate communication outside the team, perhaps diversity on one dimension is sufficient. By maintaining some degree of homogeneity on company tenure, intra-team communication may be facilitated. Homogeneity in members' age also may perform a similar function.

To date, there is no research on different combinations of diversity among a number of demographic factors. Team process may be facilitated by different composition of the team. Alternatively, team process also may be facilitated by learning and feedback, as shown by the 17-week-long study of 36 student groups described in the previous section. Table 6.1

summarizes the major findings from this body of demography research. Developing strategies to manage demographic diversity in teams will be discussed in further detail in Chapter 10.

Implications of Demographic Diversity for Temporary Groups: Research Findings

Temporary task groups are defined as those that are formed to perform a specific task or solve a specific problem and are disbanded when the task is completed or the problem is solved. Team members are usually drawn from a variety of organizational departments and levels; hence, in general, these teams may be more heterogeneous in demography (e.g., on functional backgrounds or rank) than permanent work teams. These teams often are referred to as "task forces" in organizations. Even as task forces,

Table 6.1 Major Research Findings on the Impact of Demographic Diversity on Different Types of Groups

Type of Groups	Group's Diversity Dimension	Relation-ship	Outcomes
Top Management Teams	Age Educational level Team tenure	(+)	Turnover
	Functional background Company tenure Team tenure	(+) (−)	Innovation and change Strategic planning Strategic actions
	Company tenure Educational level Functional background	(+) (−)	Firm performance
Operating Work Groups	Age Gender Group tenure Race Functional background	(−) (+)	Social integration Turnover Group cohesiveness Emotional conflict Task conflict
	Race Job level	(−) (+)	Group process Performance
Project/New Product Teams	Age Company tenure Functional background	(−) (+)	Inside team communication Outside team communication
	Team tenure Functional background	(+) (−)	Task process Innovation Performance

Note: (+) or (−) indicates whether the relationship is positive (+) or negative (−). See text for detailed discussion of positive and negative relationship for each dimension and outcome.

the life span of these teams or groups extends beyond a few hours. If it is true that the social categorization process occurs at the moment two or more individuals come into contact, and that impressions formed in the early stage have lasting effects (see Chapters 4 and 5), then the effect of demography on temporary task groups of the type found in organizations may not be too different from the effect found on permanent work groups.

The research in experimental settings using students who perform a task of some duration—usually less than an hour—still may provide some insight into this issue. Also, if the effects found with this type of temporary group are similar to those found using natural groups of a more permanent nature, the effects of demography-based social categorization and stereotyping would be further confirmed.

Research in social psychology has related various forms of group composition to a variety of individual and group outcomes. An excellent review of this research stream was contained in a paper by Jackson (1992b) and was summarized in Table 3.5 in Chapter 3. The composition variables included members' personal attributes (e.g., personality, values, attitudes, and various demographic factors) and members' technical and social skills. Four general types of outcomes were examined: (a) performance on production tasks, (b) performance on cognitive or intellectual tasks, (c) performance on judgmental tasks that require creative solutions, and (d) group cohesion and conflict. In this section, we shall focus on the research findings related to the personal attributes, especially the demographic factors, and their effects on each of the four types of outcomes.

Demographic Effects on Production Tasks

The tasks used in research studies of production tasks usually involved perceptual and motor skills. Hence, they are similar to the work of production or administrative personnel where the technology of performing the work is well known and performance criteria are proficiency and productivity. Objective standards for performance evaluation are generally available. These experimental studies examined the effect of demographic diversity; however, they did not always produce consistent results. The indications from a few studies that focused on gender (e.g., Clement & Schiereck, 1973) and race composition (e.g., Fenelon & Megaree, 1971) found performance to be higher in homogeneous than in heterogeneous groups.

Demographic Effects on Intellectual Tasks

These tasks require problem-solving, and correct answers are generally available. Hence, it is possible to objectively measure the performance of individuals or groups engaging in this type of tasks. Most professional work (e.g., accounting, engineering, or human resources) involves intellectual tasks. Professionals who perform intellectual tasks are sometimes referred to as knowledge workers. Most of the research focused on diversity in task-related abilities and how they affect performance on this type of tasks. These studies usually found performance to be higher in groups with at least one or two members possessing the ability to discover the correct answer. A number of studies (see Wood, 1987) have analyzed gender composition on performance of intellectual tasks. These studies generally found that mixed-sex groups outperform same-sex groups.

Demographic Effects on Creative Tasks

Creative tasks require solving problems with potentially many possible solutions. There is no one correct answer for these problems. The quality of the solution is often a matter of subjective judgment and is an important criterion of performance on these tasks. Creative or novel ideas and consensus about the best solution to a problem are valued. These tasks are characteristic of those performed by top management, or research and development teams. A relatively large number of studies were conducted on the relationship between group composition and creative problem solving. Reviews covering research on this topic (e.g., Hoffman, 1979; McGrath, 1984; Shaw, 1981) concluded that heterogeneous groups are often more creative and reach higher-quality decisions than homogeneous groups. It seems that demographic diversity brings different perspectives to the task. These perspectives become resources for the task. Since breadth of ideas is an important resource for this type of task, heterogeneous perspectives associated with diversity appear to be beneficial. These findings are highly consistent with those found in the research on top management teams, reported earlier in this chapter.

Demographic Effects on Group Cohesion

The most conclusive findings from experimental studies in social psychology are the effects of demographic composition of the group on cohesion and conflict in the group. In general, demographic homogeneity is related to group cohesiveness. A parallel finding is that similarity in attitudes among members of a group is related to the level of cohesiveness in the group. Reviews of this literature by Lott and Lott (1965) and Zander (1979) have consistently shown that attitudes, values, and beliefs were systematically linked to several demographic attributes, including age, sex, educational level, and college curriculum (a precursor to functional background).

Summary

Findings from experimental studies may be summarized as follows:

a. Demographically homogeneous groups tend to perform somewhat better on production tasks than diverse groups.
b. Mixed-gender groups may perform slightly better than same-gender groups on intellectual tasks.
c. Demographically diverse groups consistently perform better than homogeneous groups on creative tasks.
d. Demographically diverse groups consistently experience lower cohesion among group members than homogeneous groups.

It is interesting that diversity affects performance differently depending on the type of task being performed. At the production level (where cognitive diversity may not be critical for performance), diversity appears to have negative effects. This suggests that the lower level of cohesion in the diverse groups may interfere with the group's task performance. Diversity, however, seems to have a positive influence on intellectual and creative tasks. These results are fairly consistent with the findings from demography research on both top management teams and new product or project teams. While such teams experience lower cohesion in the presence of demographic diversity, they are also able to benefit from the cognitive resources that diverse individuals bring to the group.

Summary

This chapter began by suggesting that work groups in contemporary organizations are becoming more diverse on a number of demographic dimensions. The chapter has focused on the implications of such diversity for different types of work groups, ranging from policy making top management teams to temporary task forces that are formed for solving a specific problem. The research on work group demography has found that diversity leads to less social integration in the group, more conflict, higher turnover of group members, greater creativity and innovation, and less communication inside the group but more communication outside the group. There is also some indication from research that through group process learning and feedback, it is possible to reverse the negative impact of diversity and reap its benefits in terms of creativity and performance. However, such process learning and intervention are not yet prevalent in most organizations.

A comparison of the research using natural groups in organizations and student samples in colleges indicates a high level of consistency.

Demographic diversity affects temporary groups and permanent groups similarly. This may be due to the reinforcing properties of the social categorization and stereotyping processes. What group processes can be used to prevent the self-sealing nature of perceptions or arrest the downward spiral of negative perceptions and interactions triggered by diversity? While some preliminary evidence exists on the usefulness of process learning and feedback in diverse teams, much more research is needed to identify and test other structural and process interventions. These ideas are the focus of Chapter 10.

The reality is that organizations will face increasing diversity in the domestic workforce, and increasing use of transnational teams to operate globally. Increasing diversity will make it a greater challenge to lead and to manage. Consider the situation of the following leader in a research and development unit of a high-technology company in California (one of the states known for its labor force heterogeneity).

> I am a minority Asian. . . . I have a very diverse job—as principal investigator on a small R &D ($200k–$300k/yr), run a small project (7 people, $1.19m/yr), pursue new business, mentor, manage a diverse team (10 people, including a number of loan-ins), and provide technical consulting to a number of projects on databases and process re-engineering. The diversity makes it a little hard. . . . I have to have many styles of interaction with people. I grew up in Hawaii and am third generation Asian-American. I have inter-married with an East Indian, am of Okinawan descent (never consider myself as Japanese—we have our own culture, language, history, art, music, traditions). I have strived to give a good balance of heritage to my sons, but worry about the future for people of all colors, even white. By the way— amongst the people who work for me I have a white female, a white male Ph.D., a black male (grooming for promotion), a Filipino female, an American-Chinese female (grooming for promotion), a Taiwanese female (green card), a Vietnamese female, a Hispanic/Japanese male, and a Japanese American female (third generation). I had a white Jewish male—transferred him to a new role; recommended a promotion. My current boss is majority Cherokee (48-year-old female senior systems engineer at an aerospace company in California).

Managers have much to learn about leading such diverse groups. Assuming race or ethnicity is a strong basis for social categorization (of both self and others), this work group is not likely to experience a high level of cohesion and intra-group communication. Member satisfaction with the team may not be high. There is an increased risk of losing the more different people by virtue of their greater difference. There may be, however, a high degree of outside communication. Given that this is a research-oriented team, it may be reasonable to expect a high degree of creativity but possibly also a low level of cohesion within the team. These are speculations based on theory and extrapolations from existing research findings. Clearly, more research on such diverse teams will be invaluable for yielding knowledge and improving practice.

Chapter 7

Understanding Demographic Diversity in Organizations

One defining characteristic of work groups described in Chapter 6 is that members of work groups, especially those in "permanent" work groups, typically know each other. In some of these groups, e.g., top management and new product teams, the interactions are frequent and intense. Not surprisingly, communication within the group and group process are relevant and important outcomes in demographic analyses. Most employees in large organizations do not know or interact with many of the other people who work in their organization.

The focus of this chapter is on the entire organization, including large operating units or installations within an organization. As an entity, the organization or the operating unit may consist of multiple groups and departments. Examples of large operating units are the divisions of multi-divisional firms such as large retail stores or manufacturing plants of an automobile company. Each operating unit or installation may have from several hundred to several thousand employees. For the purpose of the current discussion, each installation may be treated as an independent organizational entity. The difference between large operating units or installations and an independent organization is that the former is part of a parent company. Therefore, a 300-bed hospital of Kaiser Permanente is an operating unit; so is the Nordstrom Store in South-Coast Plaza in Orange County, and Xerox's Palo Alto Research Center.

How are operating units of the sort described here different from work groups discussed in Chapter 6? A major difference is that the effect of demographic diversity on individuals in these large units is through depersonalized in-group attraction based on the formation of psychological groups as part of the social categorization process. The effect of diversity on the work group and members within it described in Chapter 6 is

101

through interpersonal attraction resulting from direct interaction and communication with other group members as well as psychological identification with the group.

This chapter will describe the nature of demographic diversity in the entire organization, treating the large operating unit as an independent entity in most of the discussion. The implications of organizational-level demography for individuals and groups within the organization will be drawn from demography studies using these large units or the total organization as samples.

Nature of Demographic Diversity in Organizations

One important demographic issue for the organization as a whole is the composition of the total entity comprising many individuals not known to each other on a personal level. This includes the demographic profiles of other groups or units within the organization. The organization could range from highly homogeneous to highly heterogeneous on any given demographic dimension. It could be heterogeneous on one demographic attribute such as age but highly homogeneous on another dimension such as gender or function, or it could be simultaneously homogeneous or heterogeneous on many dimensions. For example, an automobile parts manufacturing plant may be highly homogeneous in terms of the employees' functional background but may be highly heterogeneous in terms of the employees' race or ethnicity. Demographic factors that may be relevant for the total organization are similar to those considered in previous chapters, and include gender, race, age, company tenure, educational background, or functional specialization.

A second issue that may be particularly relevant for analyzing the demographic dynamic of large units is the demographic distribution across different groups, sub-units, or levels within the organization. In some organizations, the demographic patterns are markedly different in different sub-units or departments while in other organizations, demographic diversity is more evenly distributed. For example, the accounting department may consist of all women while the sales department may be heterogeneous in gender. Occupational or functional segregation by race or gender is gradually disappearing but still prevails in most organizations. For example, engineering still tends to be male-dominated while administrative functions such as public relations or human resources tend to be gender-balanced or female-dominated. Uneven distribution across different hierarchical levels is most evident with respect to the demographic factors of race and gender. It is common that in most organizations, higher levels tend to be more homogeneous on these two demographic factors than do lower levels. In fact, it is rare to see all races and both sexes evenly represented across all management levels.

In summary, organizations may vary in terms of both the overall degree of demographic diversity and the distribution of diversity across different units, departments, or levels within the organization. These differential demographic distributions and patterns can have significant implications for inter-group relations and coordination, as well as for individuals' attachment to and identification with the organization.

Implications of Demographic Diversity in Organizations: Research Findings

Research on demographic diversity in organizations has taken both the compositional and the relational approach described in Chapter 3. The compositional approach focuses on the demographic distribution of the entity and analyzes its effect on the outcomes at the organizational level. Examples of such outcomes are turnover rate and innovation. The relational approach focuses on the difference of each member from all other members in the organization (or from a selected subgroup) on a specific demographic attribute. It analyzes the effect of this difference on outcomes such as the individual's likelihood to leave the organization. The basic process that produced outcomes at both the organizational and the individual level is similar. Heterogeneity means that each member of the organization will be different from many individuals on many demographic dimensions. To the extent that individuals may use different bases for social categorization and psychological group formation, heterogeneity on multiple demographic attributes means that there will be a greater number of psychological subgroups. Accentuated differentiation and stereotyping lead to greater inter-group conflict in the organization and a lower level of psychological attachment to the organization as a whole.

Relative to groups, there were few studies of demography at the organizational level. As reported in Chapter 3, we have identified four studies that focused on the demographic compositions at the organizational level, with organization broadly defined to include operating units within a larger organization. These units are large enough that not all employees can possibly know all other employees in it or come into contact as they conduct their work duties. The research results are organized according to the outcomes: organizational attachment and turnover, communication, and social relations at work.

Organizational Attachment and Turnover

Detachment or turnover as an outcome of demographic composition is a well-established phenomenon in the research on top management teams and work units. Presumably, the "diverse" individuals who are different from others are less socially integrated and thus are more likely to leave the group when there is an opportunity to do so. Would this effect occur at the organizational level where individuals are not likely to know all other individuals and the lack of interpersonal contact should not be of relevance for feelings of inclusion or exclusion? In other words, would the composition of the larger unit influence the social psychological reactions of individuals? There is some evidence to support the demographic effect at this level as well.

Organizational attachment.

Using 151 operating units in three large organizations, one study examined the effect of diversity on five demographic factors at the unit level on the individual's psychological and behavioral attachment to the organization (Tsui, Egan & O'Reilly, 1992). These units consisted of 44 manufacturing plants, 31 hospitals, and 76 divisions of a Fortune 100 company. The manufacturing plants were part of one Fortune 100 company that operated in the industrial products, graphics, office supplies, and electronics industries. The size of these plants ranged from 125 to 2,527 with a mean of 528 employees. The hospitals were part of a state agency that provided mental health services (inpatient as well as outpatient) throughout the entire state. Size of the hospitals ranged from 145 to 3,000 employees, with a mean of 961. The divisions were from another Fortune 100 company that had businesses in computer and peripheral equipment manufacturing, data services, and financial industries. The number of employees in the divisions ranged from 51 to 3,864, with a mean of 789. The average size across all 151 units was 834 employees. These units were responsible for the actual production of products or delivery of services to customers. The head of each unit was a managing director responsible for the operation of the entire unit. In most cases, each unit was located in a different city or region from the other units. Thus, from the perspective of the employees, the unit was a separate and independent entity though they knew that they were part of a larger organization. Because of separation in terms of both physical location and administration, the relevant comparison group for each employee was the population of employees in the operating unit rather than the parent organization.

It is possible, however, that the demographic composition of the entire organization as well as the associated demographic dynamic could influence the perception and reactions of employees in the operating unit. This will be discussed in more detail in the following section. The present focus is on the influence of the demographic composition of the unit on the members' psychological and behavioral reactions. The reactions measured in this study included psychological commitment to the organization, work attendance, and intent to stay with the organization. It was expected that individuals who were most different from others in the unit on one or more of the relevant demographic attributes would report the lowest organizational attachment measured by the three indices. This is because individuals who were most different from others would be assumed either by others or themselves to also be dissimilar in attitudes, beliefs, and values. Thus, they would experience the most social isolation. Furthermore, heterogeneity means that there is less likelihood that the large operating unit would become a meaningful psychological group that binds all of its members. To the extent that an organization or unit departs from homogeneity on a particular demographic dimension, members will find that unit less satisfying as a psychological group. One manifestation of dissatisfaction is lower psychological attachment and higher frequency of voluntary absences. Also, individuals who are not psychologically attached to the organization will have a lower psychological commitment to it and a higher likelihood of leaving that unit if an opportunity presents itself. These effects of lower attachment are similar to the low social integration and turnover observed in top management teams or work-groups reported in Chapter 6.

The data for this study were collected as part of a larger study on human resource department activities. Employees would have no reason to believe that the researchers were studying issues of diversity. This is important so that the participants would not be "primed" to give answers in the survey that would confirm the hypotheses. Data were collected via a mailed survey and only a small sample of the employees in each operating unit was used. Company representatives confirmed that the demographic profile of the study sample was highly similar to the overall profile of employees in their respective companies. On the average, there were 12 people from each operating unit with a total of 1,705 employees participating in the study. With the sampling procedure employed, it is not likely that any of the 12 individuals would know the other 11 in the sample.

Five demographic factors were included in the study. They were gender, race, age, education, and company tenure. Demographic diversity was measured at the individual level as the difference between a specific person and all others in the sample on a particular demographic attribute. This is the relational demography measure described in Chapter 3. The larger the score, the more different is the individual from others in the unit. Therefore, "token" individuals will have the largest difference scores while individuals in the numerical majority will have smaller difference scores. Individuals in a unit that is homogeneous on a demographic dimension will have the smallest difference scores (in fact zero, denoting no difference from any others in the unit) on that particular dimension. For example, a man in a unit of two men and three women would have a difference score of .77 on gender, 0 for being the same as the other man and 3 for being different from each of the three women. The value of 3 is then divided by 5 and the square of the product is the final difference score on gender for this man. A man in an all-male unit has a score of .00.

The results showed that employees most different from others in the unit on race and on gender were the least psychologically attached. They were absent more often than other employees, they reported the lowest level of psychological commitment to the organization, and they expressed the highest degree of intent to leave the organization. Employees most different from others on age were most inclined to leave the organization. This finding is highly consistent with findings from studies on top management teams and small groups where turnover is most likely to occur and social integration is lowest for individuals most different from others on age.

Different effects for different groups.

A most significant finding of the above study is the asymmetrical effect of demographic diversity for individuals in different social categories. The impact appeared to be greater on men than on women, and greater on whites than on non-whites. Specifically, the psychological attachment of men declined systematically in relation to the degree to which the men were different from others on gender in the unit. The greater the difference, the lower the attachment. On the other hand, the psychological attachment of women was unrelated to the gender difference score. In other words, women who were most or least different from others in the unit on gender did not differ in their frequency of absences or intent to leave the organization. In fact, women who were more different from others in the unit on gender (i.e., they were in the more gender-heterogeneous units) expressed a slightly higher level of psychological commitment than women who were less different from others on gender (i.e., they were in the relatively less gender-heterogeneous units). Figure 7.1 is a graphic presentation of the relationship between the extent of being different in gender by an individual to others in the unit and the degree of the individual's psychological commitment to the organization. Though not presented graphically here, the profiles for frequency of absences and intent to leave the company were highly similar to that for psychological commitment shown in Figure 7.1.

A similar asymmetrical effect was found for race. For whites, those who were most different from others in the unit on race were the least psychologically attached. These whites reported the highest number of voluntary absences, expressed the lowest level of psychological commitment to the company, and were most inclined to leave the company. For the non-white employees, there was no relationship between the extent of difference and any of the three attachment measures. Non-white individuals who were in race-heterogeneous or race-homogeneous groups were similarly

Figure 7.1 Difference in Gender and Psychological Commitment to the Organization

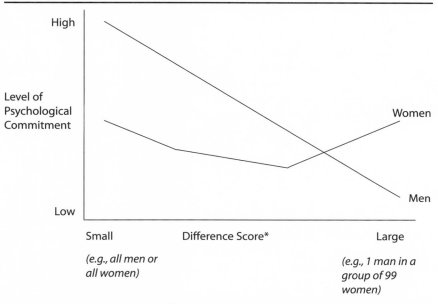

*Extent to which an individual is different from others on gender in the organization
Note: The two lines are presented for comparative illustration only. The graphs are not to scale.

attached to the organization. Figure 7.2 shows the psychological commitment of whites and non-whites as a function of the extent to which they were different from others in racial background. Again, the results for absences and intent to leave the company, not presented here, were similar to that for psychological commitment.

It should be noted that the above effects of demographic diversity were obtained after controlling, statistically, for the effects of the direct demographic attributes of the individuals. In other words, the lower attachment of men is not because the individual is a male but because the men were in an organizational unit that had a relatively large proportion of women. In fact, ignoring the demographic composition of the operating unit, men and women expressed a similar level of organizational commitment and intent to stay with the company, even though men tended to be absent less frequently than women. However, having accounted for the differential absence rates as a function of the individual's gender, men in units with more women were absent more often than men in units with fewer women. There was no difference in the frequency of absences between whites and non-whites. white employees in units with more non-white employees reported more absences than white employees in units with

Figure 7.2 Difference in Race and Psychological Commitment to the Organization

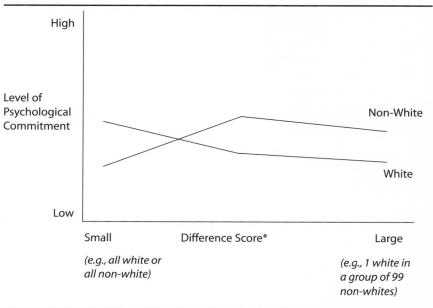

*Extent to which an individual is different from others in the organization on race
Note: The two lines are presented for comparative illustration only. The graphs are not to scale.

fewer non-whites. It is also interesting to note that, on the average, non-white employees in this study expressed a higher level of psychological commitment and a lower level of intent to leave the company than white employees even though non-white employees' attachment to the organization was not affected by the degree of racial heterogeneity in the operating units.

In addition to gender and race, this study also found some effects for age and company tenure. Individuals more different from others in age expressed a lower level of intent to stay with the company. Evidently, employees also used age as a basis for defining their psychological group. If the organization they work in is populated by people who differ from them in age (either older or younger), they find it a less attractive place to work. A different kind of result was obtained on company tenure. Those most different from others on this demographic dimension (most of these were newer employees) reported the lowest number of absences. They were, however, neither more nor less committed than employees who were similar to others on company tenure. The pressure or desire to show good attendance behavior by new employees may have dominated other concerns, including being different on other dimensions such as race or gender. Thus, a new white male employee in a mixed gender and racial group where most members are long-time employees may not feel socially integrated in terms of psychological commitment to the organization but may still maintain a good attendance record.

The most important finding of this study is the differential effect of demographic diversity on men versus women and on whites versus non-whites. This finding is significant in that earlier research has assumed that diversity affects the social and numerical minority members of the organization more than the numerical majority members. Here, it is the dominant majority, i.e., whites and males, that reported the most negative feelings when they were in settings with others who are demographically different from themselves. In fact, the highest commitment was reported by men in the gender-homogenous (i.e., all men) operating units, relative to all other groups in this sample. Similarly, white individuals in homogeneous white units reported the highest level of attachment, and it declined steadily with increasing numbers of non-whites in the operating unit.

This sample had only 10% minorities, ranging from 7% in one company to 22% in another company. This means that the white majority may begin to show psychological discomfort, as expressed by lower attachment, even when the minority proportion is very small. This study also showed that among the five demographic factors, the strongest effects were found for race and gender. Gender and race are highly visible, and, therefore, their activation in a social setting for self-categorization may be automatic in American society. The lack of interpersonal interaction makes it difficult to find out that a demographically dissimilar person may in fact be quite similar in underlying beliefs and values. The automatic nature of social categorization and stereotyping makes it even more difficult for interaction between dissimilar individuals to occur. In fact, the greater the number of dissimilar others (heterogeneous), the more heightened will be inter-group differentiation and conflict. In this way, heterogeneity reduces rather than increases interpersonal contact. Several sociologists (e.g., Blau, 1977; Kanter, 1977) have proposed that increasing heterogeneity increases contact, understanding between different groups, an,d by extension, social integration. The findings from this study suggest the opposite. Increased heterogeneity, in this study, appeared to reduce social integration, especially for whites and males.

A more severe case of decreased organizational attachment is a person's actually leaving the organization. Pfeffer and O'Reilly (1987) analyzed the turnover rate of nurses as a function of tenure distribution. A nation-wide random sample of community hospitals produced 298 hospitals for this study. Only hospitals with at least 50 registered nurses were included in the study. For each hospital, the turnover rate of nurses (number of full-time nurses who left divided by the number of full-time nurses on staff) and two indices of tenure diversity were measured. The two indices produced highly similar results. A greater value on the diversity index implies that nurses entered the hospitals at different times. After controlling for other factors that may also influence turnover (e.g., unemployment rate in the area, union status of the hospital, etc.), tenure diversity was positively associated with turnover rate. This finding again is consistent with the idea that heterogeneity increases differentiation and diminishes social integration. In this case, day of entry to the hospital appeared to have been a relevant basis for self-categorization and psychological group formation. Tenure differences not only negatively influence interpersonal attraction and cohesion in smaller work groups, they also reduce depersonalized interpersonal attraction in the larger units, leading to a higher turnover rate in these units.

Communication

Hoffman (1985) studied the question of race composition and interpersonal contact directly. Specifically, he tested the idea of whether increasing the representation of a racial minority in a group would increase the group's total frequency of interaction (Hoffman, 1985). The idea is based on the classic "contact hypothesis" (see Cook, 1978), which posits that association with people from a disliked group leads to the growth of liking and respect for that group. This is because contact should provide opportunities to discover similar beliefs and attitudes, which in turn should increase attraction between the two individuals or groups. However, many researchers also have pointed out that the case is not so simple (e.g., Allport, 1979; Hewstone & Brown, 1986). The study by Hoffman (1985) shows that contact between dissimilar individuals simply does not occur, even though there is increasing opportunity to do so (through the increased number of dissimilar others).

The study was conducted in 96 federal civilian installations in 13 Southeastern states. Installations such as the FBI, the CIA, and federal prisons and hospitals were excluded. Individuals participating in the study were all supervisory personnel. A total of 2,083 individuals participated with an average of 22 per installation. Among them 15% were females and 5% were non-white (most were blacks). The percentage of blacks ranged from 0% to 46.2% across the 96 units. The number of employees in the 96 installations ranged from 75 to 964 employees. The study report did not indicate the average size (number of employees) of the installations. Those who participated in this study represented a sample (about 20%) of the actual number of employees in the units. Because of the size and geographical range of the units, most of the respondents were strangers to each other. Thus, this sample and the operating units were quite similar to those used in the study on organizational attachment by Tsui et al.

(1992) reported above. Since the purpose of this study was to analyze inter-group communication as a function of group composition based on race, units with no black representation were excluded from the analysis. The actual composition of employees based on race in the 96 units was from 1.3% to 46.2%.

After controlling for other factors that also may influence communication (e.g., the overall size of the installation, the sex and educational level of the individuals), racial composition of the organization did not increase inter-personal communication within each installation. When these other factors were not controlled, race composition was, in fact, negatively cor-related with interpersonal communication. In other words, individuals engaged in less interpersonal interaction in the more racially heteroge-neous units. Interpersonal communication includes conversation and con-tact with one's supervisors, subordinates, or peers. Racial composition, however, was associated with increased frequency of communication at the organizational level. Individuals in the more race heterogeneous instal-lations attended more formal meetings held by the supervisory personnel and their directors. These results are not surprising when considered in light of the social categorization process. Using race as a category for self-categorization, increasing heterogeneity increases inter-group differentia-tion and reduces contact at the interpersonal level. However, attendance at formal communication meetings requires less interpersonal contact. Both minority and majority members may feel more comfortable with structured formal mechanisms to obtain the required information for con-ducting their role responsibilities than informal interpersonal contacts.

In summary, this study showed that increasing the proportion of people who are different from each other does not necessarily increase contact between these people, and, in fact, it may actually reduce communication. Both whites and blacks reported reduced interpersonal communication in these units. These results again confirmed the importance of race as a basis for social categorization and stereotyping. Increasing the proportion of the numerical minority group serves to heighten inter-group distinction. It appears that both the majority and the minority in this sample contributed to polarization of differences in the organization. Results from the study on organizational attachment reported above, however, suggest that the majority (i.e., whites) reacted more negatively to increased race diversity in the organization.

Social Relations As a Function of a Cross-Level Demographic Effect

Thus far, we have focused on the influence of demographic composition of a unit on the attitudes and behaviors of individuals in that unit. Ely's (1994) study is an excellent example of a cross-level demographic effect. She examined how female representation in the upper echelon affects professional women's social relations in lower levels of the organization. She used social identity and categorization processes to explain why and how gender distribution in upper levels would influence social relationships in lower levels. Based on the assumption that status is positively related to level, over-representation of men in higher organizational levels reinforces the lower social status of women relative to that of men. Based on the further assumption that status is valuable to both men and women, organizational level becomes a meaningful category for social identity. Women in organizations with a large proportion of men in higher organizational levels may engage in out-group favoritism with or without corresponding degradation of the in-group. In these organizations, being a woman is incompatible with desired membership in more powerful organizational groups. For (the relatively few) women who are in the top echelon, the top management team may be a stronger basis than gender for social identity. Identification with this group would provide a more positive social identity than identification with the (less powerful) women in lower levels of the firm. For women in lower levels, identification with gender also does not contribute to a positive social identity because, in this context, gender and power are incompatible. As a result, the quality of social relations between professional women in lower levels with women in both higher and same levels will be poorer than would be the case when there is a higher representation of women in the upper echelon.

These ideas were tested using 108 women lawyers in eight law firms that ranged from 50 to 200 lawyers. Four of the firms were considered male-dominated in that the percentage of women in partnership ranged from 4% to 11%. Four of the firms were considered sex-integrated with the percentage of women in partnership ranging from 15% to 29%. The percent of women lawyers in the associate position (lower level) was similar in the two types of firms, ranging from 38% to 50%. Using both interview and written surveys, the associate lawyers were asked about their perceptions and relations with other women in upper management as well as other woman associate lawyers. The results were consistent with the predictions based on social identity theory. Compared with women in firms with relatively many senior women, women in firms with few senior women reported more negative perceptions and feelings toward both senior and peer women. They were less likely to see senior women as role models, more likely to see competition in their relationship with peer women, and less likely to find social support in these relationships. This study is particularly important because it is the first study to examine demographic impact across organizational levels.

This study opens up an entirely new avenue of research on demographic issues within complex organizations. The study could be extended to examine demographic composition in lower organizational levels as a function of demographic composition in the top management team. Also, differences in demographic composition across different units of the same organizations may influence relationships and coordination across units. For example, a department with a high level of diversity and hence low social integration might affect this department's relationship with other departments with a low level of diversity with high social integration. The dynamic of different demographic composition in different parts and levels of the organization is a topic most under-researched.

Summary

The research studies reported in this chapter focus on demographic diversity at the level of the organization (or large operating unit) and provided consistent support for the negative effect of diversity on individuals and on relationships between individuals. In demographically diverse units or organizations where more people were different from each other, the following outcomes were observed. First, there was less interpersonal communication. Second, social relations were poorer. Third, psychological attachment to the organization and intent to stay with the company were lower, especially among the dominant majority and usually among high-status individuals. Fourth, higher actual turnover resulted in some cases. The demographic factors that were associated with these outcomes were gender, race, age, and company tenure. These research findings are summarized in Table 7.1.

Interestingly, none of the research studies reported in this chapter analyzed the effect of diversity in functional specialization at the organiza-

Table 7.1 Summary of Research Findings on Organizational Level Demography

Group's Diversity Dimension	Outcomes
Gender	(+) Absences (–) Psychological commitment (+) Intent to leave (–) Social relations with senior-level and peer women
Race	(+) Absences (–) Psychological commitment (+) Intent to leave (–) Interpersonal communication
Age	(+) Intent to leave the company
Company tenure Educational level	(+) Turnover

Note: (+) or (–) indicates whether the relationship is positive (+) or negative (–).

tional level. There also was no analysis of diversity in educational backgrounds or educational level. Whether the effects of these demographic factors observed at the small group level are applicable to the organizational level is a question that remains to be answered.

Synthesizing the studies across all three levels (dyad, group, and organization) in Chapters 5, 6, and 7, we conclude that diversity on the following demographic factors appears to be relevant: (1) gender, (2) race, (3) age, (4) educational level, (5) job tenure, (6) team tenure, (7) company tenure, (8) functional specialization, (9) educational background, and (10) industry experience. Effects of diversity in gender, race, age, educational level, and job tenure have been found in vertical dyads. Effects of diversity in age, gender, race, company tenure, team tenure, and functional background have been reported in various types of small groups. At the organizational level, relevant demographic factors are gender, race, age, and company tenure. Table 7.2 summarizes the relevant demographic diversity factors based on research at the various levels of analysis.

The outcomes that are affected by demographic diversity relate to various forms of social integration and resulting departure from the group or organization. In general, diversity leads to greater inter-group differentiation and lower social cohesion and attraction among individuals who are demographically different. Negative traits of the out-group and positive traits of the in-group are accentuated except where there is a clear distinction in the social status of different groups. Out-group favoritism may occur if the superior status of the out-group is clear and if the individual fits another social category that correlates with the out-group. This is the case when organizational rank is correlated with the male gender. Women may use organizational rank rather than gender to self-categorize because being part of the high-ranking group contributes to a positive social identity more than being female. These interpersonal, group, and inter-group effects occur

Table 7.2 Relevant Demographic Diversity Factors at Different Levels of Analysis

Level of Analysis	Relevant Demographic Diversity Factors
Vertical Dyad	Gender, race, age, educational level, job tenure
Horizontal Dyad	Gender, race, age, educational level
Small Group	Age, company tenure, team tenure, educational level, industry experience, functional background
Organization	Gender, race, age, company tenure educational level

as a function of the social categorization process based on particular demographic attributes and not because of the specific (ill or good) intentions of a particular group of individuals. This aggregate set of research findings also is quite clear in showing that diversity affects both the majority and the minority, i.e., potentially everyone in the organization.

Finally, the study on the demography of the law firms suggests that demographic effects occur not only in terms of the composition of the unit in which one is a member but relationships among members within this unit also are influenced by the demographic diversity outside of the unit. This suggests the relevance of the context. For example, it is possible that demographic difference in a vertical dyad may take on a different meaning depending on the composition of the group in which the particular dyad is embedded. A male working for a female supervisor may not experience the same (low) level of support and positive affect in a female-dominated group as in a gender-balanced group. Similarly, an older subordinate working for a younger supervisor may not be viewed favorably by the supervisor in a work group of primarily older subordinates, relative to another work group of primarily younger subordinates. In other words, the extent of inter-group differentiation associated with different degrees of diversity in the larger unit may provide different social psychological meaning for small groups and individuals inside the larger unit. The larger organization itself may be a social category offering different meanings to different individuals. It can modify the meaning or salience of other demographic attributes as well as the importance of these demographic patterns to individuals and groups. Chapter 9 describes an integrative framework in which we describe how the organization may serve as a context in potentially modifying the meaning and effects of demographic diversity on individuals and groups.

Conclusion

Clearly, demographic diversity is as much an organizational issue as it is an individual issue. In fact, it has become a major challenge for organizational leaders at all levels. At the top, the challenge is not only to manage the internal dynamic of the top management team itself, but also to understand and be responsive to the inter-group dynamic associated with increasing diversity along one or more demographic attributes among employees in lower levels. In this chapter, we have described, through both conceptual analysis and research data, the potential positive outcomes of demographic diversity. They include higher-quality decisions, innovation, and firm performance. These benefits are not always realized, however, due to the low cohesion, weak organizational attachment, and high turnover often observed in heterogeneous organizations. Therefore, appropriate processes are needed to minimize the inter-group conflicts that arise in diverse organizations. Some ideas on managing demographic diversity at the organizational level will be offered in Chapter 10.

Chapter 8

Demography Diversity in the International Arena: The Chinese Case

Of all the countries outside of the United States or Canada, why do we choose to focus on China in discussing demographic diversity in the international arena? The answer is simple: China is a developing economy and U.S. companies have tremendous interest in it. The U.S. is the third-largest foreign investor in China, after Hong Kong and Taiwan (Qiu & Wu, 1997). U.S. joint ventures in China are dealing with diversity issues that go far beyond skin color or gender. Let us use the example of the management team in Pharmex-Tianjin, an alliance between Pharmex, a large U.S.-based pharmaceutical company, and the government of Tianjin, China (Hambrick, Li, Xin & Tsui, 1998). The general manager is American, the deputy general manager is Chinese. The directors of finance, manufacturing, and marketing are all American while the director of personnel and the controller are Chinese. These managers form two demographic coalitions that overlap with nationality as well as a number of other demographic factors. The age gap between the two coalitions is 10 years: average age is 50 for the American managers while it is 40 for the Chinese managers. The educational gap is 5 years: 17 years on average for the Americans and 12 years for the Chinese. Differences also exist in the staff-line experience: 75% of the Pharmex coalition have primarily line management experience (marketing, manufacturing, and sales) while none of the Tianjin managers have line management experience (instead, their background is in staff areas of accounting, external relations, and human resources). This type of demographic diversity is typical in many Sino-foreign joint ventures, and the negative dynamics associated with such diversity may well account for the problems experienced by many of these management groups (Hambrick et al., 1998).

China is an interesting and relevant case for another reason. In recent years, there has been much attention and writing on the importance of relationships in doing business in China. The term *"guanxi"* (pronounced kuan-hsi) has appeared in both the popular and the academic literature to refer to a special type of relationship in China (Jacobs, 1980; Yang, 1994). It is defined as the existence of particularistic ties between two or more individuals. The particularistic ties could be family relations, past co-workers, attendance at the same school, or ancestors from the same region of the country. It is well known that relationships based on *guanxi* and the use of *guanxi* are endemic in Chinese business (Alston, 1989; Hall & Xu, 1990; King, 1991; Lockette, 1988; Yang, 1994). Since *guanxi* has instrumental value to the involved parties (Hwang, 1987; Xin & Pearce, 1994), a knowledge of *guanxi* is necessary to understand work place social relations and performance implications in both indigenous Chinese firms and multinational corporations operating in China (Tsui, 1997). In this chapter, we focus on *guanxi* in the Chinese context as a special form of relational demography.

The Meaning of *Guanxi*

The term *"guanxi"* in the Chinese language, and in the popular business magazines, is actually quite loose in its meaning. It could refer to any one of these definitions: (a) existence of a relationship between people who share a group status, (b) being related to a common third party, (c) actual connections with and frequent contact between people, (d) contact person with little direct interaction, or (e) friendship without common background. From the above list, it seems that *guanxi* could refer to both cause (e.g., common background) and effect (e.g., communication and friendship) in a relationship. These multiple meanings do not facilitate understanding or study. There is, however, a common thread among most of the definitions. That is, they refer to a certain type of interpersonal relationship, one that is personal and built on particularistic criteria. Tsui and Farh (1997) found the definition used by Jacobs (1980) to be most simple and directly comparable to the idea of relational demography. *Guanxi* is defined as the existence of direct particularistic ties between two or more individuals. This definition is therefore more comparable to relational demography than to either simple or compositional demography.

Similarities and Differences between *Guanxi* and Relational Demography

To the extent that *guanxi* signals some commonality between two or more individuals on some particularistic ties, it can be considered as a special form of relational demography. In fact, it could be considered as an indigenous Chinese term for relational demography. Equivalent terms can be found in other cultures, such as the term *blat* in Russia or *pratik* in Haiti, both of which refer to some type of instrumental–personal ties (Walder, 1986). Both *guanxi* and relational demography involve the existence of some ties between individuals. Both address the implications of such commonality or connections for interpersonal and business outcomes. There are however several important differences.

First is the basis of the relationship. *Guanxi* is based on particularistic ties, such as family ties or same schools, that are unique to the individuals. Relational demography focuses on similarity between one individual and others based on social categories that are universal, such as race, gender, or educational level. *Guanxi* bases relate to an individual's native and socioeconomic origin or background rather than physical attributes, such as age or sex. Some of these are ascribed, e.g., natal origin or place of birth, while others are achieved, e.g., where the person lived or went to school. Most of the *guanxi* bases are not directly observable but are discovered only through direct conversation with a person or introduction by a third party. Table 8.1 summarizes a set of relevant background or demographic factors for each. Of the listed bases, only three are common between the two concepts. The base of locality or native origin for *guanxi* appears to be similar to the idea of national origin or country of citizenship for relational demography. The base of past or former coworkers (for *guanxi*) may capture the same idea as the place of past employment (for relational demography). Former classmate (for *guanxi*) implies that the individuals have the same alma mater (for relational demography). It should be noted that the non-overlapping bases do not imply that either set is necessarily irrelevant or unimportant in the other context, it only means that they have not been the focus of past studies. Further research may well reveal that the bases of relational demography are equally relevant in the Chinese context and the bases of *guanxi* are similarly meaningful in the U.S. context.

A second difference shown in Table 8.1 is the type of base involved. Most of the bases of *guanxi* involve interpersonal interaction and the development of friendship. These include having worked together previously (either as coworkers or as supervisor–subordinate), having studied together (former classmate), having been neighbors, having been a teacher or student to each other, or being members of the same immediate or extended family. The only exceptions are common native origin and surname. In contrast, most of the bases for relational demography such as age, ethnicity, gender, religion, or occupation, do not necessarily imply or involve opportunities for interaction among individuals sharing the same attributes. Instead interaction may be the outcome of presumed similarity in values and attitudes based on the observed physical attributes. Another difference is that most of the bases of *guanxi* seem to involve some relationship in the past, while most of the bases for relational demography refer to an individual's current or existing characteristics.

Table 8.1 Bases of *Guanxi* and Relational Demography

Guanxi	Relational Demography
Close kin	
Distant kin	
Surname	
Former neighbor	
Former teacher–student	
Former supervisor–subordinate	
Former coworker	Place of current or past employment
Former classmate	Alma mater
Locality or native origin	National origin or country of citizenship
	Race/ethnicity
	Sex
	Age
	Education
	Religion
	Major field of study
	Military experience
	Industry experience
	Company tenure
	Team or work group tenure
	Occupation or functional specialization

From Tsui & Farh, 1997

The relevance or prevalence of different bases suggests that *guanxi* and relational demography may involve different processes in influencing interpersonal and work outcomes. The underlying process is perhaps the major difference that distinguishes *guanxi* from relational demography. In traditional Chinese society where Confucian teachings are influential, the concepts of interdependent self, roles, role obligation, and *renqing* (social obligation or interpersonal favor and generosity) in interpersonal relationships are particularly important. The following section describes the processes that link *guanxi*, different modes of interpersonal relationships, and work outcomes.

Guanxi and Modes of Interpersonal Relationships

To understand why *guanxi* is important and how it operates in Chinese societies, one must understand China's Confucian legacy. The word *"lun"* was used in Confucian ideology to refer to the concept of *guanxi*. According to Confucianism, an individual is fundamentally a social or relational being. Social order and stability depend on a properly differentiated role relationship between particular individuals (King, 1991). Confucius defined five cardinal (dyadic) role relations (called *wu-lun*):

emperor–subject, father–son, husband–wife, elder–younger brothers, and friend–friend. Yang (1993) described *wu-lun* as

> a highly formalistic cultural system . . . [requiring] each actor to perform his or her role in such a way that he or she should precisely say what he or she was supposed to say, and not to say what he or she was not supposed to say. In order to be a good role performer, the actor usually had to hide his or her free will. . . . This is why Chinese [culture] has been described to be situation-centered or situationally determined. (pp. 29–30)

Under the heavy influence of Confucianism, Chinese often view themselves as interdependent with the surrounding social context, and it is the "self in relation to other" that becomes the focal individual experience. This view of an interdependent self is in sharp contrast to the Western view of an independent self. The latter sees each human being as an independent, self-contained, autonomous entity that (a) comprises a unique configuration of internal attributes (e.g., traits, abilities, motives, and values) and (b) behaves primarily as a consequence of these internal attributes (Markus & Kitayama, 1991). As part of the emphasis on differentiated relationships, attention to others in China is highly selective with a strong tendency to divide people into categories and treat them accordingly. The bases of *guanxi* determine how others are categorized. Yang (1993) describes the three major categories of interpersonal relationships in China: *chia-jen* (family members), *shou-jen* (familiar persons such as relatives outside the family, neighbors or people in the same village, friends, colleagues, or classmates), and *sheng-jen* (mere acquaintances or strangers). These three categories of relationships have completely different social and psychological meanings to the parties involved and are governed by different sets of interpersonal rules.

The *chia-jen* (family) relationship is characterized by permanent, stable, expressive relationships in which the welfare of the other is part of one's duty. The general rule of exchange is that one does his or her best to attend to the other's needs with little or no expectation of return in the future. Such unconditional protection and loyalty cluster around the family, surrounded by circles of decreasingly potent identities of the lineage group (Redding et al., 1993). It has been well observed that one of the most distinctive features of Chinese societies is their family orientation (Bond & Hwang, 1986; Yang, 1993). In China (as in some other cultures), loyalty (and related favoritism) to family is an obligation, and it is rendered largely without an obligation of reciprocity.

The *sheng-jen* (stranger or mere acquaintance) category includes all those with whom one has no prior or current relationship or interactions. They could include members of one's local community, fellow employees who work in the same (large) company, or customers of a business. Interactions with *sheng-jen*, if any, are superficial and temporary and are dominated by utilitarian concerns, focusing on personal gains and losses. The defining characteristic of this relationship is instrumentality without affection, unlike the relationship with *chia-jen*, which involves primarily affection, or that with *shou-jen*, which has both an instrumental and an affective component. *Shou-jen*, by definition, is neither a *chia-jen* or a *sheng-jen*, but is someone with whom one has a friendship that may range from superficial to extremely intimate. A coworker or subordinate falls into this category. The relationship is a mixture of that with *chia-jen* and *sheng-jen*, and takes both expressive and utilitarian forms. Favoritism is often followed by an expectation of reciprocity (Hwang, 1987; King, 1989).

Depending on the bases of *guanxi*, an interpersonal relationship could fall into any of these three categories. In traditional Chinese settings, *guanxi* is relevant only for the *chia-jen* and *shou-jen* categories. However, recent research has found that the social identification process also operates among Chinese people (Li, 1993; Li & Hsu, 1995), and thus interpersonal attraction based on arbitrarily created similarity could occur with individuals in the *sheng-jen* category. Therefore, through the identification process, the *sheng-jen* category may be further differentiated into two groups: *sheng-jen* with common identity and *sheng-jen* without common identity. Table 8.2 summarizes the modes of interpersonal interactions with each of the four categories of relationships as well as types of *guanxi* and relational demographic bases that might be relevant for each category.

As shown in Table 8.2, family tie is the primary and only base for individuals in the *chia-jen* category. Responsibility or obligation is the dominant principle of interaction. For relationships with *shou-jen* category, a variety of bases are involved, most of which are the bases for *guanxi* and some of which are the bases for relational demography (Table 8.1). Exchanging favors and generosity are the dominant principles of interaction. Individuals in the *sheng-jen* category are treated differently depending on whether there is any commonality in background or demographic factors. People in the *sheng-jen* category will be treated with affection and be viewed positively when they share a common identity of importance. Bases of common identity could be either demographic factors or particularistic ties. Individuals in the *sheng-jen* category without common identity, on the other hand, are treated with discretion and caution.

Guanxi, Relationship Demography, and Work Outcomes

Based on the dominant modes of interaction, different mediating processes link *guanxi* and relational demography to interpersonal and work outcomes in the Chinese context (Tsui & Farh, 1997). Three mediating processes are: role obligation, reciprocity, and social identification. Figure

Table 8.2 *Guanxi* Bases and Interpersonal Relationships in the Chinese Context

Categories of Relationship	Dominant Principles of Interaction	Ways of Social Treatment	Bases for *Guanxi* or Common Identity
Family (*Chia-jen*)	Responsibility or obligation	Unconditional protection	Close kin
Familiar person (*Shou-jen*)	Exchange of favor and generosity (*renqing*)	Trust and social accommodation	Distant kin, former classmate, former teacher–student, former supervisor–subordinate, former coworker, or former neighbor
Stranger with common identity (*Sheng-jen*)	Utilitarian exchange with depersonalized affection	Favoritism	Native origin, surname, or other demographic attributes (e.g., age, sex, education, alma mater)
Stranger without common identity (*Sheng-jen*)	Utilitarian exchange without affection	Discretion and caution	None

From Tsui & Farh, 1997

8.1 is a graphic representation of how *guanxi* and relational demography affect interpersonal and work outcomes through these three mediating processes. Social identification applies to all three categories of relationships but is the primary mechanism for influencing relationships with individuals in the *sheng-jen* category. Beyond identification, role obligation mediates *quanxi* based on kinship ties and interpersonal or work outcomes. Due to role obligation, an individual will act more favorably toward a family member than toward a nonfamily member. An uncle, for example, will likely choose his nephew for a summer job in his company over another young man who may be equally or more qualified. Beyond identification, reciprocity mediates *guanxi* with *shou-jen* and outcomes. Mutuality or reciprocity in the exchange with *shou-jen* is the necessary ingredient for maintaining the relationship. Further, *shou-jen* with intimate relationships (i.e., intimate friends), may be treated as "family," and favoritism toward them could become a role obligation without anticipation of reciprocity. Finally, social identification is the primary mechanism linking *guanxi* with *sheng-jen* with common identity to the interpersonal and work outcomes.

All four categories of relationships and all three mediating processes apply to interpersonal relationships among Chinese people. However,

Figure 8.1 A Conceptual Framework of *Guanxi*, Relational Demography, and Work Outcomes in Chinese Organizations

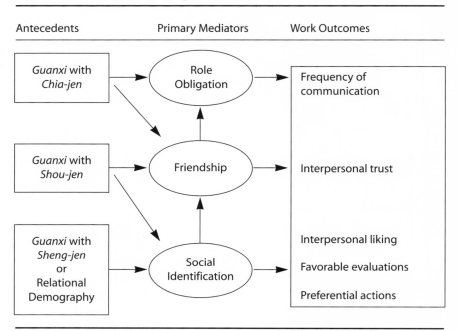

From Tsui & Farh, 1997

managers from the foreign parent in Sino-foreign joint ventures generally fall into the *shou-jen* or the *sheng-jen* categories, depending on the extent to which there exist particularistic ties or demographic similarity between the individuals in the two groups. As the example in the beginning of this chapter shows, the Chinese and the foreign managers could differ not only in nationality but also in functional background, educational level, and age. Lack of any common background between these managers creates real tension between the two coalitions and heightens identification and solidarity among the managers within each coalition (Hambrick et al., 1998).

Positive outcomes that are potentially affected by *guanxi* and relational demography include increased frequency of communication, interpersonal trust, liking, and favorable or preferential treatment. Negative outcomes could include substantive or relational conflict (Jehn, 1995), emotional or psychological detachment from the other party or the group, and actual physical withdrawal in the form of frequent absences or departure from the (employment) relationship. Systematic research on the influence of *guanxi* and relational demography in the Chinese employment setting is just beginning. We will report these research findings in the following section.

Research Evidence on *Guanxi* and Relational Demography

In this section, we report three studies that focus on vertical dyads and one study on horizontal dyads. These studies were conducted in Taiwan and in mainland China. All the studies assessed the joint effect of relational demography and *guanxi* on a variety of employment outcomes. This stream of research has focused on the dyad, both horizontal and vertical. Outcomes included interpersonal trust, quality of the relationship between the supervisor and the subordinate, supervisory judgment of subordinate performance, and subordinates' commitment to the organization.

Interpersonal Trust

Using a sample of 560 supervisor–subordinate dyads in an insurance company in Taiwan, Farh, Tsui, Xin, and Cheng (1998) analyzed the effect of both *guanxi* and relational demography on five outcomes. These outcomes are subordinate's trust in the supervisor, supervisory rating of the subordinate's performance, subordinate's actual sales performance, subordinate's organizational commitment, and intention to quit the company. In this sample, 87% of the dyads consisted of members identical in gender, 41% were similar in educational level, and 28% were similar in age. A much smaller proportion, however, had particularistic ties; 3.4% of the dyads were former classmates, 3.2% were relatives of each other, 2.9% had the same last name, 3.4% had the same natal origin, 2.1% were former colleagues, and 2.5% were former neighbors. Significant effects for both relational demography and *guanxi* were found for only one outcome: subordinate's trust in the supervisor.

The effect of relational demography is contrary to expectation. Instead of similarity-attraction, as would be predicted based on the social identification process, we found dissimilarity to be associated with a higher level of trust in the supervisor by the subordinate. Further analyses revealed that subordinates reported a higher level of trust in their supervisors when the supervisors were better educated than when the supervisors were less educated than or similarly educated as the subordinates. These findings could be unique to this cultural setting where education is valued. Therefore, better-educated supervisors were trusted more than similarly or less educated supervisors. Results for gender were also surprising. Further analysis showed that male subordinates reported the lowest level of trust in their male supervisors, relative to all other subordinates. The finding on gender could be due to the nature of the sample. The sales agents in the insurance company were primarily females. Females held the more powerful supervisory positions as well. Therefore, male subordinates trusted their male supervisors less. The results on *guanxi* confirm our expectations. Two *guanxi* bases were significantly related to trust in the supervisor as expressed by the subordinates. Trust was higher when the two members of the dyad were relatives and when they were former neighbors. These results were obtained even after controlling for the effects of relational demography as well as the simple demographics of both the supervisor and the subordinate. The Farh et al. study (1998) reported a second sample of 32 business executives and their relationship with 8 to 10 connections, yielding a total of 205 horizontal or lateral dyads. These executives were interviewed using a structured interview guide. Each executive described the primary *guanxi* base ("How did you first establish a tie with the connection?") with each connection and his or her trust in the connection and their perception of the connection's importance for his or her business success. The executives mentioned only three particularistic ties: former classmates (10.7%), relatives (4.4%), and same natal origin (2.4%). Three relational demography variables were also included: 71% of the horizontal dyads were the same gender, 43% had the same educational level, and 28% were similar in age.

Significant results were obtained on all three *guanxi* bases but for only trust in the connection as expressed by the executive for all three particularistic ties. None of relational demography variables was significant. The three *guanxi* variables accounted for 43% of the unique variance in business executives' trust in their connections. Being related, having been classmates in the past, and being of the same natal origin are important ties for the trust that these business executives expressed in their connections. These results are consistent with the ideas explicated in Figure 8.1. These connections are trusted because they fall into the *chia-jen* and *shou-jen* categories.

Quality of Supervisor–Subordinate Relationship, Subordinate Commitment to the Company, and Supervisor's Ratings of Subordinate Performance

Using a sample of 175 Taiwanese managers and their subordinates, Xin, Farh, Cheng, and Tsui (1998) investigated the effect of both *guanxi* and relational demography on several employment outcomes in the vertical dyad. Among the 175 subordinates, 44% were themselves managers. The rest of them held professional-level jobs. The companies represented by the sample were diverse: auto assembly, electronics, computers, textiles, food, chemicals, and oil refineries. In this sample, 73% of the dyads were the same gender, 19% had identical company tenure, and 18% had similar educational levels. In terms of *guanxi*, 43% reported same natal origin or dialect, 9.6% were former colleagues, 1.7% were kin, 1.1% had the same last name, and only .6% were former neighbors. Outcomes investigated in this study included the quality of the relationship between the supervisor and the subordinate as reported by both members of the dyad, the subordinate's organizational commitment, and the subordinate's performance as rated by the supervisor. Significant results were found for two *guanxi* bases and one relational demographic variable.

Similarity in company tenure, and *guanxi* in terms of having been former colleagues and speaking the same dialect (suggesting the same natal origin) were positively associated with a high-quality supervisor–subordinate relationship as perceived by the subordinate and the subordinate's commitment to the organization. Only one *guanxi* variable, i.e., having been former colleagues, and tenure similarity were positively associated with the supervisor's perception of a high-quality relationship with the subordinate. Furthermore, the study also found that *guanxi* based on former colleague-ship (but not tenure similarity) was associated with the supervisor's favorable evaluation of the subordinate's performance. In summary, this study confirmed the importance of two particularistic ties for favorable work outcomes in the vertical dyad. The lack of significance of the other particularistic ties could be due to the low proportion of their occurrence in these vertical dyads. The importance of tenure similarity is consistent with research findings in the United States. When members of the vertical dyad have worked for their company for about the same length of time, they tend to give each other a relatively high level of mutual support, a key characteristic of a high-quality relationship in vertical dyads.

The Xin et al. study (1998) also included a second sample of 168 vertical dyads in 42 state-owned plants in two cities in mainland China. At each plant, two senior managers were interviewed. Each manager nominated two subordinates, one considered most and the other least cooperative by the manager. Each of the two subordinates was also interviewed. The 42 plants were in a variety of industries, including auto assembly, auto parts, electronics, computer software, construction, textile, and paper. In this sample, 38% of the dyads were similar in company tenure, 61% identical in gender, and 42.6% similar in educational level. Common particularistic ties were not very prevalent, with 1.8% of the dyads reporting kinship ties. In addition, 4.3% were former neighbors, 5.6% former classmates, 8% had the same natal origin, and 22.1% had the same party affiliation (i.e., both belonged to the Communist Party). The same set of outcomes as in the managerial dyad sample in Taiwan was used. They include the quality of the relationship in the dyad, the subordinate's organizational commitment, and supervisory assessment of the subordinate's performance. Results showed that two *guanxi* bases were significant for all four outcomes but only two relational demography variables were significant for one of the four outcomes.

Sharing the same natal origin and having the same party affiliation were positively associated with a high-quality relationship in the dyad, as perceived by both members of the dyad, and also with commitment and performance. Similarity in company tenure and gender was positively associated with high-quality relationship in the vertical dyad as perceived by the subordinate only. This study further confirmed the importance of *guanxi* in the Chinese context but the effect of relational demography is both weak and inconsistent.

Summary

Table 8.3 summarizes the research results based on these studies. As shown, both relational demography and *guanxi* appear to be related to some work outcomes, though the effect of relational demography is relatively weak and tends to be inconsistent. A variety of *guanxi* bases were found to be instrumental in affecting various work outcomes. These outcomes include being related to each other; belonging to the same party affiliation (communism); being former colleagues, classmates, or neighbors; and sharing the same natal origin (either speaking the same dialect or ancestors were from the same province or township). The work outcomes affected by these *guanxi* bases include trust in supervisor or in the business associates (i.e., those connections with whom one has particularistic ties), a positive and supportive relationship between the supervisor and the subordinate, subordinate commitment, and favorable assessment of the subordinate's performance by the supervisor.

These findings are highly consistent with the results of studies conducted in the United States. They confirm our view that *guanxi* is a special form of relational demography and that relational demography may be meaningful in other cultural settings, at least as shown in the Chinese context.

Future Directions

Clearly, the research reported in this chapter offers preliminary but encouraging evidence about the potential relevance of demographic diversity in the international arena, as is found in the Chinese context. Even in China, much more research is needed to explore a host of other variables in different types of organizations and groups. For example, although we used the example of a U.S.–Sino joint venture to illustrate the extent of demographic diversity in the top management team, so far there has been no research on the top management teams of joint ventures. Such research should add to the knowledge that has been accumulated on top management team demography using U.S. samples. Hambrick et al. (1998) describe how the composition of the top management groups in joint ven-

Table 8.3 *Guanxi*, Relational Demography, and Work Outcomes in China

Sample	Independent Variables	Outcomes
560 Insurance agents and their supervisors (Taiwan)	Education difference Gender difference Related to each other Former neighbors	Trust in the supervisor
205 horizontal dyads (Mainland China)	Same natal origin Former classmate	Trust in the connection
175 managers and their subordinates (Taiwan)	Tenure similarity Same natal origin Former colleagues	High-quality relationship between supervisor and subordinate Subordinate commitment Subordinate performance
168 senior managers and their subordinates (Mainland China)	Gender similarity Tenure similarity Former classmate Same natal origin Same party affiliation	High quality relationship with supervisor High quality relationship between sub and supervisor Subordinate commitment Subordinate performance

Note: Only the significant relationships are reported in the above table.

tures may trigger two types of downward spirals. One downward spiral is caused by the negative dynamic associated with demographic diversity in the team. A second downward spiral is triggered by the tension and goal incompatibility between the parents. Hambrick et al. (1998) further proposed a set of process and structural mechanisms that may minimize or arrest these two downward spirals. Their framework offers a promising direction for research in a variety of cultural settings, including China. Additional mechanisms for minimizing the negative effects of demographic diversity will be described in detail in Chapter 10 on managing diversity.

Notes

This chapter draws from these papers: Tsui & Farh, 1997; Farh, Tsui, Xin & Cheng, 1998; and Xin, Farh, Cheng & Tsui, 1998.

Chapter 9

An Integrative Framework of Demographic Diversity in Organizations

The review of the demographic diversity research in Chapters 5 to 8 has shown quite clearly that diversity affects a variety of outcomes. Many of these studies used the social psychological processes of categorization and identification to help explain the relationship between diversity and outcomes. This body of research, though consisting of a set of relatively fragmented studies, provides a sound foundation for the development of an integrative framework of demographic diversity. In this chapter, we will present and describe this framework, which is graphically presented in Figure 9.1.

This framework not only includes the mediating processes that link demography to outcomes, an emphasis strongly endorsed by Lawrence (1997), but also a set of antecedents or sources of demographic diversity in organizations. It further separates out the social psychological processes that are responsible for the social outcomes (either positive or negative) from the discovery of the different knowledge, skills, and perspectives associated with demographic diversity and that are responsible for task outcomes, i.e., potential performance gains. It also addresses the role of the context in either strengthening or weakening the relevance or salience of a particular demographic factor for social categorization or identification. Finally, it identifies where intervention is useful to minimize the negative effect of diversity so that its positive potential can be realized.

Visible versus Non-visible Demographic Factors

We define demographic diversity broadly to include any characteristic that can serve as a basis for social categorization and self-identification.

Figure 9.1 Demographic Diversity: Antecedents, Moderators, Mediators, and Outcomes

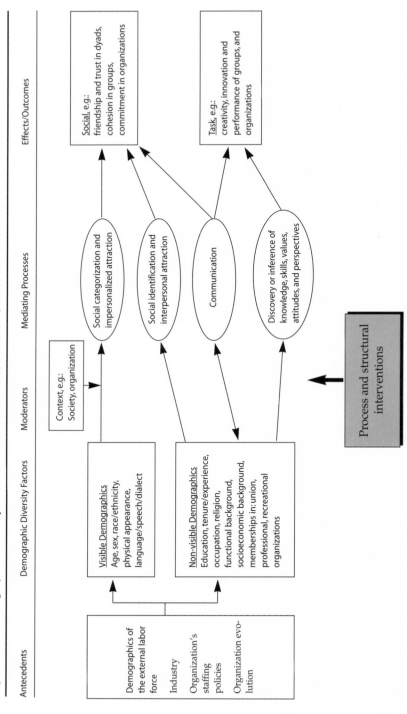

Demographic diversity comes in two types: visible and non-visible. The visible factors include age, sex, race or ethnicity, physical appearance, language, speech patterns, and dialect. Physical appearance could include weight and height, skin color, or physical disability. Language and speech pattern, including accent and dialect, not only enable understanding but they are clues to one's national or geographic origins. These visible characteristics serve as cues to trigger the stereotype associated with that category and the social categorization process whereby similar others are categorized "in" and dissimilar others are categorized "out."

The salience of a particular factor is affected by the context within which the individual is situated. For example, a fair-skinned individual would notice another fair-skinned individual in Africa and a dark-haired person would notice another dark-haired person in northern Europe. The same fair-skinned individual would not notice a fair skin color as a social category in central Europe or Canada. Therefore, the society or location is a context that moderates (i.e., strengthens or weakens) the relationship between a particular demographic factor and the social categorization process. Social categorization (of self and of the other) leads to impersonalized attraction, which in turn evokes the social identification process. Social identification occurs with people who are similar to oneself on personally meaningful or situation-induced salient social categories.

The non-visible demographic factors usually are discovered after some communication, either written or oral. For example, a recruiter would discover the educational background of a candidate, such as type of degree or alma mater, from a written resume or in an interview. Two people typically would discover their religion, occupation, natal origin, or membership in the Rotary club after some conversation, unless the origin is revealed through accent or if there are visible signs of membership through artifacts such as a badge or uniform. Similarity in meaningful social categories leads to social identification and interpersonal attraction. Identification and attraction facilitate communication. Communication leads to the discovery of other common demographic diversity factors. Communication also facilitates the discovery of knowledge, skills, or perspectives.

In summary, the two kinds of demographic factors each play a different role with the visible factors responsible for the initial social categorization and identification. While the visible factors are immediately accessible, the non-visible factors are discovered only after either direct or indirect communication and they may further strengthen or weaken the initial identification. They may also lead to new identification. Here, we are proposing that most of the knowledge and skills are associated with the non-visible demographic factors, which implies that their discovery tends to be delayed. This time ordering of the effects of the two types of demographic factors is consistent with existing research which suggests that performance gains in diverse groups often are preceded by social outcomes such as liking or conflict (Watson et al., 1993).

Mediating Processes

We identified four mediating processes, which occur in this sequence: social categorization accompanied by impersonalized attraction, social identification accompanied by interpersonal attraction, communication, and discovery of knowledge, skills, and perspectives. Social categorization is a relatively non-conscious process. It serves to provide information about the similar or dissimilar other (by invoking the stereotype associated with the social category). For example, Orientals are often assumed to be non-assertive and overweight people are often assumed to love food. Social categorization also serves to offer a level of comfort or discomfort (through the process of impersonalized attraction) in the presence of others who are similar or dissimilar on the relevant demographic attribute. For example, an Asian in New York City may choose not to eat in a restaurant with a primarily Jamaican clientele but might feel less discomfort if there is at least one other Asian in the restaurant. An older person might not want his or her hair styled in a salon that caters to teenagers but would be more likely to use it if she or he saw another older customer in the salon. An expatriate might feel very much an outsider in the host country but might feel less isolated if at least one other expatriate lived in that community. Each of these individuals have an impersonalized (though non-conscious) attraction for the similar other and "dis-attraction" or impersonalized rejection of the dissimilar others.

Social identification follows social categorization if the category is at least minimally meaningful to the individual. In the hair salon example above, the older customer would feel no discomfort if age was not a salient category for self-identity. This person would not feel particularly attracted to the other "older" customer. If age was a meaningful social category, the two "older" customers would feel an immediate affinity and might, for example, make eye contact, smile at each other, or start a conversation. Through their conversation, they may discover further commonality on the non-visible demographics or particularistic ties. They also may discover differences that may dilute the initial attraction. They may further discover knowledge, skills, attitudes, values, or perspectives that are associated or assumed to be associated with certain demographic attributes. If one of the two older people is an accountant while the other is a lawyer, inference of knowledge and skills (and of values) may result "naturally" from the knowledge of their respective occupations. If they are in completely unrelated fields, they may search for another commonality or their dissimilarity may inhibit further communication.

Communication, therefore, serves to facilitate the further discovery of commonality or differences in demographic background between the individuals. Repeated interaction with the same person, as occurs between co-workers and a customer who has a relationship with a service provider (Gutek, 1995) provides opportunities to discover even more commonality or differences. However, due to the accentuation process whereby positive attributes of the similar other are exaggerated, such communication tends to focus on discovery of further commonality and there is a selective exclusion of dissimilarities. Therefore, initial identification tends to be further solidified by the selective discovery of additional common background, experiences, and attitudes. Knowledge of the demographic profile of the other will also lead to inferred or assumed differences in knowledge, skills, or perspectives. These inferences or assumptions are based on the social stereotypes associated with particular demographic attributes. Occasionally, though rarely, communication may also serve to discover real differences in these areas.

Inferred, assumed, or discovered, diversity on certain attributes means that there may be real differences in knowledge, skills, attitudes, values, and perspectives. It is widely believed that engineers and marketers tend to see the same problem in a different light (Dearborn & Simon, 1958). Accountants and operations experts bring different knowledge and skills to the task. Individuals with different educational backgrounds and different industry experiences can offer diverse views and perspectives to a management issue. National differences exist in individualism, power distance, and tolerance for ambiguity. Diversity on knowledge, skills, and perspectives, or even attitudes and values, may affect problem solving and analyses and potential solutions or approaches to the task. Therefore, demographic diversity can mean both real and assumed differences on these task-relevant factors.

Effects or Outcomes

We organize outcomes into two broad categories: social and task. Social outcomes result primarily from the social categorization and identification processes. Task outcomes are affected by knowledge, skills, and perspectives (even attitudes and values) associated with demographic diversity as well as by the social outcomes. Social outcomes include friendship and trust at the dyad level; cohesion, commitment, and interpersonal conflict (or lack thereof) at the group level; and integration, commitment, and inter-group conflict (or lack thereof) at the organizational level. Task outcomes include creativity, innovation, and performance of the group and of the organization. Outcomes at the individual level include commitment to the group or organization, and preferential treatment by similar others in terms of favorable performance evaluations, promotions, or other forms of career advancement.

We further expect that social outcomes would facilitate task outcomes such as lower turnover and higher commitment, which reduce the cost of managing a business, and reduce work group conflict that could impede production. A high-performing work group, on the other hand, should also facilitate cohesion, since performance may enhance the self-esteem of the group or the individual. The relationship between social and task outcomes is quite complex and more likely reciprocal than independent or unrelated.

The Moderating Role of the Context

Two types of contexts are relevant for further understanding of demographic effects. First is the social or societal setting. Some demographic factors—such as gender—are important in almost any social and societal settings. Others—such as age—are almost universally important but may have different meanings; in some societies the elderly are considered wise whereas in others they are considered nonproductive and a social cost. Still other factors are important in some social or societal settings but not in others. In a society where certain social categories are highly related to status and power (e.g., religion with status in India) or where a certain social category is the primary basis of self-identity (e.g., family in China), differences on these social categories would take on considerable importance.

The social setting is also relevant where an individual is very different from others in the context. For example, being an American is more salient to an American in Russia than to another American in Canada (Buss & Portnoy, 1967). Being an American is not particularly salient to Americans interacting with other Americans in America! Therefore, the societal context may heighten the salience of a particular demographic factor. Ethnic diversity between Americans and people of other nationalities can take on a different meaning and can lead to different results depending on whether the Americans are located in Russia or in Canada. This also means that demography studies of multinational firms or joint ventures in one country may produce results that cannot be generalized to multinational firms or joint ventures in other countries.

A second relevant context is the organization within which dyads and groups are located. The effect of the organization can be twofold. First, depending on its overall "diversity climate," it can heighten differences or minimize differences between people of different social categories. People who are otherwise different would see or experience less difference in organizations with a positive diversity climate (to be discussed more in

Chapter 10). Organizations with a positive diversity climate will strive to reduce the relevance of visible demographic differences among their members and make efforts to highlight common characteristics among people who are different, often by searching for commonality on non-visible factors. Second, the organization itself can serve as a meaningful social category for identification by its members. This is especially true for organizations with a strong culture.

Some organizational theorists argue that work organizations are mini-societies that have their own distinct patterns of culture and subcultures (Morgan, 1986). One culture theorist offers the following meaning of organization as cultural entity:

> As individuals come into contact with organizations, they come into contact with dress norms, stories people tell about what goes on, the organization's formal rules and procedures, its informal codes of behavior, rituals, tasks, pay systems, jargon, and jokes only understood by insiders, and so on. These elements are some of the manifestations of organizational culture. (Martin, 1992, p. 3)

The employing organization, therefore, has the potential of offering cultural meanings to its members much like the demographic attributes of ethnicity, gender, or national origin. It potentially may have the same social psychological significance for employees as that offered by other social categories such as gender, race, education, or occupation. The organization may serve as a "super-ordinate" category for deriving self-identity by individuals. It can be a potentially attractive psychological group for some individuals. An appropriate example of the organization serving as an attractive psychological group and offering positive social identity for its members is the old IBM. The strong identification of IBM employees with their company is well documented in both academic and popular sources (Peters and Waterman, 1982). The following story (not from IBM but another "strong culture" organization) illustrates a case of a strong identification with the organization.

> We have a young woman who is extraordinarily important to the launching of a major new [product]. We will be talking about it next Tuesday in its first worldwide introduction. She arranged to have her [baby born by a] Caesarean [operation] yesterday in order to be prepared for this event, so you see—we insisted that she stay home and this is going to be televised in a closed circuit television, so we're having this by TV for her. (Martin, 1992, p. 35)

While there are many different interpretations of this story (such as the organization is not being sensitive to the woman's condition), one possibility is that the organization may be a more important social category for this woman's self-identity than her gender or her new motherhood—which might be the case if the woman requested for this broadcast to be brought to her room in the hospital. When the organization becomes a super-ordinate category for all its members, inter-group conflict and differentiation due to demographic diversity would be minimal. This occurs because the organization is the primary category for self-categorization by all its members and it becomes a meaningful psychological group that binds all individuals. Identification with the organization leads to accentuation of its positive attributes and thus further enhances the members' self-image and identity.

Frequent downsizing in recent years, however, is making the organization less and less attractive as a psychological group. Treatment of workers as labor costs rather than as assets makes it difficult for managers to convince workers they should identify with the company. Indeed, if the old psychological contract of job security in exchange for good performance and loyalty to the company is now being displaced with a more mobile and transient labor force, it would be foolish for workers to look to the firm as a source of self-identification.

When the organization is not a primary basis for social categorization, demographic factors are likely to be more relevant for members' self-identity. In these organizations, many social categories may exist, depending upon the number of members and extent of demographic diversity in the organization. Social categories could be differentiated along functional specialty, occupation, race, gender, hierarchical level, and so on. Each social category can have its own unique subculture. This differentiation increases the likelihood of increasing within-group cohesion and communication while decreasing cohesion and communication between subcultures within the larger organization.

In summary, the organization can moderate the effect of demographic diversity on outcomes depending on its own diversity climate and on whether it is a meaningful social category for identification by its members. The relevant question here is, What makes an organization an attractive psychological group? There is some indication that organizations with a "strong culture" (defined as high consensus in the beliefs and values among organizational members) are more likely to offer a positive identity for its members than organizations with a relatively weaker culture (Deal and Kennedy, 1982). Discussion of the development of a strong organizational culture is beyond the scope of this book. However, it is important to conclude with two key points. First, the organization could be a meaningful category for social identity for its members. And second, when it is used by a majority (or all) of the members of an organization for self-categorization, it is likely that the negative dynamics of demographic diversity may be minimized or may not even occur. However, research is needed to verify these conjectures.

Antecedents of Demographic Diversity in Organizations

There have been very few studies on the antecedents of diversity within firms. In Chapter 3, we discussed the lack of empirical research on the antecedents or "causes" of demographic diversity in organizations. Perhaps this reflects the assumption that diversity research is a given context and firms can do little to prevent or stop the changes taking place in the larger labor force. However, as will be discussed below, firms do have some control over the demographic composition of their internal workforce through staffing policies and managerial actions.

What makes some organizations more diverse than others? What are the sources of demographic differences among the employees of an organization? There are two potential sets of sources, one external to the organization and another internal to the organization. The external sources include the demographic composition of the labor force in the geographic area from which the organization draws its employees and the industries in which the organization operates. The increasing demographic diversity of U.S. firms is attributable largely to the increasing diversity of the U.S. labor force. Relative to some other countries, e.g., Japan, China, or Norway, the U.S. labor force is more heterogeneous in terms of race/ethnicity and national origin. Some firms are located in regions with a large minority or immigrant population, e.g., southern California or Texas. Other firms operate in industries dominated by employees with particular demographic characteristics. For example, micro-electronics, semi-conductors, and fast food industries have largely a young labor force. Some service industries, such as the hospitality industry, employ both young and immigrant workers. The composition of the external labor force can have a direct impact on the demographic composition of the firm's internal workforce. In fact, firms are expected to have an internal labor force that is roughly comparable to that of the relevant external labor market.

Some countries in Europe and Saudi Arabia, for example, "import" guest workers from other countries. These guest workers may differ from the locals not only in nationality but also in educational background and a variety of cultural values, norms, or customs. The economic development of a region could be a critical factor in the increasing heterogeneity of the labor force of that region and the organizations within it.

Firms can also influence their internal workforce composition by deliberate staffing policies. Affirmative action hiring is designed specifically to ensure sufficient representation of employees in certain categories. Equal employment opportunity is to ensure that no applicants, regardless of their social categories, are excluded from job or placement consideration. Staffing policies about external hiring and internal promotion or placement can be focused on developing an appropriate distribution of employees on both visible and non-visible demographic attributes. The irony of the current U.S. legislation is that, while firms are not to make employment decisions based on certain demographic attributes, they are also expected to have a reasonable distribution or representation of their employees on these same attributes. Employers, therefore, are expected to both use and not use demographic attributes in employment decision making. The key is how such information is used and for what purpose. In either case, the organization's staffing policies, whether deliberate or implicit, can affect the demographic diversity of its internal workforce.

Changes in the strategy and structure of the firm also introduce demographic variation over time. For example, research by Haveman (1995) found patterns of tenure distribution to be related to organizational founding, dissolution, and mergers. Keck and Tushman (1992) found changes in the demographic composition in the executive team when the organization experienced reorientation, environmental jolts, or technological discontinuities. Organizational evolution, therefore, is another source of demographic variation of workforce.

Propositions on the Integrative Framework

The proposed framework in Figure 9.1 is both comprehensive and limited. While it is clear that dimensions of demographic diversity are not substitutable (i.e., being diverse in age is not equivalent to being diverse on functional specialty), our model is limited because it does not spell out the specific effect of each demographic factor. It does not describe what knowledge or skills are associated with which demographic attribute. It does not go into the details of how social categorization and identification occur. It does not link diversity on specific attributes to each of the outcomes. And it does not include all potential moderators. The nature of the tasks performed by individuals within the group is an example of one such moderator; diversity may have a greater effect on a team with interdependent tasks among its members than on a team with members performing independent tasks. Further refinement of this framework is clearly desirable.

However, the framework is comprehensive because it incorporates a set of factors that were rarely considered in past demography or diversity research. These are the mediating processes, the contextual factors as moderators, and the antecedents of demographic diversity in the firm's internal labor force. The framework describes the processes by which demographic diversity leads to a set of social and task outcomes for the individual, the dyad, the group, and the organization as a whole. Based on this framework, we make the following propositions.

Propositions on Antecedents of Demographic Diversity

P1 Firms located in societies or geographic areas with a more demographically diverse labor force will have a more demographically diverse workforce than firms located in societies or locations with a less demographically diverse labor force.

P2 The top management teams of foreign subsidiaries of multinational firms or joint ventures will be more demographically diverse than top management teams of domestic firms or top management teams of the parent company of the multinational corporation or joint ventures.

P3 Firms that operate in industries with a demographically diverse labor force will have a more demographically diverse workforce than firms that operate in industries with a more demographically homogeneous labor force.

P4 Firms that have strong and extensive staffing policies based on equal employment and affirmative action will have a more demographically diverse workforce than firms that have staffing policies that are weak and limited with respect to equal employment and affirmative action.

P5 There will be more changes in the demographic composition of firms that have frequent strategic change, restructuring, mergers, and acquisitions.

Propositions on Mediating Processes

P6 Initial social categorization will be based more on visible than on non-visible demographic attributes.

P7 Social identification with individuals sharing common demographic attributes or with particularistic ties will be positively associated with frequency of communication with such individuals.

P8 Frequency of communication will be positively associated with demographic similarity, and communication with demographically similar individuals will be associated with discovery of further demographic commonality.

P9 Social identification and interpersonal attraction will be stronger among individuals sharing more bases of demographic similarity or particularistic ties than among individuals sharing fewer bases of demographic similarity.

P10 Demographically diverse groups will have more diversity in knowledge, skills, attitudes, values, and perspectives than demographically homogeneous groups.

Propositions on the Moderating Role of Contextual Factors

P11   Social identification based on particular demographic attributes will be stronger in societies where those particular attributes are strong bases for self-identity than in societies where such attributes are weak bases for self-identity.

P12   Social categorization based on visible demographic attributes will occur more frequency in organizations with a weak or unfavorable diversity climate than in organizations with a strong or favorable diversity climate.

P13   Social categories based on both visible and non-visible demographic attributes will be weaker when employees have a strong organizational identification than when employees have a weak organizational identification.

Propositions on Outcomes

P14   Homogeneity in social category and common identification with social category will be positively associated with friendship and trust in dyads; with low emotional conflict, high cohesion, and commitment in groups; and with commitment and inclusion in organizations.

P15   Diversity in knowledge, skills, and perspectives will be positively associated with outcomes such as task conflict, creativity, innovation, and performance of individuals, groups, and organizations.

P16   Social identification will be more strongly associated with social outcomes than with task outcomes, while diversity in knowledge, skills, and perspectives will be more strongly associated with task outcomes than with social outcomes.

Summary

The proposed framework attempts to provide an integrative view on the effect of demographic diversity on outcomes for the individual, the dyad, the group, and the organization as a whole. It shows that the normal outcomes of demographic diversity is less attraction, less likelihood of friendship formation, less trust, less cohesion between members of dyads and groups, and lower commitment to the organization. However, demographic diversity also has the promise of a greater variety of skills, knowledge, and perspectives that can facilitate creativity and performance in work groups and organizations. Yet, lower trust, cohesion, and commitment may prevent the group or the organization from realizing the potential associated with these cognitive and knowledge resources. How does a group or an organization resolve such a paradox? The answer lies in the creation of structural and process intervention, the shadowed box in

Figure 9.1. These refer to the strategies for managing diversity at the individual, group, and organizational levels. Chapter 10 describes in detail the strategies at each of these levels. The reality is that diversity is a liability until and unless processes are in place to manage the negative dynamic and to release diversity's hidden potential. In an increasingly competitive global environment, overcoming this liability may be a key to long-term survival.

Chapter 10

Managing Demographic Diversity

"Managing" diversity has become fashionable to the point that seminars, executive training, and undergraduate and MBA courses are devoted to the topic. The first question to be addressed in programs aimed at managing diversity is whether or not diversity indeed needs to be managed! Based on the research available on organizational demography, we conclude that it *is* fruitful to manage diversity. As we have already discussed, social categorization based on visible characteristics such as race/ethnicity, sex, age, and language and dialect is common, normal, and natural. We also know that, in general, people prefer to be around people who are like them. In the absence of other information, it is easy to rely on visible social categories to determine whether or not one person will like another person.

We believe that diversity can be managed in two ways. One way to manage diversity is to be aware of the social psychological processes that mediate the relationship between visible demographic characteristics and social and performance outcomes. After becoming aware of the mediating processes, one can influence and manage them to arrest the negative effects and to reap the positive benefits of diversity. A second, and more controversial, way to manage diversity is to actively manage the distribution of workers on the basis of visible characteristics much in the same way managers actively manage the distribution of workers on less visible characteristics such as prior experience, tenure, functional area, and occupation. While some managers actively manage the distribution of men and women or people of different ethnic groups, others view such a strategy as counter-productive (i.e., not focusing on getting the best possible person for the job) and argue that it is tantamount to setting quotas.

We assume that diversity is to be embraced for two good reasons. One, it is socially desirable and responsible to give equal opportunity to people of all social categories. Second, managing diversity is economically wise because of the hidden potential of diversity. In a global economy, exploiting the advantages of diversity can provide a competitive advantage in an increasingly competitive and efficient market.

We are only at the beginning stage of understanding why diversity has created both difficulties and benefits and why organizations and groups have not been able to marshal and use effectively the cognitive resources associated with having a diverse group of workers. It is also clear that we no longer need prove that diversity is beneficial; it is. Our challenge is to develop methods to capture the benefits of diversity by designing methods to overcome the negative dynamics associated with the social categorization process.

In this chapter, we suggest strategies that can move us in the direction of better understanding and constructive action. Some strategies can be derived from understanding how social categories are formed and the conditions under which they operate. Some strategies are suggested by research on specific mechanisms or processes that may reduce inter-group conflict or promote intra-group cohesion. Some of the strategies are aimed at individuals and dyads, some at groups, and others at organizations. The strategies are organized and presented in this chapter for each of these levels.

These ideas are offered with the caveat that most of the methods are based on research using college students in experimental designs or with children in elementary schools. Some methods are derived from work in teams or personal development in the organizational change domain. Thus, both new and more research is needed to verify the efficacy of many of the strategies proposed here in natural organizational work groups composed of dissimilar members. Let us begin by examining strategies used by individuals to manage demographic differences.

Personal Strategies for Managing Demographic Differences

The best place to begin is with each and every individual who finds the presence of dissimilar others to be an inevitable fact of life in today's world of work. It would be helpful for each individual to recognize that it is natural to be biased in favor of others similar to oneself and against others who are dissimilar to oneself. The most promising solution to the diversity problem is for every individual to make a commitment to address this issue. The best place to begin is not with others but with oneself.

Discovering the Primary Bases of Self-Identity

How should one begin this process of developing personal strategies to operate effectively in today's diverse world? A reasonable starting point is for all persons to understand what social categories they use to describe themselves. Each person can ask: On what basis do I categorize myself and others? From what sources do I derive my self-image and what about me makes me proud? How strong do I feel about my gender, my cultural ethnic background, my educational achievement, the kind of work I do, my religious belief, my age, where I was born and raised, where I live, and where I work? Who are my friends at work and outside of work and what is the primary social and demographic background of each? When I meet someone new for the first time, what am I most likely to notice first about the person and what am I most interested in finding out about that individual? The answers to these questions can provide some insight into the primary sources of one's own social identity and how one might react to others who do not share the primary social categories from which one's self-identity is based.

This self-knowledge will not only help us understand how we react to others who are different from us, it also can reveal why we feel the way we do about ourselves when we are in the presence of dissimilar others. Both types of reactions (reactions about others and about ourselves) are natural outcomes of our basic need to have self-esteem. Our esteem is bolstered by accentuating the positive attributes of the social group to which we belong and exaggerating the negative attributes of the "other" groups to which we do not belong. Self-esteem is enhanced when we define ourselves as members of high-status social groups. Clearly, these reactions and associated behavior triggered by the social categorization process, while useful to oneself, do not necessarily contribute to positive and productive interactions among individuals in different social categories. However, such reactions are understandable. Since we are all victims of such social psychological processes, we are all in the same boat. Empathy toward each other is a helpful step toward mutual acceptance and support.

Remembering a Simple Statistical Rule

One simple statistical rule can help people counteract the tendency to stereotype others who are strangers. On most psychological or personality characteristics (e.g., attitudes, conscientiousness, mathematical ability, loyalty, assertiveness, dominance, diligence), people are normally distributed (i.e., the distribution of the attribute fits a normal curve). Though the average person from one social category, say Asians, may be higher on an attribute such as shyness than the average person of another category, say Americans, any one Asian could be higher or lower on this attribute than an American. In other words, for any meaningful psychological or personality characteristic, there is almost always an overlapping region—sometimes a large overlapping region—between any two social categories. Figure 10.1 illustrates this point with a graph showing the average and the range of assertiveness of two categories of people. The average level of assertiveness for Category A is a score of 50 and for Category B, it is a score of 70. Therefore, members of Category A are less assertive than members of Category B. The range of assertiveness score for individuals in Category A is 20 to 80 while the range of assertiveness score for individuals in Category B is between 50 and 100. However, person A1 of group A has a score of 75 while person B2 of group B has a score of 55. Therefore, person A1 from the relatively non-assertive group is more assertive than person B2 from the relatively more assertive group. Stereotyping person A1 as non-assertive—which would happen if person A1 is categorized as belonging to Category A rather than seen as a unique individual—would lead to inaccurate expectations and treatment by others.

While Figure 10.1 shows hypothetical distributions of two fictitious categories of people, Figure 10.2 shows real distributions of men and women on a characteristic often assumed to be much more likely in men than in women, namely, mathematical ability. A meta-analysis of 100 usable sources containing 259 independent effect sizes showed that the distributions of men and women in mathematical ability were .15 standard deviations apart (Hyde, Fennema & Lamon, 1990). Although men are often considered better at math than women, it is obvious from these results that if a man and woman were each randomly selected, in many instances, the woman would have greater math ability than the man. Stereotyping every

Figure 10.1 Group vs. Individual Differences

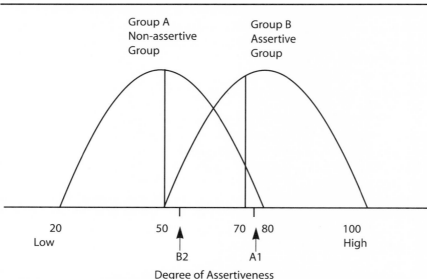

Note: A1 is an individual in Group A, B2 is an individual in Group B.

Figure 10.2 Gender Difference in Math Performance

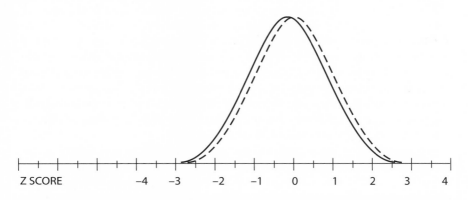

Two normal distributions that are 0.15 standard deviations apart (i.e., *d* = 0.15. This is the approximate magnitude of the gender difference in mathematics performance, averaging over all samples.)

Source: From Hyde et al., 1990, Figure 1, p. 149

woman as having less math ability than every man will clearly result in many incorrect inferences.

There is a second reason why this simple statistical rule can be useful. It provides us with a baseline to determine the likely behavior, attitudes, or tendencies of a specific individual. In other words, we can make an estimate of the probability of the person's true characteristics. Let us use an example to illustrate this point. From cross-cultural research, we know that people in collectivist cultures tend to cooperate while people in individualistic cultures tend to compete in interpersonal situations. In other words, the average person in the collectivist culture would be cooperative while the average person in the individualistic culture would be competitive. However, to assume that any single individual in a particular social group would be like the average member of that group would be an act of stereotyping. The simple statistical rule of the normal curve would remind us that we could be wrong. However, the statistical rule also suggests that chances are greater that an individual from a collectivist culture is more likely to be cooperative than an individual from an individualistic culture. The problem is not that we do not make this probable guess. The problem is that we do it too often or too well. Stereotyping an individual on a particular personality attribute or behavioral tendency based on his or her category membership is making a probable guess that the individual will be like an average individual in that group. Over 30% of the people in any particular group are, however, not the average. To avoid what is referred to as the Type I error (to assume it is when it is not), it is critical that we verify our inference (or probable guess) by observation of actual behavior of that individual. Since our perceptual process is such that we see what we believe, obtaining multiple observations of the individual and from multiple sources (if possible) would be desirable.

Along the same vein, we often make Type II errors (to assume that it is not when it is) by the stereotypic response that an individual from a collectivist culture would not be individualistic. It is probable that any one individual from the collectivist culture would be as or perhaps more individualistic than an individual from an individualistic culture. Therefore, being a skeptic about one's ability to accurately judge and observe people is a critical skill of a responsible individual.

While having multiple interactions with others and receiving information from multiple sources enable one to guard against stereotyping, it is not always possible to do this. For example, workers who interact with customers in service encounters interact primarily with strangers, i.e., people with whom they have no prior interaction and with whom they do not intend to interact in the future (Gutek, 1995). Under these circumstances it is particularly easy to apply stereotypes to these customers (and it is equally easy for the customers to stereotype service providers who are strangers to them). Therefore, it is especially important to be mindful of that possibility and retain a healthy skepticism about being able to judge these strangers accurately.

Assessing One's Vulnerability to Self-Stereotyping

It is also important to be aware of the extent to which one is vulnerable to self-stereotyping. To do so is especially detrimental to people who belong to a social category associated with negative attributes. (See Steele, 1997, for an overview of research on this topic.) For those who are in social categories that are positively stereotyped, self-stereotyping would provide an additional source of self-confidence. The inter-group dynamic associated with the self-enhancement of one group may, however, be costly to the well-being of the comparison group and make it difficult to form a productive relationship between people from the two categories. Therefore, self-stereotyping should be avoided by members of any social category. It is probably always better to have an accurate assessment of one's traits and abilities. Gaining self-esteem at the expense of others and relationships with others is of debatable merit.

Most of the research on the performance impact of self-stereotyping assumes that the stereotypes are negative in nature (see Chapter 4 for a discussion of this research), perhaps because negative stereotypes can do more damage than positive ones, including to those people who are most unlike the stereotype. For people who are sensitive to negative stereotypes associated with the social categories to which they belong, it is critical to develop an awareness of the extent to which they are vulnerable to self-stereotyping. Here is a list of questions that may help determine the extent to which one may be engaging in self-stereotyping on the basis of gender, race, religion, ethnicity, national origin, occupations, or educational background or level:[1]

a. How often do I perceive myself as typical of others who share the same social category (demographic background) as myself?
b. Do I behave or perform differently when I am in a group consisting primarily of people like myself, and groups consisting primarily of people different from myself?
c. How often do I believe that others view me or judge me based on my membership in a particular group more than based on the characteristics unique to myself?
d. How often do I think people respond to me for what I really am rather than for my membership in my primary social category?
e. How often do I think that, because of my demographic background, people around me play it safe and hold back from saying what is really on their mind?
f. How often do I wonder if people sometimes judge my ability based on stereotypes of my social group?
g. How often do I think, because of my demographic background, people put on an act of friendliness that does not match their true feelings toward me?
h. Is it easier for me to seek help from others who are similar to me on certain demographic dimensions than from people who are different?
i. Am I comfortable in entering situations where I am the sole member of my particular background?
j. When other members of my particular background embarrass themselves, do I worry about how their actions will reflect upon me?

A person who answers yes or often to many of these questions is likely to be a victim of self-stereotyping. A simple example is an Asian who believes that Asians are not assertive and is therefore reluctant to speak up in work settings. Others believing in such a stereotypic attribute of Asians would be reluctant to call upon the Asian for suggestions in a group setting. Sometimes this happens because others have the good intention of wanting to protect or respect the needs of the Asian person. Not being asked to contribute, the Asian becomes even more hesitant. Thus, the entire process becomes a self-fulfilling prophecy for everyone, and it reinforces the stereotype held by everyone (observers as well as the target person) that Asians are not assertive and this particular Asian fits the stereotype. In reality, this particular Asian could be an extremely eloquent speaker in a social setting where such stereotyping is not applicable or is less salient, such as around the family dinner table or in an Asian church discussion group.

The term "stereotype threat" (Steele, 1997), has been used to describe a situation where a negative stereotype about one's social category becomes relevant to interpreting oneself or one's behavior in an "identified-with" setting. The Asian in the example above might experience stereotype threat if he considers himself a particularly eloquent speaker, contrary to the stereotype of Asians, and is placed in a situation where others are expecting him to be reticent and quiet. Another example is an African-American who considers herself very good at math being placed in a competitive situation with others who expect African-Americans to perform poorly in math. In these types of situations, Steele (1997) and his colleagues have found that the stereotype-threatened perform less well than they do when they are not in that kind of situation.

What should those susceptible to self-stereotyping do? Once they become aware of this tendency, there are a number of possible actions. They can consciously begin to let their actions reflect their true selves. They can inform others of their true inclinations and solicit support from their friends at work. Self-regulation in the form of seeking feedback and help from others and adjusting one's behavior accordingly often results in positive impressions by others.[2] These suggestions are obviously quite straightforward and may be too obvious to dwell upon. Nonetheless, self-awareness is an excellent starting point and self-regulation is an excellent process for increasing personal and professional effectiveness in the diverse work setting.

Taking Ownership of the Problem

As some of the quotes at the beginning of the first chapter demonstrate, members of both the minority and the majority categories can feel frustrated by the diversity problem. Both can feel that members of the other category cause the problem and receive favored treatment by management. Management, by instituting diversity programs with most of the focus on structuring career paths for the historically disadvantaged groups and by providing training to supervisors on the diversity issue, essentially are taking ownership of the problem, leaving individuals waiting for something positive to happen to them. The relatively deprived ask, "When is management going to be serious about addressing this diversity problem?" The dominant majority wonders, "When will it be my turn to receive the benefits that I deserve?" The message here is that everyone believes "It is not my problem, it is yours!" It is worthwhile to reiterate that understanding differences is everyone's problem, and hence it is everyone's responsibility to address it. This means that every member should take ownership of the problem and take the initiative to resolve it.

This includes all employees (of any social category), the work group leader or supervisor, the middle manager leading the department or operating unit, and the top executive for the entire organization. For example, everyone can work to avoid placing anyone of any social category in a "stereotype threat" position. It is unfair to expect some people's work to reflect only on them and to expect other people's work to reflect on everyone in their social category. Knowing that a failure to speak eloquently will reflect on all Asians or that a failure to perform well at math will be interpreted as proof that women are not good at math puts undue pressure on people who themselves do not fit the negative stereotype.

Dyad-Level Strategies for Managing Demographic Diversity

A dyad, by definition, involves two persons who must engage in some interactions. There are a variety of actions that either or both members of the dyad may take to ensure that the interaction is positive, productive, and beneficial to both parties. Most of the strategies or actions proposed here should be applicable to both the vertical and the horizontal dyad. However, due to the power differential between the two members in the vertical dyad, some strategies may be more important than others, and one member may feel more hesitant than the other in using some strategies. Managing the demographic dynamic in a vertical dyad must involve sensitivity toward the power relationship and guard against hesitancy by either member. Further, many of the strategies at the personal level (described above) and at the group level (to be described below) should be applicable at the dyad level as well. In this section, we focus on those strategies that are particularly appropriate for dyads.

Discovering Similarities through Exploring Common Categories

From the discussions in Chapter 4, we know that categorization based on a visible attribute or known category is immediate and long lasting. The other individual will be perceived as similar or different depending on the category being used. The first step is to become aware of the category that is being used by one or the other person at the initial encounter. The next step is to explore other categories that the two members may share in common (see Pettigrew & Martin 1987). This will require a dialogue that explores each person's background and past experiences. Attention to artifacts in another person's office that may reveal educational background (diplomas); past residences (pictures); places visited (pictures, coffee mugs, coasters, or mementos); professional or recreational activities (trophies or plaques); or family status (photographs) could uncover potential background similarities. Willingness to engage in apparently non-work-related conversations could facilitate the discovery of similarities. Such dialogues also may reflect one's interest in the other party, and perceived interest should further contribute to relationship building in the dyad.

A native Hispanic and a Philippine immigrant may seem to have little in common but it is quite likely that both are Catholics. A middle-aged Caucasian and a black person of similar age may both be Vietnam veterans. Japanese and Jewish persons may have a similar passion for their alma mater. It is possible, and in fact quite probable, that between any two individuals, there may be more similarities than differences on many of the social categories that have been found to influence interpersonal outcomes. In exploring common categories, each party also can discover the primary category for social identity used by the other party as well as the other party's vulnerability to self-stereotyping. Such information would reveal the unique person in the other, and interaction could be based on the true selves rather than on a "stereotypically constructed self." Being understood and treated according to one's true self rather than as a categorical self should facilitate mutual acceptance and high-quality relationship in the dyad.

Building Intimacy through Self-Disclosure

When faced with another person who is different from oneself on some meaningful or salient attribute or known background characteristic, the social categorization process operates. It leads to an inference of differences between self and the other person on a host of other non-observable attributes, including attitudes, values, and preferences presumed to be associated with individuals in the social category invoked. One of the outcomes of perceived dissimilarity is reduced interaction and psychological distance between the two members. This psychological distance does not facilitate the development of a high-quality relationship in the dyad, either vertical or horizontal. One way to reduce this psychological distance is a willingness to provide information about oneself. Social psychologists have suggested that healthy relationships build on the openness between the two parties (Jourard, 1964, 1968). Research has linked self-disclosure to perceived trustworthiness (Melinger, 1956; Wheeless & Grotz, 1977) and to the development of close relationships (Wheeless, 1978; Wheeless & Grotz, 1977). By sharing information about one's dispositions, attitudes, and values, one expresses one's trust in the other party. Such self-disclosure can lead the other person to similar disclosures. In a vertical dyad, the subordinate may be hesitant to initiate self-disclosure, not knowing how the supervisor may react to this behavior. Therefore, self-disclosure by the supervisor may be particularly important establishing a climate of mutual openness between the two members. In a horizontal dyad, self-disclosure by either party should facilitate openness in the dyad. In the study by Xin et al. (1998), researchers found self-disclosure by the supervisors (in the

Taiwan sample) to be associated with subordinates' perceptions of the quality of the relationship with the supervisor and subordinate's commitment to the organization. Therefore, self-disclosure may be a useful strategy for building an intimate relationship in the dyad. One must, of course, guard against too much disclosure or inappropriate disclosure. Further, some people may not be comfortable with disclosure of very personal and intimate information. There might be cross-cultural differences about the extent and type of information that should or can be disclosed to those who are not family members or confidants. Other strategies to be discussed here, such as self-regulation and self-monitoring, would be helpful to assess whether self-disclosure is helping or hurting the relationship in the dyad.

Meeting Expectations through Self-Regulation and Self-Monitoring

In the previous section on personal strategies, we introduced the idea of self-regulation and feedback-seeking to guard against the tendency of self-stereotyping. The self-regulation process (e.g. Tsui & Ashford, 1994) can be especially useful in fostering a productive, supportive, and beneficial relationship with another individual who can be a supervisor, a peer, a subordinate, or a customer. It begins with finding out and understanding the expectations that each party has for the other. These expectations could be about job goals and duties, about style and frequency of interaction, about resources and support to be shared, and about future behavior. Either or both parties should also seek feedback from the other regarding perceptions, opinions, and views of the other party's behavior in meeting expectations. Negative feedback focuses on information about what behavior should be changed or how a person can improve. Positive feedback focuses on what a person does well instead. Seeking negative feedback conveys a sense of sincerity and eagerness to be responsive to the other party's needs and expectations. It further conveys that one is secure and confident and not afraid of discovering or revealing one's weakness to the other party. Research has confirmed both the substantive and the impression management functions of seeking negative feedback using a direct inquiry strategy (Ashford & Tsui, 1991; Tsui, Ashford, St. Clair & Xin, 1995).

Social psychological research has further demonstrated the importance of adjusting one's behavior in response to the behavioral cues of the other party. This is referred to as "self-monitoring" (Snyder, 1979). Research studies with sales personnel (Marshall, Palmer & Weisbart, 1979) have found that individuals who monitor their behavior to adapt to the expectations and style of the customers are more successful in getting sales than those sales personnel who do not. Self-monitoring involves being observant and attentive to the verbal and non-verbal cues of the other party, and adapting one's behaviors, both verbal and non-verbal, accordingly. It is the process that is specific to an interaction episode while self-regulation is the process that is focused on the relationship as a whole, including understanding expectations, seeking feedback on evaluations, and adjusting behavior to reduce any discrepancies.

Group Strategies for Managing Demographic Diversity

Besides individual- and dyad-level strategies for managing demographic diversity, social categorization and social identity theory suggest a variety of group-level strategies. It is possible, for example, to provide structural mechanisms that will supercede inter-group differences by creating a necessity for group members to cooperate in order for them to succeed as individuals. It is also possible to provide a super-ordinate category that serves as a basis for social categorization by all members of the group. We shall first describe several structural mechanisms as group level strategies to deal with the diversity problem, and then discuss several interpersonal skills that might facilitate awareness, understanding, and acceptance of differences among individuals in the group as well as improve group process and performance.

Creating a Superordinate Goal

Many experimental studies over the years have shown that the assignment of a superordinate goal can decrease inter-group conflict (e.g., Sherif, 1966; see also Hewstone & Brown, 1986; Kramer, 1991). A superordinate goal is one that neither group can attain on its own and that supercedes any other goals the groups may have. Superordinate goals work best if they are significant to each member of the group. The survival of an organization may be one superordinate goal. Defining the competitor as a common enemy and then beating the enemy is an example of another super-ordinate goal. The design of a new product by a team composed of members from engineering, marketing, manufacturing, etc. may also serve as yet another super-ordinate goal for the people from each of these functional areas.

Unfortunately, the effect of a superordinate goal may last only for the duration of the task. For example, conflict between the engineering and manufacturing divisions may re-appear once the survival crisis is over. Similarly, the harmony between a group of Catholics and a group of Protestants may exist only during the process of solving a problem that is of great concern to both groups. It is not likely that such harmony will endure once the problem is solved and the problem-solving team is disbanded. A one time intervention of this nature is, therefore, not sufficient. A series of cumulative superordinate goals is required. The presence of a super-ordinate goal in essence has the same effect as the creation of a new in-group. As long as this new in-group provides positive social identity through achieving the individually meaningful superordinate goal, intra-group conflict should be reduced.

Structured Interdependence and Cooperation

In the mid-1970s, a group of researchers tested an innovative idea by using structured classroom arrangements to promote interpersonal attraction, self-esteem, happiness, and, most importantly, academic performance in racially integrated schools. The classroom was structured in such a way that competitiveness was incompatible with success and that success could occur only as a result of cooperative behavior among the students in a group. This is in great contrast to the traditional classroom where the students are rewarded when they individually outperform their classmates. In the cooperative classroom, the students could succeed only by paying attention to their peers and by helping and teaching each other. How did this come about? The following description illustrates the cooperative classroom:

> The upcoming lesson happened to be a biography of Joseph Pulitzer. We created a biography of Joseph Pulitzer that consisted of six paragraphs. The first paragraph was about Pulitzer's ancestors and how they came to this country; the second described his childhood and growing-up years; the third covered Pulitzer as a young man, his education, and his early employment; the fourth told of his middle-aged years and how he founded his newspaper; and so forth. Each major aspect of Pulitzer's life was contained in a separate paragraph.
>
> We mimeographed our biography, cut it into six one-paragraph sections, and gave each child in the six-person learning group one of the paragraphs. Thus each learning group had within it the entire biography of Joseph Pulitzer, but each child had no more than one-sixth of the story. In order to learn about Pulitzer, the students had to master their paragraph and teach it to the others in their group. For example, David was responsible for Pulitzer as a young man, Marianne for Pulitzer as a child, and so forth. Each student took his paragraph, read it over a few times, and then joined his counterparts from the other groups. That is, David, who had Pulitzer as a young man, consulted with Bonnie, Ted, Jane, and Carl, who had also been given Pulitzer as a young man. They could use each other to rehearse and to be sure they understood the important aspects of that phase of Pulitzer's life.
>
> A short time later the children went back to their groups, where they were informed that they had a certain amount of time to teach that knowledge to each other. They were also told that at the end of that time (or soon thereafter) each person would be tested on his knowledge of Pulitzer's *entire* life. Clearly the students had to depend on one another to learn all their material. The

process is highly reminiscent of a jigsaw puzzle, with each student possessing a single vital piece of the big picture. Because of this resemblance, we came to refer to our system as the "jigsaw" model. (Aronson, Blaney, Stephan, Sikes & Snapp, 1978, pp. 26–27)

The jigsaw technique was instituted in several classrooms for six weeks. The effectiveness of this technique was compared to classrooms using traditional (competitive) methods that were taught by effective teachers. The findings are quite consistent. Children in the jigsaw classroom, compared to children in the traditional classroom,

- grew to like their group-mates more than others in the classroom,
- started to like school better,
- increased their self-esteem,
- performed as well or better,
- cooperated more and saw their classmates as learning resources.

These attitudinal and behavioral changes were observed of black, white, and Chicano children. What is most interesting about this experiment is that cooperativeness was not treated as an attitude but as a skill. The students were taught how to cooperate and to see that cooperativeness is the most productive strategy to become successful as an individual. It could be viewed that the learning task becomes a super-ordinate goal for all groups.

The researchers also were quick to point out that the students must be taught how to work cooperatively because such a skill does not come naturally in this individualistic, competitive culture. A team-building exercise in the learning group before the curriculum materials are tackled is essential to provide the students with the skills to become comfortable and familiar with the new method of learning. The researchers also found that group size should be no less than three but no more than seven, with five or six an ideal size. A small size would limit the opportunity to learn while a large size would reduce the chance for members to speak, and, hence, their interest level would drop. Group composition is also an important factor. The jigsaw group should ideally contain both sexes, different racial or ethnic groups, and members who are different in personality and in ability. Such diversity extends the potential learning resources available to each member. A jigsaw member is challenged to develop empathy and tolerance and learns to work toward common goals with persons different from himself or herself on a number of dimensions. Developing skills to work with people who are different from oneself is the ultimate challenge for each individual in the diverse work setting that we are in now. Some of these skills are described below.

Interpersonal Skills in Groups

There are a number of basic skills for relating to others in a group, many of which were discussed by Aronson et al. (1978), considering conditions necessary for the success of the jigsaw classroom. Many skills are useful in any group setting but three skills are particularly important in diverse groups: listening skill, helping skill, and skill in observing and evaluating group process.

Listening Skill.

Research has shown that we are generally very poor listeners and that we are much worse when we face people who are different from us or who do not speak with the same accent or tone. The irony is that we are all capable of being good listeners. Some of us have received training in such skills. Others of us are good at it only if we want to be. Therefore, it is not a matter of ability, but a matter of motivation. In a small group where there is a clear hierarchy of social status, the high status people are listened to more than the low status people. This occurs with listeners of both higher and lower social status. The lower status people lose motivation because the signals are quite clear that others do not listen even if they try to speak. The members of the lower status group, unknowingly and unintentionally, collude with members of the higher status group in reducing their own involvement and commitment in the group.

Is the responsibility for changing this dynamic on the higher status group? By now, it should be clear that the answer is no. It is everyone's responsibility to do so. The individuals in the lower social status (or those with stereotypic attributes suggesting that they will not speak or cannot speak clearly) must also participate in changing the listening skills for themselves. In other words, every member of a social category in the small group is responsible for elevating the listening skill of the entire group.

Helping Skill.

A related and equally important interpersonal skill in the group is the helping skill. The idea here is that each member of the group must demonstrate his or her value to the group by extending help to others rather than expecting to be helped by others. Each person must take the initiative to see what help others need. Others then reciprocate such initiative. For the group leader, his or her responsibility is to reward and reinforce helping behavior and to discourage or ignore competitive behavior. Reward must be based on how much an individual helps others rather than how often an individual comes out on top. In the jigsaw classroom experiment, the researchers used a Broken Squares Game to teach such helping behavior.

> All group members receive six pieces of a puzzle. They are told that the object of the game is for each person to end up with a completed square. The pieces each person needs are distributed among his teammates, so he is not going to be able to complete his puzzle alone. Nor can he simply take a piece he needs from someone else. He can only give away one of his own pieces to help another group member complete his or her square. To encourage each person to be actively helpful to others instead of waiting to see who can help him, no communication is allowed. This means a participant cannot ask or signal for someone to pass him a piece. For each member of the group to end up with a completed square, *all other* members must take the initiative. They must see what pieces others require and reach over to give those pieces to them. In other words, the emphasis is on giving and cooperating. (Aronson et al., 1978, p. 38).

At the end of the game, the participants discussed their feelings and observations of the process of how their groups worked. The participants saw quite clearly that they were more successful and felt better when they received help from others. These feelings begin with the individuals first taking the initiative and responsibility to help others.

Skill to Observe and Evaluate Group Process.

A third skill that is particularly valuable in diverse groups is the skill to observe and evaluate group process. In homogeneous groups, interpersonal liking and attraction make it easy for people to trust each other, to listen to each other, and to disagree openly and freely. In diverse groups, the opposite would occur. Therefore, group members must develop the skills to watch for signs of process breakdown. Group members must focus on such questions as:

- Are we listening to each other?
- Are we encouraging everyone to participate?
- Are we treating each other with kindness and respect?
- Are we sticking to the task?
- Are we refraining from saying something in fear that it may offend a specific individual or individuals?
- Are we truly understanding each other?
- Are we helping each other to succeed in our individual tasks?
- Are there any symptoms of stereotyping (self and others) among us?

The above questions should be asked by every individual member of the group, especially at the beginning stage of a new group. Since the social categorization process occurs at the early stage of the group's life, to differentiate roles at this early stage would reinforce differentiation and hamper group process. Every member must learn the skill and take the responsibility for ensuring that premature categorization does not occur. Active listening, helping skills and group observation and evaluation skills are necessary elements of effective group process in any group, especially in diverse groups.

The importance of process learning and feedback is demonstrated by the 17-week longitudinal study discussed in Chapter 6. The study found that diverse groups performed worse at the beginning, but after 17 weeks, they caught up and, in fact, out-performed the homogeneous groups. In this experimental study, students were given feedback on their group process several times throughout the 17 weeks. It appears that students in diverse groups benefited from this process feedback and were able to capture the cognitive resources that diverse members brought to the group. Once process problems (i.e., inter-group conflict, not listening, not trusting) in diverse groups are resolved, the groups are able to realize the benefits of diversity and perform better than homogeneous groups. Since the homogeneous groups also received such process feedback, their relatively lower level of performance gain suggests that cognitive resources may be more limited in the homogeneous groups.

Attention to Group Composition

To avoid the formation of coalitions along the line of demographic factors, forming a team with a high level of heterogeneity on a variety of demographic factors might be a fruitful strategy. Let us use the example of an international joint venture management team. Membership in the parent company is a natural division between top management group members in a joint venture. Overlapping parent company membership with nationality would heighten inter-group distinction. Therefore, instead of appointing all expatriates from the United States for a U.S.–China joint venture, some expatriates could be from Europe, Australia, or other parts of Asia. Nationality may diffuse the strength of parent company affiliation. Further, the joint venture could appoint some members with relatively short tenure with the parent company. These members are less likely to have developed a strong identification with the parent company. The idea here is to bring some alternative demographic variables to help reduce the potential conflict surrounding the original division. A team with heterogeneity on a number of dimensions may avoid division along any one factor. Given people's need for inclusion, the team itself could become a possible category for developing one joint identity.

Organizational Strategies for Managing Demographic Diversity

A variety of strategies have been proposed to help organizations manage today's diverse workforce (see, for example, Cox, 1993; Fernandez, 1991; Jackson & Associates, 1992; Levinger, 1987; Thomas, 1991 for many structural and process solutions). In this section, we focus primarily on approaches that are derived more directly from social identity theory and the related social categorization process. The key question is how to change the primary basis for social identification by members of a diverse group so that inter-group differentiation could be minimized and intragroup cohesion could be maximized.

The Organization As a Superordinate Category

One way the organization can help to manage diversity is to strive to increase the salience, relevance, and importance of the organization as a social category for deriving social identity by its membership. An organization is a bounded social category itself in that it provides one identity for its employees. The organization is also characterized by interdependence among its members in that the success of each member and the organization as a whole depends on the contribution of each individual within it. To the extent that the organization can enhance the social identity of its members, i.e., it becomes a meaningful psychological group, ingroup cohesion and cooperation will occur and inter-group differentiation will not (see Brewer, 1994). To the extent that organizational members use the organization as a primary social category in defining themselves, accentuation of positive features of the organization should occur and such positive evaluation should extend to other members in the group. Depersonalized in-group attraction should replace inter-group conflict. When this form of re-categorization is successful, in-group loyalty will be transferred from the original subgroups to the organization as a whole. Gaertner, Dovidio, Anastasio, Bachman, and Rust (1993) refer to this as the "common in-group identity model."

Experimental studies by social psychologists have identified situational factors that can enhance the perceptual salience of a new combined work group and reduce the salience of subgroup identities (see, for example, Gaertner et al., 1993; Brewer, 1994, 1997). Consistently, these studies found that when participants perceive the combined team as a single entity rather than as an aggregate of two or more separate groups, evaluations of former out-group members become more positive.

Merging the subgroups into a single common category that replaces or dominates the original category differentiation can create super-ordinate categories. For example, the former People's Express Airline referred to all employees as associates and did not make distinctions on the basis of employees' occupation or job function. If the organization is successful in replacing a person's occupation or function as a primary category for self-identity, that person should identify as a People's Express employee first and as a pilot or maintenance engineer second. Companies that have been successful in developing the organization as a super-ordinate category for its members' identity include IBM, Hewlett Packard, Federal Express, Johnson and Johnson, and Lincoln Electric. Most of these companies would also be considered by Peters and Waterman (1982) to be "strong culture" companies.

Just merging two groups to form a new group does not guarantee that the new group will become a meaningful social category for identification. Similarly, being a member of an organization does not necessarily make that organization an important basis for an individual's social identity. As discussed in Chapter 7, in many organizations, subgroup differentiation occurs regularly and inter-group conflict is prevalent. These cleavages can occur along a variety of categories, including the employees' departmental affiliation, functional specialization, geographic location, hierarchical level, company tenure or demographics such as gender or race. What differentiates organizations that are successful in serving as a super-ordinate category for their members' social identity from those organizations that are less successful? What may differentiate them the most is the extent of organizational socialization that members receive. Extensive socialization is used by the military (the well-known boot camp experience) or by occupations such as law and medicine that have successfully developed a strong social identity among their members.

In order to develop a strong social identity, socialization typically begins before the individual joins an organization. These organizations often make entry difficult and employ a stringent selection process. Being selected to join is a measure of success in and of itself. Upon entry, the new employees (usually collectively as a group) undergo an intensive socialization process. There is usually an extensive coverage of the company's history, tradition, norms and values, products and services, and missions and goals. The CEO often makes a personal appearance to signal the importance of the new member. The company emphasizes that its success is to be the employee's super-ordinate goal. In return, the employee is promised fair return, is provided with extended benefits, and in general shown concern. Individual identity is de-emphasized, and, instead, a collective identity is reinforced. The meta-purpose of this intense socialization is to immerse and submerge the self into the organization as an in-group, i.e., to depersonalize the self. Depersonalization of self-perception becomes the basic process underlying "group cohesion, ethnocentrism, cooperation and altruism, emotional contagion and empathy, collective behavior, shared norms and mutual influences, etc." (see Turner, 1985, pp. 99–100). When this occurs, the organization becomes a meaningful and important psychological group.

In some U.S. companies, such as IBM or Hewlett-Packard, company-wide socialization programs are used extensively to persuade employees to define themselves in terms of the organization rather than categories such as the employees' occupation or the department where he or she works. Such a kind of collective socialization strategy has been shown to lead to higher internalization of organizational goals in research studies (see Van Maanen & Schein, 1979). As such intense socialization is common practice in Japanese and Korean companies, in these countries, the company may well be "a super-ordinate category for self-identification among employees, leading employees to submerge their personal interests to organizational objectives" (see Tsui, 1994).

When the organization becomes a meaningful social category for social identification by its employees, there will be high levels of in-group cohesion, mutual trust, open communication, and reciprocal support. Strong initial socialization is one method to promote the organization as a super-ordinate category. There are a number of other methods as well (e.g., job rotations), though their effects are not as strong as initial socialization. This is because the effect of social categorization (of self and others) based on demographic factors occurs at the initial stage of a group formation (or when an individual joins an existing group). Early socialization provides the new members a particular frame to engage in this initial categorization and interferes with categorization based on other categories or categories that members bring with them to the new group. All of this contributes to a supportive environment for "diverse" people and in effect is a relatively unobtrusive way to manage diversity.

An organization can reach out to underrepresented groups by beginning to socialize future employees through a process Pettigrew and Martin (1987) call tithing. Although a traditional tithe is 10%, a tiny fraction of that amount could, as Pettigrew and Martin note, have a large effect on a local labor market. The firm would simply allocate some money to help educate and train future employees, providing special workshops and activities, some onsite, as well as tuition grants and the like. This money would be targeted at high school and college students from underrepresented groups. By contributing to their education and training through various programs, the company can begin socializing those young people to see the company as a source of identification.

While corporations may be able to increase minority representation and identification with the company by providing financial support and special programs for youngsters they have targeted as future employees, providing special programs for the same underrepresented groups when they are employees can have two negative unintended consequences. One, belonging to a formal subgroup like Hispanic engineers might reduce one's identification with the organization. Second, belonging to a group like Hispanic engineers probably makes it easier for other employees to categorize Hispanic engineers as a group separate from the company as a super-ordinate category. That is, others may identify themselves but not Hispanic engineers as part of the psychological organization. Needless to say, identifying anyone as an "affirmative action hire" can also serve to remove that person from the psychological group that is the organization.

Before we close this section, it is important to note two caveats. When we discuss the possibility of the organization serving as a primary social category for employees, we do not endorse such a strong identification that the person loses all identity as an individual. We are not talking about brainwashing or total submersion in a culture or becoming part of a cult. Second, it is worth noting that trends in corporate restructuring (e.g., downsizing, becoming "lean and mean," using an increasing number of part time, temporary, and contract workers) work against the kind of corporate identification that we are discussing. In order to foster identification with the company the strong culture generally needs to support workers and increase their self-worth. In addition, the values implicit in the culture probably need to correspond to the person's own values.

Creating Cross-Cutting Categories

The strategy of creating a super-ordinate category presumes that it is possible to decrease the salience of other categories that members have previously used as important bases for social identity. There are at least two reasons why this presumption of being able to eliminate some of these other group identities may be naïve (see Brewer, 1994). First, people's need for inclusion may not be satisfied by identification with the organization as a whole. The organization may be too large to provide intimate support at the interpersonal level. Therefore, individuals will still look for groups at the more proximal level for satisfying this need. Psychological groups along basic categories, such as one's departmental affiliation, immediate workgroup, or ethnicity, or along race and gender demarcation within the work group may provide needed social support. A second reason is that individuals also have a need to be distinctive. This means that they want to have some basis for differentiating themselves from all other individuals in the (large) organization. Large, diverse, and highly inclusive social organizations are not likely to provide the conditions necessary to engage strong social identification. Such psychological needs push people to establish subgroup identification even in the presence of a strong identification with the organization.

Further, an organization of any reasonable size could not operate without some differentiation along functional, product, or regional lines. Some hierarchical distinction is inevitable. With increasing diversity, there is increasing likelihood of differentiation along racial, gender, and age categories. How does the organization prevent any of these categories from dominating other categories or even the organization itself as a category? Dominance occurs especially when certain categories of people enjoy greater power and social status in the organization and when they converge with categories that involve a societal dominance structure. For example, men are a dominant category if men hold all high-level positions. The engineering department would become a dominant category if it has the largest budget and the loudest voice in the company's decision-making process. The idea of creating "cross-cutting categories" is proposed as a strategy to keep the categories in balance and under control.

The idea is to bring some alternative categorization into play to help reduce the conflict surrounding the original division. Suppose a product is having difficulty in the market place although its design is basically sound. The issue is with marketing and manufacturing. A special task force is created to address this problem. Two representatives are chosen from marketing and two from manufacturing. One marketing representative and one manufacturing representative are responsible for research and bringing to the task force all the financial information related to design, production, distribution, and advertising. These two become the financial experts for the task force. The other marketing and manufacturing reps are responsible for researching and bringing to the task force all the information about competition. What are the competitors' approaches to manufacturing and marketing of similar or related products? These two become the competitor experts for the task force. This crosscutting role and category assignment ensures that marketing will not look at the problem only from a marketing perspective, and manufacturing only from a manufacturing perspective. These crosscutting role assignments would likely result in less inter-group differentiation (based on function) and less in-group bias following contact in a cooperative team experience (see Marcus-Newhall, Miller, Holtz & Brewer, 1993). Such cooperation is achieved without necessarily deliberate efforts to reduce social categorization by function.

The idea of crosscutting categorization is quite straightforward at one level, but research on the efficacy of such a method to reduce inter-group conflict is still relatively new. It appears that it could provide a useful guide in the assignment of roles to members of groups or task forces to prevent the situation where roles are consistent with non-role social categories, and thus perpetuate a differentiation along demographic lines.

Beyond Contact: The Importance of a Positive Diversity Climate

One outcome of crosscutting role assignments is that members of different social groups are forced to engage in more frequent contact than they would if roles are convergent with other non-role social categories. It is interesting that one of the earliest theories to reduce inter-group conflict is by increasing contact between opposing groups (see Cook, 1978; Kanter, 1977). The belief is that contact allows people to discover that they have more similar values and attitudes than they had assumed based on different demographic or background attributes. This discovery leads to mutual understanding and liking and over time neutralizes the initial negative feelings. However, social psychological research has shown convincingly that contact alone is not sufficient. In fact, it can enhance or deepen intergroup hostility. Some of the relevant research findings are reported in Chapter 7. For example, Hoffman (1985) showed that increasing the number of minorities led to decreased informal communication between the minority and majority members of the organization. Cook (1978) proposed that the positive outcomes of contact (i.e., favorable attitudes toward out-group members or change from less favorable to more favorable) would occur only under certain facilitating conditions. We refer to these conditions as elements of a positive diversity climate. Creation of such a climate is the final strategy that we describe in managing demographic diversity at the organizational level.

Years of social psychological research have identified the following conditions to be important in ensuring that inter-group contact will bring positive results. In other words, these conditions contribute to a positive diversity climate that will facilitate the success of all the strategies described in this chapter—at the personal, dyad, group, and organizational levels. The focus of the contact idea here is on increasing inter-group harmony or reducing inter-group differentiation and not necessarily on promoting interpersonal liking. The question is "under what conditions would increased contact lead to understanding, acceptance, and harmony between otherwise highly differentiated groups?" Five such conditions are suggested here.

- First, contact would lead to communication, understanding, and acceptance of members of the other category if members of different (demographic) categories are equal in status. Therefore, efforts to increase the status of the lower status categories are essential. As an illustration, international joint ventures may minimize division within the management team along national lines by balancing position level with assignments. In the case of the Pharmex–Tianjin joint venture discussed in Chapter 8, the general manager is from one partner, the deputy general manager is from the other partner. The director of finance is American while the controller (a comparable position) is Chinese. Therefore, managers from both partners hold positions of comparable status.
- Second, contact would facilitate inter-group relations if the characteristics of the out-group member disconfirm the prevailing out-group

stereotype. However, paradoxically, if the out-group member is too atypical of the out-group, that person will be seen as an exception rather than the rule. Thus attitude toward the out-group as a whole will not change, though attitude toward that particular individual may improve (Pettigrew, 1979). Therefore, disconfirming evidence is a difficult condition to achieve since the person should be both like and unlike a typical member in his or her group.

- Third, the contact situation encourages and perhaps even requires cooperation in the achievement of a goal. The jigsaw classroom success attests to the importance of structured interdependence for cooperative effort.
- Fourth, the situation enables an intimate level of interaction so that individuals can get to know each other as individuals rather than superficially (as stereotypic category members).
- Fifth, the larger context (e.g., organizational policies and practices) favors or promotes a group equality norm.

In summary, the above five conditions are considered the basic elements of a positive diversity climate. Organizational leaders must see to it that such facilitating conditions exist for diversity efforts to succeed at all levels: individual, group, and organization. Table 10.1 summarizes the strategies described in this chapter for each of three levels.

Summary

Managing the dynamic of demographic diversity must occur at every level of the organization: the individual, the dyad, the group, and the organization. Everyone in the organization must take the initiative and assume the responsibility to understand what demographic diversity is, what it means for people in different social categories, and how it affects the individual, the group, and the organization as a whole. Some of the strategies can be employed at the discretion of the individual, the dyad, or the group. Others require structural intervention by the leadership of the organization. These strategies should be applicable to managing diversity within domestic work settings or the international arena. Among all the strategies discussed in this chapter, we believe the most important and fundamental is the strategy, "Taking ownership of the problem." Managing diversity must begin with me, me in whatever role or position I hold and whatever location I am in. If I am an employee, I practice the individual, dyad, and group strategies. If I am a manager, I practice all of the strategies as well as those organizational strategies I have the power to initiate. Members of any category should embody such readiness. Through owning the problem and taking the initiative in addressing it, we have the

Table 10.1 Strategies for Managing Demographic Diversity in Organizations

Personal-Level Strategies
  • Self-discovery of primary categories for self-identity
  • Wise application of a simple statistical rule
  • Control over self-stereotyping
  • Ownership of the problem and initiative to make a difference

Group-Level Strategies
  • Creation of cumulative super-ordinate goals
  • Structured interdependence and cooperation
  • Interpersonal skills for effective group process

Organizational-Level Strategies
  • Organization as a super-ordinate category
  • Cross-cutting categories and role assignments
  • Provision of a positive diversity climate

hope of arresting the negative effects of diversity, reaping the benefits of cognitive resources associated with diversity, and improving the quality of life for everyone.

Notes

1. This list of questions was adapted from an instrument developed by Kent Harber at the University of Michigan and Claude Steele (Stanford University) as part of the research project on assessing vulnerability to self-stereotyping and academic performance among college students; an overview is provided in Steele (1997).

2. The idea of self-monitoring or self-regulation is based on work by Tsui and her colleagues published in 1991, 1994, and 1996. They found active feedback seeking by managers from others at work (e.g., superiors, peers, and subordinates) to be positively associated with perception of the manager's effectiveness by these other groups.

Chapter 11

Directions for Future Research

Research on organizational demography has a short history—less than fifteen years—though diversity has been a concern to researchers and managers interested in race, ethnicity, and gender since the Civil Rights Amendment of 1964. As indicated in earlier chapters, knowledge about diversity is derived from both laboratory studies using student samples and field studies using natural work groups in organizations. Diversity research has focused primarily on race and gender while demography research has a broader mission, not specifically focused on legally protected categories. More specifically, demography research often focuses on age, tenure, and functional specialization. The major findings from research studies focusing on demographic diversity have been summarized in earlier chapters. However, we need to learn much more. In this chapter, we discuss five demographic issues that are in need of more research. Following that we propose and describe several research methods that can further our insight and knowledge about the dynamics of demographic diversity in complex organizations.

Before researchers can expect an employee in a company, a supervisor of a functional work group, a general manager responsible for a large operating unit, or the chief executive officer of a company to care about research on this topic, we need solutions that have been tested and shown to be effective. For example, before companies embrace the notion that they should try to match the race and sex of service providers with their customer base, it is important to find out if this is effective in increasing sales as well as how it affects employees. Research helps to identify, to verify, and to refine workable and effective solutions. To help us identify, verify, and refine solutions, we still need more understanding of how diversity is affecting individuals, groups, and companies. We all have a stake in this problem. This chapter provides some suggestions to those researchers who are devoting their professional work to this topic.

171

Important Demographic Issues Requiring More Research

Diversity in Involvement Teams

To date, demography research of organizational work groups has focused on either the top management team or the new product or project teams (see Chapter 6 for a discussion of this stream of research). These groups compose a very small proportion of an organization's workforce. In reality, the majority of employees are in work groups involved in the actual production of goods or delivery of services or in staff units providing administrative or logistic support to these front line work groups. There is a paucity of research on these operating work groups or units. We do not know the demographic composition of most work groups. Historically, occupations and work groups have been segregated along racial and gender lines and there is some evidence that work is also segregated by age (see for example, Greenberger and Steinberg, 1986). Presumably, through structural intervention, today's work groups are more integrated. Structural integration, however, brings with it problems of social integration. Management attention to diversity has focused primarily on structural integration. It is now time to pay attention to the social integration of diverse work groups.

Operating work groups in some or perhaps most firms are organized along the traditional model with one supervisor responsible for the operations of the unit. There is, however, an increasing use of autonomous or semi-autonomous work teams with employees having greater discretion over the work to be performed and greater involvement in the governance and management of the team and its work. Lawler, Mohrman, and Ledford (1992) provide data on the use of employee involvement teams in Fortune 1000 companies. Both types of work groups, whether organized along the traditional model or along the (newer) involvement model, face a similar challenge. They are becoming more demographically diverse.

A major difference between these traditional and semi-autonomous groups is the amount of interpersonal interaction required of the members in the group. In the traditional work group, employees perform their own work. Because supervisors judge their performance, they tend to orient toward and communicate with their supervisor. Reward is based on individual achievement. Interpersonal interaction is typically not critical for the success of the group as a whole. In the involvement teams, by contrast, members are responsible for and evaluated on the success of the entire team. Interpersonal interaction is critical for the team to perform well. Such teams have many of the features of the jigsaw classroom described in Chapter 10. For such teams to succeed, cooperation and mutual helpfulness are essential. Diversity in the involvement teams could hamper the development of intra-group cohesion and in-group attraction that is necessary for effective group process. In general, analyzing and understanding the influence of demographic diversity on the process and performance of involvement teams is a diversity issue that is in need of systematic research.

Cross-Level and Cross-Group Compositions

A second demographic issue also deserving more research is the effects of different demographic distributions in different parts and levels in the organization on the individual employee's experiences and inter-group relations. The study of woman lawyers described in Chapter 6 (Ely, 1994) is an example of a research study that analyzed cross-level effects. That study focused on the attitudes and perceptions of professional women in lower levels of the organization toward other women in the company in response to different compositions of men and women in the upper echelon. That study did not analyze the reactions of women toward men and the reactions of men toward both women and men in response to varying gender composition in top management. Since social categorization and stereotyping applies to everyone (i.e., both men and women), we would gain much from understanding the reaction of men as well as that of women. The research also suggests that organizational-level data on demographic distribution are needed. No studies have utilized an entire organization's demographic data. Given that most companies have computerized personnel information systems and that the method for indexing demographic distributions of an employee population has been developed, such research is both possible and desirable. Organizational resistance to revealing serious demographic gaps will be a major challenge to be overcome by researchers. Collaboration between managers and researchers is clearly critical for progress in organizational demography research.

Demographic Diversity As a Context

A third demographic issue that pertains to the work group is to understand how the demographic diversity of the work group as a whole influences the quality of the relationship between pairs of individuals in the group, especially individuals who differ on specific demographic attributes. In Chapter 5, we described how the quality of the relationship between the supervisor and a subordinate might be enhanced by both similarity and difference in the dyad on attributes such as age, educational level, or tenure. Clearly, the vertical dyad does not exist in a vacuum. It is embedded in a work group or unit with many other individuals and with varied degrees of demographic diversity. For example, would the quality of a dyad consisting of a female supervisor and a male subordinate be better or worse in a work group consisting primarily of women (a situation of relative homogeneity in gender) than in a work group consisting of a mix of men and women (a situation of relative heterogeneity in gender)? In other words, would the presence of other men increase or decrease the female supervisor's liking of and support for the male subordinate? According to inter-group theory, heterogeneity generally leads to greater inter-group differentiation and conflict. Therefore, in a work group with a relatively high heterogeneity in gender, the relationship between the female supervisor and the male subordinate should be worse than in a work group that is more homogeneous in gender composition. Work group heterogeneity, following this logic, would accentuate the negative attraction between members of the dyad that differ in gender, in race, or in age. Other theories would make other predictions; for example, according to Blau (1977), greater heterogeneity should decrease the salience of gender. Gutek's (1985) sex-role spillover perspective makes the same prediction. Sex roles are less likely to be invoked when men and women are evenly represented in a group. Such cross-level analysis could provide a much deeper understanding of the complex dynamics associated with diversity than research that focuses on a single level, which is the major approach in existing demography research.

Category-Specific Effects

A fourth issue for demography research is the extent to which findings are consistent across social categories versus category-specific. Some dependent variables are more relevant for some social categories than others (e.g., amount of sexual harassment is much more relevant to gender than other social categories), but other dependant variables (e.g., productivity, social integration, turnover) should be relevant across social categories. While we know that certain findings (e.g., heterogeneity is associated with greater turnover) apply to multiple social categories, we need to see if there are limits to generalizability. Are there, for example, social categories in which greater heterogeneity is not associated with greater turnover? And if so, how do they differ from the social categories where the two are related?

Context-Specific Salience of Demographic Categories

A fifth research issue is how do social categories become salient or important in organizations? Why is *guanxi* important in China and not in the United States? Is it simply a result of more mobility in the United States so that kinship and geography are more remote for Americans than Chinese? Or are there more complex social processes, including religious background, that we must consider? Why is religion more salient in

Northern Ireland than in the United States? Or is it? It makes sense to think that social categories that are salient in the broader culture will, by extension, also be important in organizations in that culture. But is it also true that individual organizations can create their own social categories, demographic dimensions that are salient there but not elsewhere? It seems likely that any dimension important to the organization is likely to become a social category. For example, in companies where seniority or tenure is important, it is likely to be a social category that influences behavior and attitudes. Where seniority and tenure do not bring special privileges, that factor may be less important.

A related issue is how social categories become manifested in organizational units, i.e., when a psychological group becomes a physical group. Despite a plethora of efforts (including legal mandates) to integrate work organizations, it appears that work units can become associated with particular social categories. For example, in one organization, the janitorial department is all Hispanic whereas in another organization it is primarily black. In one firm, the accounting department is mostly Asian, whereas in another it is primarily female. One human resources department is mostly ethnic minority whereas another is predominately white female. While we know that people like to be around people like themselves, it would appear that other forces must contribute to this sorting of social categories along work groups or functional units.

Summary

Chapter 10 provided a discussion of a variety of strategies to manage diversity by individuals, groups, and the organizations as a whole. As already indicated, most of the ideas were derived from social psychological research using student subjects in elementary schools or colleges. Research is needed to evaluate the applicability and usefulness of these strategies in work organizations. For example, would structured interdependence facilitate cooperation and helpful behavior in involvement teams? Do crosscutting role assignments improve team cohesion and performance in real groups as it was found among student groups in experimental settings? What types of social categories are most vulnerable to self-stereotyping and what are the consequences of self-stereotyping in work settings? Do organizations inadvertently discourage their most talented employees from underrepresented categories by creating situations of "stereotype threat" for these employees? To answer some of these questions requires action research that introduces interventions (i.e., the strategies), observes their process over time, and records their outcomes.

By identifying the above issues as needing more research, it is not our intention to suggest that no other topics deserve research attention as well. In fact, research on both demography and diversity is alive and well. Social psychologists, management scholars, and diversity experts are working on various aspects of the general issue, using a variety of research methods and drawing on a variety of theoretical frameworks. This is an important area that affects the life of all and has captured the attention of many scholars.

Research Design and Methods

Existing demography research utilizes two common methods. A summary of research methods used in extant demography studies is contained in Chapter 3. One method is asking employees in work units about their experiences and perceptions through interviews or written surveys. Their responses then are related to some measures of demographic diversity of the unit or of the individual's demographic difference from others in the unit. A second method is obtaining company records on the demographic composition of a group (e.g., the top management team) and using these data to develop some measures of demographic diversity of the group. The diversity measures are related to outcomes such as turnover rates in the groups, which also are obtained through company records. This method does not involve asking the individuals, and thus the research tends to be limited to measures that can be obtained from public records or with the permission of the appropriate corporate official. Both research methods are limited in that they focus on "what is" now in terms of current work group composition and current outcomes. These methods do not allow the researcher to find out "what could be" if changes in work group composition or its internal structure were introduced.

To answer "what could be" requires an experimental design. A true experiment requires random assignment of people or groups to conditions, some of which receive some kind of treatment or intervention. While experiments most often are conducted in research laboratories, it is not impossible to do true experiments in work organizations. For example, work groups could be randomly assigned to work under structured interdependence or under a traditional hierarchical structure. In the structured interdependece condition, work would be designed in such a way so that no one person could be successful without the cooperation and help of others in the group. The experiences and performance of the interdependent group could then be compared to the group organized more traditionally.

Experiments are useful whenever the natural setting does not contain the elements of a situation that may produce desired results. For example, what mix of employees with what types of demographic backgrounds would provide the best balance of cognitive resources for certain types of tasks? Would the learning of interpersonal skills and feedback on group process used in the 17-week experiment described in Chapter 6 lead to performance gains in diverse work groups in work organizations? Experimentation would provide answers to these questions.

For a lot of reasons, including the difficulty in getting permission and actually carrying out the experiment, conducting a true experiment in an organization is a rare event. More likely is the possibility of doing a quasi-experiment. A variety of quasi-experimental designs have been described along with their strengths and weaknesses (Campbell and Stanley, 1966; Cook and Campbell, 1979). Whereas quasi-experiments are quite common in the evaluation of a variety of interventions, they are still quite rare in business organizations. Clearly, more experimentation, including quasi-experiments, is desirable in organizations.

The irony is that managers engage in quasi-experiments often. They are experimenting whenever they introduce a new method or try a new approach without full knowledge or confidence that the new methods will work. However, statistically sound conclusions cannot be drawn unless there is a systematic research design that includes careful measurement of process and results, and control of other factors that might also influence the outcomes that are expected to emerge from the new method being introduced.

A third research method that has great promise of yielding useful knowledge for understanding demographic dynamics involves the utilization of a company's human resource records. Many organizations have computerized their human resource records, which may include employment history, performance appraisals, career movements within the firm, absences, grievances or disciplinary records, and sometimes even attitude and performance data of the employees' work units. These databases could be integrated and utilized to evaluate the relative demographic compositions of different units or levels and the relationship of these demographic profiles to employee and work unit outcomes such as attitudes, absences, performance, or turnover. Cross-level effects could be examined as well. Most companies treat these data as highly confidential. Individual privacy can be assured when the analyses are performed at the unit level with individuals' data aggregated and their identification concealed. There may be concerns, however, about legal issues. Could analyses performed with firm records be subpoenaed during litigation for sex discrimination or race discrimination, for example? While concerns about legal liability need to be addressed, cooperation between universities and firms in the analysis of data have the potential of yielding a gold-mine of data for researchers and information useful to managers as well.

Using a company's existing records has the advantage of not interfering with the on-going activities of individuals in the work units. This method involves the least disruption of existing work structure and procedures, in contrast to the experimental method where new procedures or systems being introduced may modify the structure as well as the nature of the relationship among individuals within the group. Thus, experiments entail maximum researcher intervention while use of company records entails minimum intervention. A method falling somewhere in between these two extremes involves a researcher observing the on-going processes and interactions among individuals and groups as they engage in their normal work routines. This method is called the non-participant observer method. The researcher appears on the work site and observes the group as unobtrusively as possible. This may done in such a way that employees are not aware that they are being observed. Clearly, this is not always possible. The purpose is to minimize interference by the presence of the researcher/observer.

This method is most useful in recording and analyzing interaction patterns of individuals in diverse work groups, including management teams, project teams, committees or task forces, and customer-service provider pairs, as well as operating work groups structured along either the traditional or the involvement model. The researcher could observe the extent and nature of interpersonal communication, power dynamics, and friendship patterns within the group. The researcher refrains from participating in any discussions and declines to comment on the group process even if requested by the group members. Objectivity and neutrality by the researcher are critical requirements of this method.

Conclusion: Partnership and Collaboration for New Knowledge

Conducting research in organizational settings requires the cooperation of company officials and employees. Academic research cannot succeed without this cooperation and support. While university-based laboratory research can explore many interesting topics having to do with demographic diversity, social categorization, and self-identification, the results of such studies ultimately need to be tested in the field. Organizational research is of necessity a collaborative enterprise between the academic researcher and the practicing manager. It is only through this partnership that we gain new knowledge about the nature of demographic diversity and its effects on individuals, groups, and organizations.

Chapter 12

Conclusion

Based on the available research findings from experimental studies using student samples but drawing primarily from results of published research using organizational studies with natural work groups, we conclude that demographic factors both facilitate and hinder communication, understanding, acceptance, and attraction between individuals and groups. They facilitate these outcomes among people who are similar to each other but hinder them among people who are different. These dynamics occur because of the social categorization and stereotyping processes described in Chapter 4. We find quite convincing the research showing that diversity facilitates creative problem solving and organizational innovation while homogeneity hinders them. We also proposed, based on research in educational settings and change literature, that the negative dynamics associated with diversity can probably be overcome by structural and process interventions. Whether demographic diversity is a liability or an asset depends therefore on the willingness of people in organizations to develop an understanding of demographic dynamics and on the initiative of people to take actions to capitalize on the cognitive resources that diverse individuals bring to the organization.

One implication of the social identity theory and the related social categorization process is that individuals prefer much more to be with others who are similar to themselves than with others who are different. This perspective, however, ignores another basic need of an individual—a person's need to be separate or different. The need for a "separate identity" or a need for "uniqueness" is discussed extensively by psychologists like Fromm (1955) and Maslow (1962). Being unique also is one aspect of an individual's self-identity or self-concept. Fromkin (1969, 1976) provides an excellent discussion and research evidence on the importance of uniqueness to self-esteem. This basic need of people suggests that diversity provides more opportunities for individuals to be different or unique. Thus, differences can become an asset for the individual.

179

This chapter is devoted to a discussion of how diversity is an asset to both the organization and the individual. It is an asset to the organization because differences represent resources on which the organization can draw. A lot of different people mean a lot of different forms of resources. Diversity is also an asset to the individual—in part because it is also a source of an individual's resources. He or she may have a skill, ability, or set of experiences that no one else has. But diversity is also an asset to individuals because differences represent different forms of uniqueness that help the individual to thrive psychologically.

Demographic Diversity As an Organizational Asset:
The Value of Differences

The benefits of diversity to the organization have been discussed in many diversity books and articles, some of which were described in Chapter 1. A number of experts agree, for example, that diversity could give the firm a competitive edge in the market place (Cox and Blake, 1991). By deploying their diverse talents in different markets, some firms turned around their declining economic performance while others increased sales noticeably. We will not reiterate in detail the very considerable potential benefits to the organization except to summarize them succinctly into three categories below.

Diversity As an Economic Resource

Today, white men constitute a little less than 50% of the current labor force. white men, therefore, represent only a portion, and an increasingly small portion, of the total human resource pool that the employer can draw upon. There are two simple reasons why it is economically rational to take advantage of the diverse labor pool. First, by including the broad range of the civilian adult population, employers would be drawing from a much larger human resource pool than they would by focusing only on the traditional white male workforce. Other things being equal, a bigger pool of applicants means a better selection. Take an example of an employer wanting some specific skill. Because women and most ethnic minorities were excluded from acquiring this skill in the past, the employer typically had, say, a labor pool of 1,000 people from which to draw. Let us say that about 10% of those people in the labor pool are highly qualified for the job. The employer needs 200 people, so the 100 highly qualified are hired (assuming that the employer has a perfectly valid selection device!) and another 100 less qualified people are hired. But now the rules of the game have changed. The country embarks on a great experiment in equal employment opportunity. Now women and ethnic minorities are allowed to acquire this skill, and many of them do. Now the labor pool increases to about 2,000 people from which the employer can draw, 10% of whom are highly qualified. The employer still needs about 200 people but now can hire 200 highly qualified people. While this example is greatly simplified (for example, selecting from a large pool of people can cost more than selecting from a more limited pool), the example contains a large kernel of truth that seems to have been lost in the rhetoric about affirmative action and equal opportunity. By providing more people access to needed skills and abilities, employers have more, not less, choice. By providing opportunity for everyone to compete for the most select universities and jobs, employers should have a more, not less, talented pool from which to choose. Employers that are competitive in attracting applicants from this larger and/or more talented pool of people should have more skilled, not less skilled, employees.

There is a second reason why employers should take advantage of diversity in the labor pool. Employers can save money in the long term by addressing the negative dynamic created by the social categorization process early and systematically rather than late and on an ad hoc basis. Intergroup conflict diverts people's energy away from engaging in productive work. The employer will find good returns to the economic investments to help individuals and groups to understand the meaning of diversity and to learn the skills to relate to others who are different. These investments can take the form of specific diversity training or structural and policy changes that foster the positive effects of diversity. The focus of this investment should be on everyone rather than just managers and supervisors or the people who are in the minority categories. Progress on solving the diversity problem will be hastened if everyone in the organization acquires an understanding and assumes an ownership of the problem. Willingness to deal with it directly and openly on the part of all people from all backgrounds is the most economic approach for addressing the diversity problem.

Diversity As an Intellectual Resource

Diversity and demography research described in Chapters 5, 6, and 7 has shown quite clearly that people with different backgrounds bring different perspectives to the tasks they perform and to the groups to which they belong. These different perspectives may mean a different way of perceiving, analyzing, and understanding the task or the problem being addressed. They may result in different alternatives or solutions to a problem or approaches to performing a job. These different points of view are invaluable for addressing problems that may not have a clearly correct or incorrect answer and for problems that affect a lot of different people. Differing perspectives allow exploration of many more options. Considering many different perspectives also implies that there will be more extensive discussion of the problem and its solutions. The extensive discussion becomes a process of engaging the members and developing a commitment to the solution that is finally adopted. The tendency to accept a solution prematurely by highly cohesive groups can lead to disastrous decisions. In his discussion of "groupthink," Janis (1982) provided numerous examples of political fiascoes caused by the failure of highly cohesive, homogeneous groups to consider alternatives. Diversity brings not only intellectual resources but also prevents the group from becoming myopic and closed-minded.

Diversity As a Social Resource

People with different backgrounds bring with them a variety of social and cultural characteristics that can enrich the social interaction and experiences of everyone in the group. Some people spend a great deal of money, and travel to far away places to experience the diversity of different cultures. Demographic diversity can bring the world to one's immediate social or work group. All it takes for this to happen is for individuals to be willing to ask others for their views, their perspectives, their past experiences, and to listen well. Everyone, not only the majority toward the minority, but also the minority toward the majority, as well as one minority group toward other minority groups, should show such willingness and interest. Variety adds spice to life, and sharing develops understanding, appreciation, and acceptance among potentially vastly different peoples.

Demographic Diversity As a Personal Asset:
The Value of Uniqueness

The most valuable aspect of diversity is perhaps the differences among people who are different. Each group and each individual is unique on some demographic attributes. To the extent that being unique is a basic need of humans, diversity provides an opportunity for the satisfaction of this basic human motivation. People seek uniqueness or differentiation from others through the choice of names, clothing, dates, mates, beliefs, performance, or, sometimes, even deviant actions. People want to be noticed and to be recognized as individuals rather than just as undifferentiated members of a group or as exemplars of a social category. Nothing is more annoying to white women and ethnic and racial minorities of both sexes than to think that an employer's interest is probably due to one's sex, race, or ethnicity. No one wants to be sought after as a social category, someone to make a firm "look good" in managing diversity. No one wants to be invited to apply for a job just so a firm can say there were women or minorities being considered for a job, even though there is no serious interest in one's candidacy. This is especially the case since women and minorities who are eligible to be considered for highly placed nontraditional jobs are probably relatively more unique and individualistic than both other women and minorities and the more traditional job candidates for these jobs.

Being unique is also a source of self-esteem for the individual. Studies have shown that there is a decline in self-esteem when individuals find themselves among others who are extremely similar to themselves on attitudes (see, for example, Ganster, McCuddy, and Fromkin, 1977). This is especially true for individuals who have a high need for uniqueness. For these individuals, uniqueness is threatened or perceived to be lost when one is extremely similar to others in the comparison group.

In a demographically diverse group, almost everyone is different or unique on some demographic attributes. The opportunity to be noticed is especially high for those individuals who are different from others on multiple attributes. For example, a tall, young, Asian female who speaks with a Cambridge accent will probably catch others' attention quite easily. A person with an unfamiliar accent may be difficult to understand but he or she may get extra attention because it takes more effort to be understood. These unique attributes could be valuable resources for the individual.

Some individuals even take advantage of their uniqueness through calling attention to it or exaggerating it. For example, a minority individual might preface his or her comments by saying "I am different, therefore, my idea is different. Perhaps my idea can provide a different way of looking at this problem." Statements like these are likely to draw more attention to what one has to say than would directly stating a point of view.

By drawing attention to one's uniqueness, one is also increasing the awareness of one's difference from others in the group. This might increase inter-group differentiation. However, it is possible to be both unique and similar by discovering categories in which one is distinct from others and identifying categories in which one is similar to others (see Pettigrew & Martin, 1987). No matter how different two people may seem, they are likely to share some interest or experience, if one takes the trouble to search for commonality. And, conversely, no matter how similar two people seem to be, they too probably share some unusual common interest. It is not all that uncommon to find that two young, white, male professionals share a talent as excellent dessert chefs, something that neither would expect of the other, or that two minority women managers share a passion for fast sports cars.

Pointing out areas of uniqueness and commonality requires an awareness of the primary categories that are important sources of social identity for others and exploring categories that might be potentially meaningful for both others and self. Exploring similarities among otherwise different individuals and identifying differences among otherwise similar individuals are parts of the process involved in managing diversity.

In summary, the need for uniqueness co-exists with the need for being similar to others. This is one paradox of human nature. Yet, both are important needs, and demographic diversity in one's primary social or work group makes it more possible to satisfy both needs than when these groups are homogeneous in nature.

The End Is Where It Begins

Now we have come to the end of this book, but as Winston Churchill said, "This is not the end, this is not even the beginning of the end. It is, perhaps, the end of the beginning." We hope this book will stimulate further research on demographic diversity and will encourage organizations to truly "manage diversity" to create more cohesive, productive, and creative diverse groups. You may even find that your life will be changed by your efforts to understand why differences between individuals and groups are useful, interesting, and valuable to both you and the groups to which you belong.

References

Abrams, D. & Hogg. M. (1990). *Social identity theory: Constructive and critical advances*. New York: Springer-Verlag.

Alexander, J., Nuchols, B., Bloom, J. & Lee, S.Y. (1995). Organizational demography and turnover: An examination of multiform and nonlinear heterogeneity. *Human Relations*, 48, 1455–1480.

Allison, P.D. (1978). Measures of inequality. *American Sociological Review*, 43, 865–880.

Allport, G.W. (1979). *The nature of prejudice*. Cambridge/Reading, MA: Addison-Wesley.

Alston, J.P. (1989, March–April). *Wa, guanxi* and *inhwa:* Managerial principles in Japan, China, and Korea. *Business Horizons*, pp. 26–31.

Ancona, D.G. & Caldwell, D.F. (1992). Demography and design: Predictors of new product team performance. *Organizational Science*, 3, 321–341.

Argyris, C. (1957). *Personality and organization*. New York: Harper & Row.

Aronson, E., Blaney, N., Stephan, C., Sikes, J. & Snapp, M.B. (1978). *The jigsaw classroom*. Beverly Hills, CA: Sage.

Ashford, S.J. & Tsui, A.S. (1991). Self-regulation for managerial effectiveness: The role of active feedback seeking. *Academy of Management Journal*, 34(2), 251–280.

Ashforth, B. & Mael, F. (1989). Social identity theory and the organization. *Academy of Management Review*, 14, 20–39.

Bantel, K.A. (1993). Top team, environment, and performance effects on strategic planning formality. *Group and Organization Management*, 18, 436–458.

Bantel, K.A. & Jackson, S.E. (1989). Top management innovations in banking: Does the composition of the top team make a difference? *Strategic Management Journal*, 10, 107–124.

Baron, J.N., Mittman, B.S. & Newman, A.E. (1991). Targets of opportunity: Organizational and environmental determinants of gender integration within the California Civil Service, 1979–1987. *American Journal of Sociology*, 96, 1362–1401.

Baskett, Glen D. (1973). Interview decisions as determined by competency and attitude similarity. *Journal of Applied Psychology*, 57, 343–345.

Bem, S.L. (1981). Gender schema theory: A cognitive account of sex typing. *Psychological Review*, 88(4), 354–364.

Blau, P. M. (1977). *Inequality and Heterogeneity*. New York: Free Press.

Bond, M.H. & Hwang, K.K. (1986). The social psychology of Chinese people. In Bond, M.H. (ed.), *The psychology of Chinese people*, 211–266. New York: Oxford University Press.

Brewer, M.B. (1979). In-group bias in the minimal intergroup situation: A cognitive-motivational analysis. *Psychological Bulletin*, 86, 307–324.

Brewer, M.B. (1994). Managing diversity: Can we reap the benefits without paying the costs? In Jackson, S., Ruderman, M., and Tornow, W. (eds.), *Work team dynamics and productivity in the context of diversity*. American Psychological Association.

Brewer, M.B. (1997). The social psychology of intergroup relations: Can research inform practice? *Journal of Social Issues*, 53(1), 197–211.

Brewer, M.B. & Miller, N. (1984). Beyond the contact hypothesis: Theoretical perspectives on desegregation. In Miller, N. and Brewer, M.B. (eds.), *Groups in contact*, 281–302. San Diego, CA: Academic Press.

Bryne, D. (1971). *The attraction paradigm*. New York: Academic Press.

Bryne, D., Clore, G.L., Jr., & Smeaton, G. (1986). The attraction hypothesis: Do similar attitudes affect anything? *Journal of Personality and Social Psychology*, 51, 1167–1170.

Bryne, D., Clore, G.L., Jr., & Worchel, P. (1966). The effect of economic similarity–dissimilarity as determinants of attraction. *Journal of Personality and Social Psychology*, 4, 220–224.

Bullock, C. (1976). Interracial contact and student prejudice: The impact of southern school desegregation. *Youth and Society*, 7 (March), 271–309.

Burt, R.S. (1982). *Toward a structural theory of action*. NY: Academic Press.

Buss, A.H. & Portnoy, N.W. (1967). Pain tolerance and group identification. *Journal of Personality and Social Psychology*, 6, 106–108.

Campbell, D.T. & Stanley, J.C. (1966). *Experimental and quasi-experimental designs for research*. Chicago: Rand-McNally.

Campion, M.A., Medsker, G.J. & Higgs, A.C. (1993). Relations between work group characteristics and effectiveness: Implications for designing effective work groups. *Personnel Psychology*, 4, 823–850.

Chemers, M.M., Oskamp, S., & Costanzo, M.A. (1995). *Diversity in organizations: New perspectives for a changing workplace*. Thousand Oaks: Sage Publications.

Clement, D.E. & Schiereck, J., Jr., (1973). Sex composition and group performance in a visual signal detection task. *Memory and Cognition*, 1, 251– 255.

Cook, S.W. (1978). Interpersonal and attitudinal outcomes in cooperating interracial groups. *Journal of Research and Development in Education*, 12, 97–113.

Cook, T.D. & Campbell, D.T. (1979). *Quasi-experimentation: Design and analysis for field settings*. Chicago: Rand–McNally.

Cox, T.H. (1991). The multicultural organization. *Academy of Management Executive*, 5, 34–47.

Cox, T.H. (1993). *Cultural divxersity in organizations: Theory, research, and practice*. San Francisco, CA: Berrett-Koehler.

Cox, T.H. & Blake, S. (1991). Managing cultural diversity: Implications for organizational competitiveness. *Academy of Management Executive*, 5, 45–67.

Cox, T.H., Lobel, S.A. & McLeod, P.L. (1991). Effects of ethnic group cultural differences on cooperative and competitive behavior on a group task. *Academy of Management Journal*, 34, 827–847.

Cross, E.Y. & White, M.B. (1996). The diversity factor: Capturing the competitive advantage of a changing workforce. Chicago: Irwin Professional.

Deal, T. & Kennedy, A. (1982). *Corporate cultures: The rites and rituals of corporate life*. Reading, MA: Addison-Wesley.

Dearborn, D.C. & Simon, H.A. (1958). Selective perceptions: A note on the departmental identification of executives. *Sociometry*, 21, 140–144.

Dockery, T.M. & Steiner, D.D. (1990). The role of the initial interaction in leader–member exchange. *Group and Organizational Studies*, 15, 395–413.

Eisenhardt, K.M. & Tabrizi, B.N. (1995). Accelerating adaptive processes: Product innovation in the global computer industry. *Administrative Science Quarterly*, 1, 84–110.

Ely, R.J. (1994). The effects of organizational demographics and social identity on relationships among professional women. *Administrative Science Quarterly*, 39, 203–238.

Fairhurst, G.T. (1993). The leader–member exchange patterns of women leaders in industry: A discourse analysis. *Communication Monographs*, 60, 321–351.

Fairhurst, G.T. & Snavely, B.K. (1983). A test of the social isolation of male tokens. *Academy of Management Journal*, 26, 353–361.

Farh, J.L., Tsui, A.S., Xin, K. & Cheng, B.S. (1998). The influence of relational demography and *guanxi*: The Chinese case. *Organization Science*.

Fenelon, J.R. & Megaree, E.I. (1971). Influence of race on the manifestation of leadership. *Journal of Applied Psychology*, 55, 353–358.

Fernandez, J.P. (1991). *Managing a diverse work force*. Lexington, MA: Lexington Books.

Finkelstein, S. & Hambrick, D.C. (1990). Top-management team tenure and organizational outcomes: The moderating role of managerial discretion. *Administrative Science Quarterly*, 484–503.

Fiske, S.T. (1987). On the road: Comment on cognitive sterotyping literature in Pettigrew and Martin. *Journal of Social Issues*, 43, 113–118.

Fiske, S.T. (1993). Controlling other people: The impact of power on stereotypes. *American Psychologist*, 48, 621–628.

Fromkin, H.L. (1969). Affective and valuational consequences of self-perceived uniqueness deprivation: I. Hypotheses and methodological prescriptions. Paper no. 261. Institute for Research in Behavioral, Economic, and Management Sciences. Lafayette, IN: Purdue University.

Fromkin, H.L. (1976). The search for uniqueness and valuation of scarcity: Neglected dimensions of value in exchange theory. Paper no. 558. Institute for Research in the Behavioral, Economic and Management Sciences. West Lafayette, IN: Purdue University.

Fromm, E. (1955). *The sane society*. New York: Rinehart.

Fullerton, H.N., Jr. (1987). Labor force projections: 1986 to 2000. *Monthly Labor Review* (September), 19–29.

Gaertner, S., Dovidio, J., Anastasio, P., Bachman, B. & Rust, M. (1993). The common ingroup identity model: Recategorization and the reduction of ingroup bias. In Stroebe, W. & Hewstone, M. (eds.), *European Review of Social Psychology*. Vol. 4, 1–26. Chichester, England: Wiley.

Ganster, D.L., McCuddy, M.K. & Fromkin, H.L. (1977). Magnitude of similarity and self-esteem: Replication and extension with uniqueness theory. Paper no.

592. Institute for Research in the Behavioral, Economic, and Management Sciences. West Lafayette, IN: Purdue University.

Giles, M.W. & Evans, A. (1986). The power approach to intergroup hostility. *Journal of Conflict Resolution*, 30: 469–486.

Graen, G. & Cashman, J.F. (1975). A role-making model of leadership in formal organizations: A development approach. In Hunt, J.G. and Larson, L.L. (eds.), *Leadership Frontiers*, 143–165. Kent, OH: Kent State University Press.

Graen, G., Orris, J.B. & Johnson, T.W. (1973). Role assimilation in a complex organization. *Journal of Vocational Behavior*, 3, 395–420.

Greenberger, E. & Steinberg, L. (1986). *When teenagers work*. New York: Basic Books.

Gutek, B.A. (1985). *Sex and the workplace*. San Francisco: Jossey-Bass.

Gutek, B.A. (1995). *The dynamics of service: Reflections on the changing nature of provider/customer interactions*. San Francisco: Jossey-Bass.

Hall, R.H. & Xu, W. (1990). Run silent, run deep: Cultural influences on organizations in the Far East. *Organization Studies*, 11, 569–576.

Hambrick, D., Li, J.T., Xin, K. & Tsui, A.S. (1998). *Composition and processes of international joint venture management groups: A new perspective on alliance effectiveness*. Paper presented at the International Research Conference on Management and Organizations in China. Hong Kong University of Science and Technology, January.

Hambrick, D.C., Cho, T.S. & Chen, M.J. (1996). The influence of top management team heterogeneity on firms' competitive moves. *Administrative Science Quarterly*, 4, 659–684.

Hambrick, D.C. & Mason, P.A. (1984). Upper echelons: The organization as a reflection of its top managers. *Academy of Management Review*, 9, 193–206.

Harrison, D.A., Price, K.H., & Bell, M.P. (1998). Beyond relational demography: Time and the effects of surface- and deep-level diversity on work group cohesion. *Academy of Management Journal*, 41 (1), 96–107.

Haveman, H. 1995. The demographic metabolism of organizations: Industry dynamics, turnover, and tenure distributions. *Administrative Science Quarterly*, 40: 586–618.

Hayles, R. (1997). The diversity directive: Why some initiatives fail and what to do about it. [Madison, WI.]: ASTD/American Society for Training and Development; New York: McGraw-Hill.

Heilman, M.E., Block, C. & Lucas, J.A. (1992). Presumed incompetent? Stigmatization and affirmative action efforts. *Journal of Applied Psychology*, 77, 536–544.

Herriot, P. (1995). *Competitive advantage through diversity: Organizational learning from difference*. London: Sage.

Hewstone, M. & Brown, R. (1986). Contact is not enough: An intergroup perspective on the contact hypothesis. In Hewstone, M. and Brown, R. (eds.). *Contact and conflict in intergroup encounters*, 1–44. Oxford: Basil Blackwell.

Hinkle, S. & Brown, R.J. (1990). Intergroup comparisons and social identity: Some links and lacunae. In Abrams, D. and Hogg, M.A. *Social identity theory*, 48–70. New York: Springer-Verlag.

Hoffman, E. (1979). Applying experimental research on group problem solving to organizations. *Journal of Applied Behavioral Science*, 15, 375–391.

Hoffman, E. (1985). The effect of race ratio composition on the frequency of organizational communication. *Social Psychology Quarterly*, 48(1), 17–26.

Hoffman, L.R. (1979). Applying experimental research on group problem solving to organizations. *Journal of Applied Behavioral Science*, 15, 375–391.

Hogan, E.A. (1987). Effects of prior expectations on performance ratings: A longitudinal study. *Academy of Management Journal*, 30, 354–368.

Hogg, M.A. & Abrams, D. (1988). *Social identifications: A social psychology of intergroup relations and group processes*. New York: Routledge.

Hogg, M.A, & McGarty, C. (1990). Self-categorization and social identity. In Abrams, D. and Hogg, M.A. *Social identity theory*, 10–27. New York: Springer-Verlag.

Hwang, K.K. (1987). Face and favor: The Chinese power game. *American Journal of Sociology*, 92, 944–974.

Hyde, J.S., Fennema, E. & Lamon, S.J. (1990). Gender differences in mathematics performance: A meta-analysis. *Psychological Bulletin*, 107(2), 139–155.

Ibarra, H. (1992). Homophily and differential returns: Sex differences in network structure and access in an advertising firm. *Administrative Science Quarterly*, 3, 422–447.

Jackson, S.E. (1992a). Consequences of group composition for the interpersonal dynamics of strategic issue processing. In Shrivastva, P., Huff, A. and Dutton, J. (eds.), *Advances in strategic management*, 8, 345–382. Greenwich, CT: JAI Press.

Jackson, S.E. (1992b). Team composition in organizational settings: Issues in managing the increasing diverse work force. In Worchel, S., Wood, W., and Simpson, J.A. (eds.), *Group process and productivity*, 138–173. Newbury Park: Sage Publications.

Jackson, S.E. & Associates (1992). (eds.). *Diversity in the workplace: Human resource initiatives*. New York: Guilford Press.

Jackson, S.E., Brett, J.F., Sessa, V.I., Cooper, D.M., Julin, J.A. & Peyronnin, K. (1991). Some differences make a difference: Individual dissimilarity and group heterogeneity as correlates of recruitment, promotion, and turnover. *Journal of Applied Psychology*, 76, 675–689.

Jackson, S.E., May, K.E. & Whitney, K. (1993). Understanding the dynamics of diversity in decision making teams. In Guzzo, R.A., and Salas, E. (eds.) *Team decision-making effectiveness in organizations*. San Francisco, CA: Jossey-Bass.

Jackson, S.E. & Ruderman, M.N. (1995). *Diversity in work teams: Research paradigms for a changing workplace*. Washington, DC: American Psychological Association.

Jackson, S.E., Stone, V.K. & Alvarez, E.B. (1993). Socialization amidst diversity: Impact of demographics on work team oldtimers and newcomers. In Cummings, L.L. and Staw, B.M. (eds.), *Research in Organizational Behavior*, 15.

Jacobs, J. (1989). *The revolving door*. Stanford: Stanford University Press.

Jacobs, J.B. (1980). The concept of *guanxi* and local politics in a rural Chinese cultural setting. In Greenblatt, S.L., Wilson, R.W. & Wilson, A.A. (eds.), *Social interaction in Chinese society*, 209–236. New York: Praeger.

Jameison, D. & O'Mara, J. (1991). *Managing work force 2000: Gaining the diversity advantage*. San Francisco: Jossey-Bass.

Janis, I.L. (1982). *Groupthink*. Boston, MA: Houghton Mifflin Company.

Jehn, K.A. (1995). A multimethod examination of the benefits and detriments of intragroup conflict. *Administrative Science Quarterly*, 40 (2), 256–282.

Johns, G. (1978). Attitudinal and nonattitudinal predictors of two forms of absence from work. *Organizational Behavior and Human Performance*, 22, 431–444.

Johnston, W.B. (1991). Global work force 2000: The new world labor market. *Harvard Business Review*, 69 (March/April), 115–129.

Johnston, W.B. & Packer, A.H. (1987). *Workforce 2000: Work and workers for the 21st century.* Indianapolis: Hudson Institute.

Jourard, S.M. (1968). *Disclosing man to himself.* Princeton, NJ: Van Nostrand.

Jourard, S.M. (1964). *The transparent self: Self-disclosure and well-being.* Princeton, NJ: Van Nostrand.

Judge, T.A. & Ferris, G.R. (1993). Social context of performance evaluation decisions. *Academy of Management Journal*, 36, 80–105.

Kanter, R.M. (1977). Some effects of proportions on group life: Skewed sex ratios and responses to token women. *American Journal of Sociology*, 82, 965–990.

Kanter, R.M. (1991). Transcending business boundaries: 12,000 world managers view change. *Harvard Business Review* (May–June), 151–164.

Katz, R. (1982). The effects of group longevity on project communication and performance. *Administrative Science Quarterly*, 27, 81–104.

Keck, S. & Tushman, M. (1988). A longitudinal study of the change in group demographies. *Academy of Management Proceedings*, 175–179.

Keck, S. & Tushman, M. (1993). Environmental and organizational context and executive team structure. *Academy of Management Journal*, 36, 1314–1344.

King, A.Y. (1989). An analysis of *renqing* in interpersonal relations. In Yang, K.S. (ed.), *The psychology of the Chinese.* Taipei, China: Kui-Kuan Books.

King, A.Y. (1991). Kuan-hsi and network building: A sociological interpretation. *Daedalus*, 120, 63–84.

Koberg, C.S., Boss, R.W. & Goodman, E.A. (1998). Factors and outcomes associated with mentoring among health-care professionals. *Journal of Vocational Behavior* (53 (1), 58–72.

Konrad, A. & Gutek, B.A. (1987). Theory and research on group composition: Applications to the status of women and ethnic minorities. In Oskamp, S. and Spacapan, S. (eds.), *Interpersonal processes: The Claremont symposium on applied social psychology*, 85–121. Beverly Hills: Sage.

Konrad, A.M., Winter, S. & Gutek, B.A. (1992). Diversity in work group sex composition: Implications for majority and minority members. In Tolbert, P. and Bachrach, S.B. (eds.), *Research in the sociology of organizations*, 10, 115–140. Greenwich, CT: JAI Press.

Kossek, E.E. & Lobel, S.A. (1996). *Managing diversity: Human resource strategies for transforming the workplace.* Cambridge, MA.: Blackwell Business.

Kramer, R.M. (1991). Intergroup relations and organizational dilemmas: The role of categorization process. In Staw, B.M. and Cummings, L.L. (eds.), *Research in Organizational Behavior*, 13, 191–228. Greenwich, CT: JAI Press.

Kulik, C.T, & Holbrook, R.L. (1998). Demographics in service encounters: Effects of racial and gender congruence on perceived fairness. Paper presented at Academy of Management Meetings, San Diego, CA.

Lawler, E.E., III, Mohrman, S.A. & Ledford, G.E., Jr. (1992). *Employee involvement and total quality management: Practices and results in Fortune 1000 companies.* San Francisco, CA: Jossey-Bass.

Lawrence, B.S. (1988). New wrinkles in the theory of age: Demography, norms, and performance ratings. *Academy of Management Journal*, 31, 309–337.

Lawrence, B.S. (1997). The black box of organizational demography. *Organization Science*, 1, 1–22.

Laws, J.L. (1979). *The second X: Sex role and social role*. New York: Elsevier.

Leach, J. (1995). *A practical guide to working with diversity: The process, the tools, the resources*. New York: AMACOM.

Leidner, R. (1993). *Fast food, fast talk*. Berkeley and Los Angeles: University of California Press.

Levinger, G. (1987). Black employment opportunities: Macro and micro perspectives. *Journal of Social Issues*, 43(1), 1–156.

Li, M.C. (1993). Analysis of Chinese self–other relations: A fairness judgement perspective. *Indigenous Psychological Research in Chinese Societies*, 1, 267–300.

Li, M.C. & Hsu, C.S. (1995). In-group favoritism and development of communal identity: The case of college students in Taiwan. *Indigenous Psychological Research in Chinese Societies*, 4, 150–182.

Liden, R.C. (1985). Female perceptions of female and male managerial behavior. *Sex Roles*, 12(3–4), 421–432.

Liden, R.C., Wayne, S.J. & Stilwell, D. (1993). A longitudinal study on the early development of leader–member exchanges. *Journal of Applied Psychology*, 78, 662–674.

Lincoln, J.R. & Miller, J. (1979). Work and friendship ties in organizations: A comparative analysis of relational networks. *Administrative Science Quarterly*, 24, 181–199.

Linton, R. (1940). A neglected aspect of social organization. *American Journal of Sociology*, 45, 870–886.

Linton, R. (1942). Age and sex categories. *American Sociological Review*, 7, 589–603.

Lippmann, W. (1922). *Public opinion*. New York: Macmillan.

Lockett, M. (1988). Culture and problems in Chinese management: A preliminary study. *American Sociological Review*, 28, 55–69.

Loden, M. (1996). *Implementing diversity*. Chicago: Irwin Professional.

Loden, M. & Rosener, J. (1991). *Work force America! Managing employee diversity as a vital resource*. Homewood, IL: Business One Irwin.

Longshore, D. (1982). School racial composition and white hostility: The problem of control in desegregated schools. *Social Forces*, 61 (September), 73–78.

Lott, A.J. & Lott, B.E. (1965). Group cohesiveness and interpersonal attraction: A review of relationships with antecedent and consequent variables. *Psychological Bulletin*, 64, 259–302.

Lynch, F.R. (1997). *The diversity machine: The drive to change the "white male workplace."* New York: Free Press.

Magjuka, R.J. & Baldwin, T.T. (1991). Team-based employee involvement programs: Effects of design and administration. *Personnel Psychology*, 4, 793–812.

Marcus-Newhall, A., Miller, N., Holtz, R. & Brewer, M.B. (1993). Cross-cutting category membership with role assignment: A means of reducing intergroup bias. *British Journal of Social Psychology*, 32, 125–146.

Markus, H.R. & Kitayama, S. (1991). Culture and the self: Implications for cognition, emotion, and motivation. *Psychological Review*, 98, 224–253.

Marshall, R.A., Palmer, B.A. & Weisbart, S.N. (1979). The nature and significance of the agent–policyowner relationship. *CLU Journal* (January) 44–53.

Martin, J. (1992). *Cultures in organizations: Three perspectives*. New York: Oxford University Press.

Maslow, A.H. (1962). *Toward a psychology of being*. New York: Van Nostrand.

McCain, B.E., O'Reilly, C.A., III & Pfeffer, J. (1983). The effects of departmental demography on turnover: The case of a university. *Academy of Management Journal*, 26, 626–641.

McGrath, J.E. (1984). *Groups: Interaction and performance*. Englewood Cliffs, NJ: Prentice-Hall.

McIntire, S., Moberg, D.J. & Posner, B.Z. (1980). Preferential treatment in preselection decisions according to sex and race. *Academy of Management Journal*, 23, 738–749.

Melinger, G.D. (1956). Interpersonal trust as a factor in communication. *Journal of Abnormal and Social Psychology*, 52, 304–309.

Meyer, A.D., Tsui, A.S. & Hinings, C.R. (1993). Configuration approaches to organizational analysis. *Academy of Management Journal*, 36, 1175–1195.

Michel, J.G. & Hambrick, D.C. (1992). Diversification posture and top management team characteristics. *Academy of Management Journal*, 35, 9–37.

Milliken, F.J. & Martins, L.I. (1996). Searching for common threads: Understanding the multiple effects of diversity in organizational groups. *Academy of Management Review*, 21, 402–433.

Mintzberg, H. (1973). *The nature of managerial work*. New York: Harper and Row.

Mittman, B.S. (1992). Theoretical and methodological issues in the study of organizational demography and demographic change. In Tolbert, P. and Bachrach, S.B. (eds.), *Research in the sociology of organizations*, 10, 3–54. Greenwich, CT: JAI Press.

Morgan, G. (1986). *Images of organization*. Beverly Hills, CA: Sage Publications.

Morris, J.H. & Sherman, J.D. (1981). Generalizability of an organizational commitment model. *Academy of Management Journal*, 24, 512–526.

Morrison, A.M. & Von Glinow, M.A. (1990). Women and minorities in management. *American Psychologist*, 45(2), 200–208.

Murray, A.I. (1989). Top management group heterogeneity and firm performance. *Strategic Management Journal*, 10, 125–141.

Murray, M. (1982). The middle years of life of middle class black men. Unpublished manuscript, Psychology Department, University of Cincinnati.

Newell, S. (1995). *The healthy organization: Fairness, ethics, and effective management*. New York: Routledge.

Nieva, V.F. & Gutek, B.A. (1980). Sex effects on evaluation. *The Academy of Management Review*, 5, 267–276.

Nkomo, S.M. (1992). The emperor has no clothes: Rewriting race in organizations. *Academy of Management Review*, 17, 487–513.

Ohlott, P.J., Ruderman, M.N. & McCauley, C.D. (1994). Gender differences in managers' developmental job experiences. *Academy of Management Journal*, 37, 46–67

O'Reilly, C.A. (1989). Corporations, culture, and commitment: Motivation and social control in organizations. *California Management Review* (Summer), 9–25.

O'Reilly, C.A., III, Caldwell, D.F. & Barnett, W.P. (1989). Work group demography, social integration, and turnover. *Administrative Science Quarterly*, 34, 21–37.

O'Reilly, C.A., III, Snyder, R.C. Boothe J.N. (1993). Effects of executive team demography on organizational change. In Huber, G. and Glick, W. (eds.), *Organizational change and redesign: Ideas and insights for improving performance*, 147–175. New York: Oxford University Press.

Parsons, T. (1942). Age and sex in the social structure of the United States. *American Sociological Review*, 7, 604–616.

Pelled, L.H. (1996a). Demographic diversity, conflict, and work group outcomes: An intervening process theory. *Organization Science*, 6, 615–631.

Pelled, L.H. (1996b). Relational demography and perception of group conflict and performance: A field investigation. *The International Journal of Conflict Management*, 7, 236–246.

Pelled, L.H., Eisenhardt, K.M., & Xin, K.R. (1999). Exploring the black box: An analysis of work group diversity, conflict, and performance. *Administrative Science Quarterly*, 230–246.

Peters, T, & Waterman, R. (1982). *In search of excellence: Lessons from America's best run companies*. New York: Harper & Row.

Pettigrew, T. & Martin, J. (1987). Shaping the organization context for black American inclusion. *Journal of Social Issues*, 43, 41–78. NY and London: Plenum Press.

Pettigrew, T.F. (1979). The intergroup contact hypothesis reconsidered. In Hewstone, M. and Brown, R. (eds.), *Contact and conflict in intergroup encounters*, 169–195. Oxford: Basil Blackwell.

Pfeffer, J. (1981). Management as symbolic action: The creation and maintenance of organizational paradigms. In Staw, B. and Cummings, L.L. (eds.), *Research in Organizational Behavior*, 3, 1–52. Greenwich, CT: JAI Press.

Pfeffer, J. (1983). Organizational demography. In Cummings, L.L. and Staw, B.M. (eds.), *Research in Organizational Behavior*, 5, 299–357. Greenwich, CT: JAI Press.

Pfeffer, J. & Moore, W.L. (1980). Average tenure of academic department heads: The effects of paradigm, size, and departmental demography. *Administrative Science Quarterly*, 25, 387–406.

Pfeffer, J. & O'Reilly, C.A., III. (1987). Hospital demography and turnover among nurses. *Industrial Relations*, 26, 158–173.

Pfeffer, J., & Salancik, G.R. (1978). *The external control of organizations: A resource dependence perspective*. New York: Harper & Row.

Prasad, P. et al. (1997). *Managing the organizational melting pot: Dilemmas of workplace diversity*. Thousand Oaks, CA: Sage Publications.

Presthus, R. (1978). *The organizational society*. New York: St. Martin's.

Priem, R.L. (1990). Top management team group factors, consensus, and firm performance. *Strategic Management Journal*, 6, 469–478.

Qiu, L.D. & Wu, C. 1997. *Investment strategies*. In *Research reports on doing business in China: Current issues*, 111–134. Hong Kong University of Science and Technology.

Ragins, B.R. & McFarlin, D.B. (1990). Perceptions of mentor roles in cross-gender mentoring relationships. *Journal of Vocational Behavior*, 37, 321–339.

Redding, S.G., Norman, A. & Schlander, A. (1993). The nature of individual attachment to the organization: A review of East Asia variations. In Dunnette, M.D. and Hough, L.M. (eds.), *Handbook of industrial and organizational psychology,* vol. 4, 647–688. Palo Alto, CA: Consulting Psychology Press.

Riordan, C.M. & Shore, L.M. (1995). Demographic diversity and employee attitudes: An empirical examination of relational demography within work units. *Journal of Applied Psychology*, 82, 342–358.

Rollins, J. (1985). *Between women: Domestics and their employers*. Philadelphia: Temple University Press.

Saltzstein, G.H. (1986). Female mayors and women in municipal jobs. *American Journal of Political Science*, 30, 140–164.

Schein, E. (1985). *Organizational culture and leadership*. San Francisco: Jossey Bass.

Schneider, B. (1987). The people make the place. *Personnel Psychology*, 40, 437–453.

Schneider, B. & Bowen, D.E. (1985). Employee and customer perceptions of service in banks: Replication and extension. *Journal of Applied Psychology*, 70, 423–433.

Schneider, B., Parkington, J.J. & Buxton, V.M. (1980). Employee and customer perceptions of service in banks. *Administrative Science Quarterly*, 25, 252–267.

Schreiber, C.T. (1979). *Changing places: Men and women in transitional occupations*. Cambridge, MA: MIT Press.

Selbert, R. (1987). Women at work. *Future Scan*, 554 (November 16), 1–3.

Shannon, C.E. & Weaver, W. (1949). *The mathematical theory of communication*. Urbana: University of Illinois Press.

Shaw, M.E. (1981). *Group dynamics: The psychology of small group behavior*. 3rd ed. NY: McGraw-Hill.

Sherif, M. (1966). *Group conflict and cooperation*. London: Routledge & Kegan Paul.

Simmons, M. (1996). *New leadership for women and men: Building an inclusive organization*. Aldershot, Hampshire, England; Brookfield, VT USA: Gower.

Smith, K.G., Smith, K.A., Olian, J.D., Sims, H.P., Jr., O'Bannon, D.P. & Scully, J.A. (1994). Top management team demography and process: The role of social integration and communication. *Administrative Science Quarterly*, 39, 412–438.

Snyder, M. (1979). Self-monitoring processes. In Berkowitz, L. (ed.), *Advances in experimental social psychology*, vol. 12, 86–124. New York: Academic Press.

Spencer, S.J. & Steele, C.M. (1994). Under suspicion of inability: Stereotype vulnerability and women's math performance. Working paper, psychology department, Stanford University, Palo Alto, California.

Steele, C.M. (1997). A threat in the air: How stereotypes shape intellectual identity and performance. *American Psychologist*, 52(6), 613–629.

Steele, C.M. & Aronson, J. (1994). Contending with a stereotype: African-American intellectual test performance and stereotype vulnerability. Working paper, psychology department, Stanford University, Palo Alto, California.

Sutton, C.A. & Woodman, R.W. (1989). Pygmalion goes to work: The effects of supervisor expectations in a retail setting. *Journal of Applied Psychology*, 74, 943–950.

Taagepera, R. & Ray, J.L. (1977). A generalized index of concentration. *Sociological Methods and Research*, 5, 367–374.

Tajfel, H. (1981). *Human groups and social categories: Studies in social psychology*. Cambridge: Cambridge University Press.

Tajfel, H. (1982). *Social identity and intergroup relations*. Cambridge: Cambridge University Press.

Tajfel, H. & Turner, J.C. (1986). The social identity theory of intergroup behavior. In Worchel, S. and Austin, W.G. (eds.), *Psychology of intergroup relations*, 7–24. Chicago: Nelson-Hall.

Tayeb, M.H. (1996). The management of a multicultural workforce. Chichester; New York: Wiley.

Teachman, J.D. (1980). Analysis of population diversity. *Sociological Methods and Research*, 8, 341–362.

Thomas, D.A. (1990). The impact of race on managers' experiences of developmental relationships. *Journal of Organizational Behavior*, 11, 479–492.

Thomas, R.R. (1991). *Beyond race and gender: Unleashing the power of your total work force by managing diversity*. New York: AMACOM.

Thomas, R.R. (1996). *Redefining diversity*. New York: AMACOM.

Tolbert, P. & Bacharach, S.B. (1992). (eds.). *Research in the sociology of organizations*. Greenwich, CT: JAI Press.

Tolbert, P.S. & Oberfield, A.A. (1991). Sources of organizational demography: Faculty sex ratios in colleges and universities. *Sociology of Education*, 64, 305–315.

Tsui, A.S. (1994). Reputational effectiveness: Toward a mutual responsiveness framework. *Research in Organizational Behavior*, 16, 257–307.

Tsui, A.S. (1997). The human resource challenge in China: The importance of *guanxi*. In Ulrich, D., Losey, M.R. and Lake, G. (eds.), *Tomorrow's HR management: 48 thought leaders call for change*, 337–344. New York: John Wiley & Sons.

Tsui, A.S. & Ashford, S.J. (1991). Reactions to demographic diversity: Similarity-attraction or self-regulation. *Academy of Management Best Papers Proceedings*, 240–244.

Tsui, A.S. & Ashford, S.J. (1994). Adaptive self-regulation: A process view of managerial effectiveness. *Journal of Management*, 20(1), 93–121.

Tsui, A.S., Ashford, St. Clair & Xin, K. (1995). Dealing with discrepant expectations: Response strategies and managerial effectiveness. *Academy of Management Journal*, 38(6), 1515–1543.

Tsui, A.S., Egan, T.D. & O'Reilly, C.A., III. (1992). Being different: Relational demography and organizational attachment. *Administrative Science Quarterly*, 37, 549–579.

Tsui, A.S., Egan, T.D. & Porter, L.W. (1994). Performance implications of relational demography in vertical dyads. Presented at the national meeting of the Academy of Management, Dallas, Texas.

Tsui, A.S., Egan, T.D. & Xin, K. (1995). Diversity in organizations: Lessons from demography research. Paper presented at the CGS/CMC conference on "Diversity in Organizations," February 12, 1994, Claremont, California.

Tsui, A.S. & Farh, J.L. (1997). Where *guanxi* matters: Relational demography and *guanxi* in the Chinese context. *Work and Occupations*, 24, 56–79.

Tsui, A.S. & O'Reilly, C.A., III. (1989). Beyond simple demographic effects: The importance of relational demography in supervisor–subordinate dyads. *Academy of Management Journal*, 32, 402–423

Tsui, A.S., Xin, K.R. & Egan, T.D. (1995). Relational demography: The missing link in vertical dyad linkage. In Jackson, S., Ruderman, M. and Tornow, W. (eds.), *Diversity in work teams: Research paradigm for a changing workplace*, 97–129. Washington, DC: American Psychological Association.

Turner, J.C. (1982). Towards a redefinition of the social group. In Tajfel, H. (ed.), *Social identity and intergroup relations*, 15–40. Cambridge: Cambridge University Press.

Turner, J.C. (1985). Social categorization and the self-concept: A self cognitive theory of group behavior. In Lawler, E.J. (ed.), *Advances in group processes: Theory and research*, vol. 2, 77–121. Greenwich, CT: JAI Press.

Turner, J.C., & Associates. (1987). *Rediscovering the social group: A self-categorization theory*. New York: Basil Blackwell.

Van Maanen, J. & Schein, E.H. (1979). Toward a theory of organizational socialization. In Staw, B.M. (ed.), *Research in organizational behavior*, vol. 1, 209–264. Greenwich, CT: JAI Press.

Vecchio, R.P., Griffeth, R.W. & Hom, P.W. (1986). The predictive utility of the vertical dyad linkage approach. *Journal of Social Psychology*, 126, 617–625.

Wagner, W.G., Pfeffer, J. & O'Reilly, C.A., III. (1984). Organizational demography and turnover in top-management groups. *Administrative Science Quarterly*, 29, 74–92.

Wakabayashi, M., Graen, G. & Uhl-bien, M. (1990). The generalizablilty of the hidden investment hypothesis in leading Japanese corporations. *Human Relations*, 43(11), 1099–1116.

Walder, A.G. (1986). *Communist neo traditionalism: Work and authority in Chinese industry*. Berkeley: University of California Press.

Waldman, D.A. & Avolio, B.J. (1986). A meta-analysis of age differences in job performance. *Journal of Applied Psychology*, 71, 33–38.

Walker, B.A. & Hanson, W.C. (1992). Valuing differences at Digital Equipment Corporation. In Jackson, S.E. (ed.), *Diversity in the work place*, 119–137. New York: Guilford Press.

Watson, W.E., Kumar, K. & Michaelsen, L.K. (1993). Cultural diversity's impact on interaction process and performance: Comparing homogenous and diverse task groups. *Academy of Management Journal*, 36(3), 590–602.

Watson, W.E. & Michaelsen, L.K. (1988). Group interaction behaviors that affect group performance on an intellective task. *Group and Organization Studies*, 4, 495–516.

Werner, C. & Parmelee, P. (1979). Similarity of activity preferences among friends: Those who play together stay together. *Social Psychology Quarterly*, 42, 62–66.

Wharton, A.S. & Baron, J.N. (1987). So happy together? The impact of gender segregation on men at work. *American Sociological Review*, 52, 574–587.

Wheeless, L.R. 1978. A follow-up study of the relationship between trust, disclosure, and interpersonal solidarity. *Human Communication Research*, 6, 143–157.

Wheeless, L.R. & Grotz, J. (1977). The measurement of trust and its relationship to self-disclosure. *Human Communication Research*, 3, 250–257.

Wiersema, M.F. & Bantel, K.A. (1992). Top management team demography and corporate strategic change. *Academy of Management Journal*, 35, 91–121.

Wiersema, M.F. & Bantel, K.A. (1993). Top management team turnover as an adaptation mechanism: The role of the environment. *Strategic Management Journal*, 14, 485–504.

Wiersema, M.F. & Bird, A. (1993). Organizational demography in Japanese firms: Group heterogeneity, industry dissimilarity, and top management team turnover. *Academy of Management Journal*, 36, 996–1025.

Williams, K.Y. & O'Reilly, C.A., III. (1998). Demography and diversity in organizations: A review of 40 years of research. *Research in organizational behavior*, 20, 77–140. Greenwich, CT: JAI Press.

Wood, W. (1987). Meta-analytic review of sex differences in group performance. *Psychological Bulletin*, 102, 53–71.

Xin, K.R., Farh, J.L., Cheng, B.S. & Tsui, A.S. (1998). *Guanxi* and vertical dyads: Evidence from Taiwan and the PRC. Paper presented at the Research Conference on Management and Organizations in China, January 15–17, Hong Kong University of Science and Technology.

Xin, K.R. & Pearce, J.L. (1996). *Guanxi*: Connections as substitutes for female institutional support. *Academy of Management Journal*, 39: 1641–1658.

Yang, K.S. (1993). Chinese social orientation: An integrative analysis. In Cheng, L.Y., Cheung, F.M.C. and Chen, C.N. (eds.), *Psychotherapy for the Chinese: Selected papers from the first international conference*, 19–56. Hong Kong: The Chinese University of Hong Kong.

Yang, M.M. (1994). *Gifts, favors and banquets: The art of social relationships in China.* Ithaca, NY: Cornell University Press.

Yount, K.R. (1991). Ladies, flirts, and tomboys: Strategies for managing sexual harassment in an underground coal mine. *Journal of Contemporary Ethnography,* 19(4), 396–422.

Zander, A. (1979). The psychology of group processes. In Rosenzweig, M.R and Porter, L.W. (eds.), *Annual Review of Psychology*, 417–451. Palo Alto, CA: Annual Reviews.

Zenger, T.R. & Lawrence, B.S. (1989). Organizational demography: The differential effects of age and tenure distributions on technical communication. *Academy of Management Journal*, 32, 353–376.

Index

About the Authors

Anne S. Tsui (Ph.D, University of California, Los Angeles, 1981) has been professor and head of the Department of Management of Organizations and [Wei Lun Senior Fellow] at the School of Business and Management, Hong Kong University of Science and Technology, since 1995. Before that, she was on the faculty of the Graduate School of Management, University of California, Irvine (1988-1995) and was on the faculty at the Fuqua School of Business, Duke University (1981-1988).

She is the editor of the Academy of Management Journal (1997-1999), a fellow of the Academy of Management, and founding director of the Hang Lung Center for Organizational Research, which explores management and organizational issues in the Chinese context. She also serves or has served on the editorial review boards of a number of leading scholarly journals in the field of management.

Dr. Tsui has a variety of research interests, including managerial and leadership effectiveness, performance assessment, human resource department effectiveness, self-regulation, employee-organization relationship, and demographic diversity. Most of her research programs were or are supported by grants from such agencies as the Office of Naval Research, National Science Foundation, Research Grants Council of Hong Kong, internal university grants, or grants from corporate or private foundations. After moving to Hong Kong, she began a new research program studying the phenomenon of *guanxi* in the Chinese context as well as the effectiveness of international joint venture leadership teams. Her research findings have been published in a number of leading academic journals. Several of her publications have received awards; her article on the theme of this book, "Being Different: Relational Demography and Organizational Attachment" (published in Administrative Science Quarterly, 1992) won the Outstanding Publication in Organizational Behavior Award in 1993 and, five years later, the ASQ Scholarly Contribution Award in 1998.

Barbara A. Gutek (Ph.D. University of Michigan, 1975), is McClelland Professor and head of the Department of Management and Policy, University of Arizona. Major research interests are the delivery of services and sexual harassment and discrimination. Author or editor of eleven books and over eighty articles, Dr. Gutek has received research grants from the National Institute of Mental Health and the National Science Foundation. A fellow in the American Psychological Association and American Psychological Society, she is a past president of the Society for the Psychological Study of Social Issues and served a term on the Board of Governors of the Academy of Management. In 1994, she received two awards from the American Psychological Association: The Division 35 Heritage Award for a "substantial and outstanding body of research on women and gender" and the Committee on Women in Psychology Award as a "Distinguished Leader for Women in Psychology." In 1994, she also received the Sage Scholarship Award from the Academy of Management. Dr. Gutek has also served as an expert witness in cases of sexual harassment and sex discrimination in the United States.